LAW
&
MENTAL
HEALTH
PROFESSIONALS

MICHIGAN

Law & Mental Health Professionals Series

Bruce D. Sales and Michael Owen Miller, Series Editors

ALABAMA: Bentley, Pippin, and Reaves
ARIZONA: Miller and Sales
CALIFORNIA: Caudill and Pope
CONNECTICUT: Taub
DELAWARE: Britton and Rohs
FLORIDA: Petrila and Otto
GEORGIA: Remar and Hubert
MASSACHUSETTS, 2ND ED.: Brant
MICHIGAN: Clark and Clark
MINNESOTA: Janus, Mickelsen, and Sanders
NEVADA: Johns and Dillehay
NEW JERSEY, 2ND ED.: Wulach
NEW YORK: Wulach
PENNSYLVANIA: Bersoff, Field, Anderer, and Zaplac
TEXAS, 2ND ED.: Shuman
VIRGINIA: Porfiri and Resnick
WASHINGTON: Benjamin, Rosenwald, Overcast, and Feldman
WISCONSIN: Kaplan and Miller
WYOMING: Blau

LAW & MENTAL HEALTH PROFESSIONALS

MICHIGAN

Beth K. Clark
Charles R. Clark

American Psychological Association
Washington, DC

Published by
American Psychological Association
750 First Street, NE
Washington, DC 20002

Copies may be ordered from
APA Order Department
P.O. Box 92984
Washington, DC 20090-2984

Typeset in Palatino by GGS Information Services, York, PA
Cover Designer: Rubin Krassner, Silver Spring, MD
Printer: Edwards Brothers, Inc., Ann Arbor, MI
Project Manager: Debbie K. Hardin, Reston, VA

The opinions and statements published are the responsibility of the authors, and such opinions and statements do not necessarily represent the policies of the APA.

Library of Congress Cataloging-in-Publication Data
Clark, Beth K.
    Law and mental health professionals. Michigan / by Beth K. Clark, Charles R. Clark.
        p. cm. — (Law & mental health professionals series)
    ISBN 1-55798-715-7 (alk. paper)
    1. Mental health personnel—Legal status, laws, etc.—Michigan. 2. Mental health laws—Michigan. 3. Forensic psychiatry—Michigan. I. Clark, Charles R. II. Title. III. Series.
    KFM4526.5.P73 C58 2000
    344.774'04—dc21

                                                                        00-038096

Printed in the United States of America
First Edition

Contents

Editors' Preface

The Need to Know the Law

For years, providers of mental health services (hereinafter mental health professionals or MHPs) have been directly affected by the law. At one end of the continuum, their practice has been controlled by laws covering such matters as licensure and certification, third-party reimbursement, and professional incorporation. At the other end, they have been courted by the legal system to aid in its administration, providing such services as evaluating the mental status of litigants, providing expert testimony in court, and engaging in therapy with court-referred juveniles and adults. Even when not directly affected, MHPs find themselves indirectly affected by the law because their clients sometimes become enmeshed in legal entanglements that involve mental status issues (e.g., divorce proceedings or termination of parental rights hearings).

Despite this pervasive influence, most professionals do not know about, much less understand, most of the laws that affect their practice, the services they render, and the clients they serve. This state of affairs is particularly troubling for several reasons. First, not knowing about the laws that affect one's practice typically results in the MHPs not gaining the benefits that the law may provide. Consider the law relating to the incorporation of professionals. It confers significant benefit, but only if it is known about and applied. The fact that it has been enacted by the state legislature does not help the MHP, any more than an MHP will be of help to a distressed person who refuses to contact the MHP.

Second, not knowing about the laws that affect the services they render may result in incompetent performance of, and liability for, the MHP either through the civil law (e.g., malpractice law) or through criminal sanctions. A brief example may help underscore this point. When an MHP is asked to evaluate a party to a lawsuit and testify in court, the court (the law's term for the judge) is asking the professional to assess and testify about whether that litigant meets some legal standard. The court is often not concerned with the defendant's mental health per se, although this may be relevant to the MHP's evaluation of the person. Rather, the court wants to know whether the person meets the legal standard as it is set down by the law. Not knowing the legal standard means that the MHP is most likely evaluating the person for the wrong goal and providing the court with irrelevant information, at least from the court's point of view. Regretfully, there are too many cases in which this has occurred.

Third, not knowing the law that affects the clients that MHPs serve may significantly diminish their capability for handling their clients' distress. For example, a client who is undergoing a divorce and a child custody dispute may have distorted beliefs about what may happen during the legal proceedings. A basic understanding of the controlling law in this area will allow the therapist to be more sensitive in rendering therapy.

The Problem in Accessing Legal Information

Given the need for this information, why have MHPs not systematically sought it out? Part of the reason lies in the concern over their ability to understand legal doctrines. Indeed, this is a legitimate worry, especially if they had to read original legal materials that were not collected, organized, and described with an MHP audience in mind. This is of particular concern because laws are written in terms and phrases of "art" that do not always share the common law definition or usage, whereas some terms and phrases are left ambiguous and undefined or are used differently for different legal topics. Another part of the reason is that the law affecting MHPs and their clients is not readily available—even to lawyers. There are no compendiums that identify the topics that these laws cover or present an analysis of each topic for easy reference.

To compound the difficulty, the law does not treat the different mental health professional disciplines uniformly or always specify the particular disciplines as being covered by it. Nor does the law emanate from a single legal forum. Each state enacts its own rules and regulations, often resulting in wide variations in the way a topic is handled across the United States. Multiply this confusion by the one hundred or so topics that relate to mental health practice. In addition, the law within a state does not come from one legal source. Rather, there are five primary ones: the state constitution; state legislative enactments (statutes); state agency administrative rules and regulations; rules of court promulgated by the state supreme court; and state and federal court cases that apply, interpret, and construe this existing state law. To know about one of these sources without knowing how its pronouncements on a given topic have been modified by these other sources may result in one's making erroneous conclusions about the operation of the law. Finally, mental health practice also comes under the purview of federal law (constitutional and statutory law, administrative rules and regulations, and case law).

Federal law authorizes direct payments to MHPs for their services to some clients, sets standards for delivery of services in federal facilities (e.g., Veterans Administration hospitals), and articulates the law that guides cases that are tried in federal courts under federal law.

Purposes of This Series

What is needed, therefore, is a book for each state, the District of Columbia, and the federal jurisdictions that comprehensively and accurately reviews and integrates all of the law that affects MHPs in that jurisdiction (hereinafter state). These materials should be written so that they are completely understandable to MHPs, as well as to lawyers. To accomplish these goals, the editors have tried to identify every legal topic that affects mental health practice, making each one the subject of a chapter. Each chapter, in turn, describes the legal standards that the MHP will be operating under and the relevant legal process that the MHP will be operating within. If a state does not have relevant law on an issue, then a brief explanation of how this law works in other states will be presented while noting the lack of regulation in this area within the state under consideration.

This type of coverage facilitates other purposes of the series. Although each chapter is written in order to state exactly what is the present state of the law and not argue for or against any particular approach, it is hoped that the comprehensiveness of the coverage will encourage MHPs to question the desirability of their states' approach to each topic. Such information and concern should provide the impetus for initiating legislation and litigation on the part of state mental health associations to ensure that the law reflects the scientific knowledge and professional values to the greatest extent possible.

In some measure, states will initially be hampered in this proactivity because they will not know what legal alternatives are available and how desirable each alternative actually is. When a significant number of books in this series is available, however, it will allow for nationally oriented policy studies to identify the variety of legal approaches that are currently in use and to assess the validity of the behavioral assumptions underlying each variant and, ultimately, lead to a conclusion as to the relative desirability of alternate approaches.[1] Thus, two other purposes of this book are to foster comprehensive analyses of the laws affecting

---

1. Sales, B. D. (1983). The legal regulation of psychology: Professional and scientific interactions. In C. J. Scheirer & B. L. Hammonds (Eds.), *The master lecture series: Vol. 2. Psychology and law* (pp. 5–36). Washington, DC: American Psychological Association.

MHPs across all states and of the validity of the behavioral assumptions underlying these laws, and to promote political, legislative, and legal action to change laws that are inappropriate and impede the effective delivery of services. Legal change may be required because of gaps in legal regulation, overregulation, and regulation based on invalid behavioral and social assumptions. We hope that this process will increase the rationality of future laws in this area and improve the effectiveness and quality of mental health service delivery nationally.

There are three remaining purposes for this series. First, although it will not replace the need for legal counsel, this series will make the MHP an intelligent consumer of legal services. This ability is gaining importance in an era of increasing professionalization and litigiousness. Second, it will ensure that MHPs are aware of the law's mandates when providing expert services (e.g., evaluation and testimony) within the legal system. Although chapters will not address how to assess clinically for the legal standard, provider competency will increase because providers now will be sure of the goals of their service (e.g., the legal standard that they are to assess for) as well as their roles and responsibilities within the legal system as to the particular topic in issue. Third and finally, each book will make clear that the legal standards that MHPs are asked to assess for by the law have typically not been translated into behavioral correlates. Nor are there discussions of tests, scales, and procedures for MHPs to use in assessing for the behavioral correlates of the legal standards in most cases. This series will provide the impetus for such research and writing.

Content and Organization of Volumes

Each book in this series is organized into eight sections. Section 1 addresses the legal credentialing of MHPs. Section 2 deals with the different business forms for conducting one's practice, insurance reimbursement, and tax deductions that clients may receive for using mental health services. With the business matters covered, the book then turns to the law directly affecting service delivery. Section 3 covers the law that affects the maintenance and privacy of professional information and discusses the law that limits service delivery and sets liability for unethical and illegal behavior as a service provider. Sections 4 through 8 consider each area of law that may require the services of MHPs: adults, minors, and families; other civil matters; topics that apply similarly in both civil and criminal cases; criminal matters; and voluntary and involuntary receipt of state services by the clients of mental health services.

Collectively, the chapters in these sections represent all topics pertaining to the law as it affects MHPs in their practices. Two caveats are in order, however. First, the law changes slowly over time. Thus, this volume will be updated on a regular basis. As MHPs become more involved in the legal system, new opportunities for involvement are likely to arise. To be responsive to these developments, revisions will also contain additional chapters reflecting these new roles and responsibilities.

Some final points about the content of this book are in order. The exact terms that the law chooses are used in the book even if they are a poor choice from an MHP's point of view. Where terms are defined by the law, that information is presented. The reader will often be frustrated, however, because, as has already been noted, the law does not always define terms or provide detailed guidance. This does not mean that legal words and phrases can be taken lightly. The law sets the rules by which MHPs and their clients must operate; thus, the chapters must be read carefully. This should not be too arduous a task because chapters are relatively short. On the other hand, such brevity will leave some readers frustrated because chapters may appear not to go far enough in answering their questions. Note that all of the law is covered. If there is no law, however, there is no coverage. If a question is not answered in the text, it is because Michigan law has not addressed the issue. Relatedly, if an obligation or benefit is created by a professional regulation (i.e., a rule of a professional organization) but is not directly recognized by the law, it is not covered. Thus, for example, professional credentials are not addressed in these volumes.

Finally, we want to point out that, in some instances, the pronoun "he" is used generically to refer to both genders. Most notably, the pronoun is used when quoting directly from the law. Legal language is generally consistent in its preference for using the masculine form of the pronoun; it is not always feasible to attempt a rewording.

Bruce D. Sales
Michael Owen Miller
Series Editors

Authors' Preface

This book is principally a treatment of state law applicable to mental health professionals (MHPs). A comprehensive treatment of federal law, which is also relevant to the actions of MHPs, is beyond the scope of this work, because it would expand it by volumes or require a more limited treatment of the subject. The sources of state law treated in this work include the state constitution, state statutes, state administrative rules, state judicial decisions, and state judicial rules.

The Michigan Constitution establishes the framework for state government and describes various individual rights that occupy a high degree of importance in Michigan. Citations to the Michigan Constitution appear in the following form: MICH. CONST. art. I, § 1. This reference indicates that the citation is to the first article in the Michigan Constitution. The Constiution is available on the state of Michigan's internet Website at www.state.mi.us.

Citations to state statutes, which result from legislation passed by the Michigan Senate and House of Representatives, appear in the following form: M.C.L. § 7600. This particular citation is a reference to the bound volumes of statutes published by West Publishing Company, titled *Michigan Compiled Laws Annotated*. The laws are enumerated by section. The *Michigan Compiled Laws* are also now available on the Michigan legislature's Internet Website at www.michigan.legislature.org.

This compilation of statutes and the Michigan Constitution contain additional useful material. The compilers attempt to include a citation and a one-sentence summary of any reported cases that have discussed the statute or constitutional provision in question. A researcher may use these case annotations to begin research on how the statute or constitutional provision has been interpreted by the courts. The compilations also contain references to prior statutes that have been repealed. A review of these repealed statutes may be necessary to understand an earlier judicial opinion interpreting them or to resolve an ambiguity in the intent of the legislature in changing the statute.

State administrative rules are created by the state agencies operating under the authority delegated to them by the legislature to carry out specific agency functions. For example, the legislation creating the Bureau of Occupational and Professional Regulation does not list all types of professional misconduct, but gives it the authority to make administrative rules regarding this issue. These rules do not appear in the volumes of statutes but instead are located in the *Michigan Administrative Code,* published by the Michigan Legislative Council. References to the administrative code appear in the following form: R 418.51. The adminsitrative rule referred to by this citation can be found by referring to the above volumes and their yearly supplements. However, the *Administrative Code* was last compiled in 1979, and finding updates is extremely unwieldy. Up-to-date administrative rules can now be found much more easily on the Internet at the state government administrative code Website: www.state.mi.us/orr.

State judicial decisions are the product of judge-made law. Reported decisions are typically those of appellate courts. They consist of decisions of the Michigan Court of Appeals, to which decisions of trial courts typically are appealed, and of the Michigan Supreme Court. Citations to these decisions appear in the following format: May v. Leneair, 297 N.W.2d 882, 99 Mich. App. 209 (1980). This particular citation tells the reader that the case refers to two parties named May and Leneair, and that the report of the decision appears in volume 297 of the second edition of the *Northwestern Reporter* on page 882. The decision also appears in volume 99 of *Michigan Appeals* on page 209 and refers to a 1990 decision by the Court of Appeals. A decision by the Michigan Supreme Court would be cited as *In re* Daniel, 759 Mich. 287 (1996) (Mich. being the abbreviation for *Michigan Reports*).

State judicial rules, as contrasted with judicial decisions, are the product of judges acting in a legislative rather than a judicial capacity. In this role, judges make rules of general application in the courts, not usually in the context of deciding cases. The Michigan Supreme Court promulgates court rules that relate to civil procedure, criminal procedure, civil appellate procedure, and practice in other courts. Most rules can be found in *Michigan Court Rules,* published by the West Publishing Company. They appear in the following form: MCR § 2.3. Other rules may be found in the *Michigan Rules of Evidence,* which appear as MRE.

Articles of relevance to a particular issue from various bar journals have been cited. They appear in the following form: Author, Title of article, 58 MICH B.J. 168 (1979).

Michigan is divided into 57 judicial circuit courts, most of which comprise one county (some circuits comprise several less populated counties). These courts hear civil, criminal, and family cases. In each circuit, there are one or more district courts which serve as the trial court for criminal misdemeanors and civil claims below $10,000. District court judges are the arraigning magistrates for felonies, and they conduct hearings to bind over felonies for trial in circuit court. These hearings are called preliminary examinations. Most counties have their own probate courts, which hear juvenile, wills and estates, trusts, guardianship and conservatorship, and civil commitment issues. As this book was in press, the state was engaged in a process of court consolidation whereby district and circuit courts were being combined, and a new family division was being developed. Currently piloted in several jurisdictions, the family division judges hear all cases involving juveniles, custody and parenting time, and certain probate matters. Thus, one judge would be able to hear all matters pertaining to a particular family, rather than have cases split between the probate, juvenile, and circuit courts. One of the best references for both the structure of the Michigan court system and the names and addresses of all judges is the annual directory issue of the *Michigan Bar Journal,* published by the Michigan Bar Association in Lansing. This directory also includes names and addresses of all attorneys who are members of the Michigan Bar and a great deal of other useful information.

In addition to the above courts, there are four state appellate courts. The first appellate district includes Lenawee, Monroe, and Wayne counties. The second district includes Genesee, Macomb, Oakland, and Shiawassee counties. The third appellate district consists of Allegan, Barry Berrien, Branch, Calhoun, Cass, Hillsdale, Jackson, Kalamazoo, Kent, Livingston, Muskegon, Ottawa, St. Joseph, Van Buren, and Washtenaw counties. The fourth district includes all of the other counties in the state.

Although the focus of this work is on state rather than federal law applicable to MHPs in Michigan, occasional reference is of necessity made to federal decisions interpreting or limiting state law. The citations to these decisions are from the U.S. District Court (F. Supp. or F. Supp. 2d), the U.S. Court of Appeals (F. or F.2d), and the U.S. Supreme Court (U.S., S. Ct., or L.Ed.). As is the case with the reports of state decisions, the number preceding the reporter is the volume number and number following is the page. References to federal legislation appear in the form 26 U.S.C. § 213(a) (1987). This particular citation to the United States Code, the repository of federal legislation, is from title 26, section 213(a), current as of 1987. In addition, there are citations to treatises and law review articles. These references may provide a fuller background of an issue of interest to MHPs.

Finally, although some of the chapters were updated until the manuscript went to press, the reader should consider the entire volume current as of June 1999.

Acknowledgments

A great number of people contributed to the completion of this volume. We would particularly like to thank our chapter reviewers, whose careful and erudite suggestions and criticisms were indispensable. They are Cynthia Botsford, JD, Robert Erard, PhD, Carol Engels, JD, Doris Foley, Lisa Halushka, JD, Carol Holden, PhD, Augustus Hutting, JD, Hon. John Kirkendall, Lonny Loy, CPA, Robert Ludolph, JD, Margo Nichols, JD, Sally Rutzky, JD, Thomas Sparks, JD, David Vore, PhD, and Patricia Watson, PhD. In addition, attorneys Jack Klarr, Merry Rosenberg, and Howard Marderosian were helpful sources of information.

Shelly Wyatt, our constantly optimistic and supportive APA editor, kept the faith that this book would actually get done, which went a long way to ensuring that it did. The hard work of the authors who completed their volumes before us provided a template that made our work much easier. The *Handbook on Liability Law for Michigan Mental Health Professions*, written by Edward B. Goldman, JD, and published by the Michigan Psychological Association, was helpful in many areas.

Finally, we give our thanks for their patience, and our love, to Pete and Laura, two great kids who, even though they have to see two psychologists every day, have turned out just fine.

Legal Credentialing

1.1

Licensure and Regulation of Mental Health Professionals

The Michigan Public Health Code[1] provides for the general licensing procedures and the regulation of most medical and mental health professionals. The licensing or certification and regulation of professionals, including MHPs, is supervised and administered by the Department of Consumer and Industry Services (hereinafter, Department), assisted by a state board for each profession. Licensing of polygraph examiners is regulated by the Occupational Code, which is administered by the Office of Commercial Services. School psychologists and school counselors are regulated by the Department of Education. This chapter will review the laws and administrative regulations that govern the health professions generally and thus are relevant to MHPs. Specific licensing laws for each mental health profession and the regulations (administrative rules) established by corresponding state boards are covered in subsequent chapters in this section. The administrative rules supplement, and in some cases may differ slightly from, the law, so it is important for MHPs to be aware of both.

(A) Licensing

All licenses are issued by the Department after an applicant meets the requirements of a particular profession. The purpose of licensing is to "safeguard the public health and protect the public from incompetence, deception and fraud."[2] Licenses are valid for life

---

1. M.C.L. § 333.1101 et seq.
2. Hill v. Highland Park Gen. Hosp., 263 N.W.2d 362, 80 Mich.App. 334 (1977).

unless revoked or suspended. However, to practice his or her profession, each licensee must also renew the license with the Department periodically. There is a 60-day-grace-period after the expiration of a license. If it is not renewed within the 60 days it is considered null and void, that is, the person is no longer licensed.[3] Health professionals must display their certificate of licensure prominently and in a place visible to the public.[4] In addition, each licensee who is in private practice must give a pamphlet provided by the Department outlining the procedure for filing a complaint to any patient who requests it.[5]

Anyone who is licensed must meet a number of general criteria. They must[6]

1. be at least 18;

2. be of good moral character;

3. have sufficient education or experience as prescribed by the law or rules to promote safe and competent practice and informed consumer choice;

4. have a working knowledge of English;

5. pay the appropriate fees;

6. establish that disciplinary proceedings before a similar board elsewhere are not pending;

7. establish that if sanctions have been imposed by any other state or country that are similar to Michigan's law and rules, they are not in force at the time of the application;

8. disclose where else he or she has ever been licensed;

9. disclose any felony convictions or misdemeanor convictions punishable by a maximum of 2 years of imprisonment or involving the illegal delivery, possession, or use of alcohol or a controlled substance.

A board may also require an applicant to take an examination.

Temporary licenses can be granted to an applicant who has completed all the requirements for licensure except the examination. A temporary license is valid for 18 months and the person must practice only under the supervision of a full licensee. The temporary license must be voided if the applicant fails the examination.[7] Boards can grant limited licenses if it is determined that the limitation is consistent with a person's ability to practice in a

---

3. M.C.L. § 333.16201.
4. M.C.L. § 333.16191.
5. M.C.L. § 333.16239.
6. M.C.L. § 333.16174; M.C.L. § 333.16177.
7. M.C.L. § 333.16181.

safe and competent manner, is necessary to protect the health and safety of patients or clients, or is appropriate to promote the efficient and effective delivery of services.[8] Applicants licensed in another state may receive a Michigan license provided that state's standards are substantially equivalent to those of this state.[9]

(A)(2) Supervision Requirements

For some licenses (see, e.g., chapter 1.5) supervision is required. Supervision is defined as the overseeing or participation in the work of another person by a licensed health professional.[10] Direct communication between the health professional and his or her supervisor must be continuously available, either in person or by telephone or other electronic means. The supervisor must be available on a regularly scheduled basis to review the practice of the supervisee, to provide consultation, to review records, and to further educate the person in the performance of his or her functions.

(B) State Professional Boards

Board members are appointed by the governor, with the advice and consent of the senate.[11] Members of each board are appointed for four-year-terms, and may not serve more than two terms and one partial term.[12] A majority of the board members must be licensed in the profession which that board licenses and the board must include at least one public member.[13] The boards elect a chairperson and are provided with administrative staff by the department. Only a board may create rules and establish standards for education and training, and only a board can approve educational programs that meet its standards.[14]

---

8. M.C.L. § 333.16182.
9. M.C.L. § 333.16186.
10. M.C.L. § 333.16109(2).
11. M.C.L. § 333.16121.
12. M.C.L. § 333.16122.
13. M.C.L. § 333.16125.
14. M.C.L. § 333.16148.

(C) Health Professional Recovery Committee

Michigan provides services for health professionals whose practice is impaired because of substance abuse or mental health problems. These services are provided by a private contractor that has demonstrated its knowledge and experience in providing services to impaired health professionals. The private contractor is overseen by a health professional recovery committee that resides in the department. The committee consists of a health professional member appointed by each board, in consultation with the appropriate professional organizations, and two public members, one of whom has training or experience in the treatment of addictive behavior.[15] Each member serves for 2 years and may not serve more than 2 terms.[16]

(D) Professional Misconduct

A board has grounds for a disciplinary investigation if one or more of the following exists:[17]

1. negligence or failure to exercise due care, including negligent delegation to, or supervision of, employees, whether or not injury results;[18]

2. a condition that impairs, or may impair, the ability to safely and skillfully practice, including

   a. incompetence;

   b. substance abuse;

   c. a mental or physical inability reasonably related to and adversely affecting the ability to practice in a safe and competent manner;

   d. being declared mentally incompetent;

---

15. M.C.L. § 333.16165.
16. M.C.L. § 333.16166.
17. M.C.L. § 333.16221.
18. A physician was liable for a mistaken diagnosis because he negligently failed to make a proper examination of the patient. Johnson v. Borland, 26 N.W.2d 755, 317 Mich. 225 (1947).

    A physician was not negligent in allowing intervals to elapse between visits, where the patient needed no attention during the intervals, but was negligent in doing so when the attention was needed and the frequency of visits was a question for the physician to determine, if he used his ordinary judgment. Fortner v. Koch, 261 N.W. 762, 272 Mich. 273 (1935).

e. conviction of a misdemeanor punishable for a maximum of 2 years, or a misdemeanor involving the illegal delivery, possession, or use of a controlled substance, or a felony;

f. lack of good moral character;

g. conviction of a criminal offense involving criminal sexual conduct;

h. conviction of a misdemeanor or felony involving fraud in obtaining fees;

i. deliberate placement of inaccurate information regarding diagnosis, treatment, or cause of condition in a patient's record or deliberate destruction or alteration of a patient record in order to conceal the licensee's responsibility for the patient's illness, injury, or death;[19]

j. final adverse administrative action taken by a board of another state, by the U.S. military, by the federal government, or by another country; and

k. conviction of a misdemeanor that is reasonably related to or adversely affects the ability to practice in a safe and competent manner.

3. fraud or deceit in obtaining or renewing a license;

4. permitting the use of the license by an unauthorized person;

5. practicing outside the scope of the license;

6. obtaining, selling, prescribing, giving away, or administering drugs unlawfully;

7. false or misleading advertising;

8. dividing fees for referrals or accepting kickbacks;

9. fraud or deceit in obtaining third-party-payments or misrepresenting to a patient;

10. betrayal of a professional confidence;

11. promotion of an unnecessary drug, device, treatment, procedure or service for personal gain or requiring someone to buy or secure such a service from somewhere in which the licensee has a financial interest;

12. failure to report a name or address change within 30 days of the change;

13. a violation of an administrative rule;

14. failure to comply with a subpoena from the board, respond to a complaint or appear at a conference or hearing;

---

19. M.C.L. § 750.492a.

15. failure to pay an installment assessment within 60 days of notification by the appropriate board;

16. failure to meet one or more of the requirements for licensure or registration;[20] and

17. failure to follow the informed consent procedures required by law for women seeking an abortion.[21]

(E) Reporting of Professional Misconduct

If a licensed health professional has knowledge that another licensee has committed a violation, the professional must report the person's name and their conduct to the Department. The report is confidential and the person reporting cannot be held civilly liable for reporting. Failure to report can be a cause of administrative action. This requirement does not apply when a licensee discovers a violation while providing professional services to the person who has transgressed or discovers the violation while serving on a committee that is assigned a professional review function (such as association ethics committees).[22] A licensee who has reasonable cause to believe that another licensee is impaired must also report.[23]

(F) Proceedings in Cases of Professional Misconduct

Anyone can make an allegation of professional misconduct, which is kept confidential, to the Department.[24] The Department then does a preliminary evaluation to determine whether there is a reasonable basis to believe there has been a violation. If so, the Department requests authorization to investigate from the relevant board chair, who must grant or deny authorization within 7 days. While the Department investigates violations, each board has a statutorily established disciplinary subcommittee, which is a standing committee of each board and acts upon the results of the investigation. Within 90 days of initiating an investigation, the Department must do one or more of the following:

---

20. M.C.L. § 333.16174.
21. M.C.L. § 333.17015 and M.C.L. § 333.170515.
22. M.C.L. § 333.16222.
23. M.C.L. § 333.16223.
24. M.C.L. § 333.16231 et seq.

1. issue a formal complaint;
2. conduct a compliance conference;
3. issue a summary suspension of the license, which stops the licensee from practicing;
4. issue a cease-and-desist order;
5. dismiss the complaint; or
6. extend the investigation not more than 30 days.

At any time during the investigation the Department can schedule a compliance conference. This conference can include the licensee, his or her attorney, one or more Department staff members and one member of the board who is not on the disciplinary subcommittee. The conference is an informal procedure designed to try to reach an agreement.[25] If an agreement is reached, the Department submits a written statement outlining the terms, or a stipulation and final order, or a recommendation for dismissal to the disciplinary subcommittee. If no agreement is reached, or the disciplinary subcommittee rejects the recommendation, a hearing before an examiner must be scheduled, though the Department may continue to try to reach a new agreement with the licensee.[26]

When a complaint is made, the licensee must be notified and has 30 days to respond in writing. Failure to respond is treated as an admission of the allegations. Many cases are settled at this early stage. However, if the complaint is not settled, the Department must hold a formal hearing, at which the licensee can be represented by legal counsel. The Department is represented by an assistant attorney general and the hearing is presided over by an administrative law judge known as a hearings examiner. A physical or mental examination of the licensee may be required.[27] After taking testimony,[28] the hearings examiner determines whether there are grounds for action and issues a Proposal for Decision which is sent to the disciplinary subcommittee for consideration. The hearings examiner cannot recommend or impose penalties.[29] Licenses can be summarily suspended after consultation with the board chair on an emergency basis if the public welfare or safety requires it and suspension is mandatory if a licensee has been convicted of a felony, a 2-year-misdemeanor, or

---

25. R 338.1608.
26. M.C.L. § 333.16231a.
27. M.C.L. § 333.16236.
28. In proceedings to revoke a license, a physician has the right to notice, hearing, statement of charge, cross-examination, production of witnesses, and fair determination on evidence. Hanson v. Michigan State Bd. of Registration in Medicine, 236 N.W. 225, 253 Mich. 601, *cert. denied,* 52 S.Ct. 19, 284 U.S. 637 (1931).
29. M.C.L. § 333.16231a.

a misdemeanor involving the illegal delivery, possession, or use of a controlled substance.[30] However, typical procedure is that the board's disciplinary subcommittee reviews the recommended findings of fact and conclusions of law from the hearings examiner. The committee is required to consult with the chairperson of the licensing board. It may request the hearings examiner to take additional testimony or evidence. It may also revise the findings of fact and conclusions as necessary. If a preponderance of the evidence is supported by the facts and conclusions, the disciplinary subcommittee can impose the appropriate sanctions. However, the disciplinary subcommittee has the power to adopt, modify, or reject, in whole or in part, the recommendations of the hearings examiner.[31] All action must be completed within 1 year of the initiation of the investigation.[32] Professionals can request a rehearing or reconsideration if they specifically set forth the reasons for, and the scope of, the requested relief. This rehearing may or may not be granted.[33]

Information pertaining to any investigation or compliance conference is considered confidential. However, the Department does publish a list of the names and addresses of professionals who have been disciplined and must report any disciplinary action to the Department, the commissioner of insurance, the state and federal agencies responsible for fiscal administration of federal health care programs, and the appropriate professional associations. A professional whose license has been revoked or suspended must give notice of this to each patient who contacts him or her for service during the revocation or suspension, and must notify each patient seen during the 120 days immediately preceding the disciplinary action.[34] Any consultants or expert witnesses who assist the Department in an investigation or hearing have immunity from damages in any suit.

(G) Penalties for Professional Misconduct

The penalties that may be imposed by the disciplinary subcommittee are probation, limitation, suspension or revocation of the license, restitution, community service, or a fine of up to $250,000. The licensee may also be required to successfully complete an

---

30. M.C.L. § 333.16233.
31. R 338.1630.
32. M.C.L. § 333.16237.
33. R 338.1633.
34. M.C.L. § 333.16241.

educational or training program, a treatment program, and/or a mental, physical, or professional competence examination.[35] Licenses can be reinstated if, after a hearing, the board is satisfied by clear and convincing evidence that the person is of good moral character, is able to practice with reasonable skill and safety, and should be permitted in the public interest to resume practice. The professional is placed on probation for 1 year under whatever conditions are set by the board. Persons whose license has been revoked cannot apply for reinstatement for 5 years and must retake the licensing examination.[36]

Professionals who are impaired because of mental illness or substance abuse problems may be accepted into the health professional recovery program providing they acknowledge their impairment, and voluntarily withdraw from, or limit the scope of, their practice as deemed necessary by the health professional recovery committee, and agree to participate in a treatment plan.[37]

(H) Unauthorized Practice of a Profession

Anyone not authorized to practice a profession who does practice or holds him- or herself out as being able to practice is guilty of a felony.[38] Anyone who practices a profession when his or her license is suspended or revoked or who aids an unlicensed person to practice a profession, is also guilty of a felony. Anyone not authorized who uses a title regulated by the Department is guilty of a misdemeanor.[39]

---

35. M.C.L. § 333.16226.
36. M.C.L. § 333.16247.
37. M.C.L. § 333.16170.
38. M.C.L. 333.16294.
39. M.C.L. § 333.16296.

1.2

Licensure and Regulation of Psychiatrists

The licensure and regulation of psychiatrists is governed by statutory law[1] and administrative rules that establish[2] a State Board of Medicine, establish qualifications and procedures for the licensure of physicians, define the practice of medicine, regulate the conduct of physicians, and recommend sanctions for violations of the statute. Physicians are also regulated by the general licensing law that governs all boards and professions (see chapter 1.1). In Michigan, physicians who are osteopathic physicians are regulated by the Board of Osteopathic Medicine and Surgery.[3] There is no separate licensure provision pertaining to the practice of psychiatry; the law is a generic one that regulates the practice of medicine or osteopathic medicine without regard to specialty. Only a person licensed under this law may practice medicine or use the title *physician*. Physician assistants are also regulated under this law.

(A) Board of Medicine

A state Board of Medicine is a part of the Department of Consumer and Industry Services and exists under the auspices of that Department. The Board of Medicine is composed of 19 members: 10 physicians, 1 physician assistant, and 8 public members. A

---

1. M.C.L. § 333.17011 et seq.
2. R 338.2301 et seq.
3. M.C.L. § 333.17501 et seq.; R 338.101 et seq.

physician member must have practiced for at least 2 years immediately prior to his or her appointment.[4]

B) Licensure

To qualify for a full license as a physician, an applicant must have completed the requirements for a degree in medicine and completed a period of postgraduate education to attain proficiency.[5] Administrative regulations developed by the Board further define the requirements of a physician.[6] The degree in medicine must be from a program that is not less than 130 weeks and does not award credit for correspondence courses. Minimum core curriculum and postgraduate training requirements are listed in the rules. Postgraduate clinical training programs must be at least 2 years in duration and accredited by an organization approved by the Board. The Board accepts the 3-part National Board of Medical Examiners Examination (NBME), the 2-part Federal Licensing Exam (FLEX), and the 3-part U.S. Federation of State Medical Boards Exam (USMLE). Passing scores on the FLEX and the USMLE are 75% for each part.[7]

B)(1) Exceptions to Licensing

An educational limited license can be granted for graduates of medical school who are still in training. The educational limited license requires practice and training only in a hospital or institution approved for training by the Board and is renewable for not more than 5 years.[8] A clinical academic limited license can be granted to a person who has graduated from an approved medical school and has been appointed to a teaching or research position in an academic institution. This person can practice only under the supervision of a fully licensed physician.[9]

B)(2) Licensure of Foreign Medical School Graduates

Persons who have graduated from a medical school outside the United States or Canada may be granted a license if they have[10]

1. been in practice no more than 10 years since completing their degree;

---

4. M.C.L. § 333.17021.
5. M.C.L. § 333.17031.
6. R 338.2301 et seq.
7. R 338.2314.
8. M.C.L. § 333.17012.
9. M.C.L. § 333.17030, R 338.2327a.
10. M.C.L. § 333.17501 et seq.; R 338.101 et seq.

2. completed not less than 3 years of postgraduate clinical training at an institution that has an affiliation with a medical school that is listed in the directory published by the World Health Organization; and

3. received a passing score on Board-approved examinations.

(B)(3) Continuing Medical Education Requirements

The rules require that in order to renew his or her license, the physician must have attended 150 hours of continuing education credit in the 3 years prior to renewal in courses approved by the Board.[11]

(C) Regulation

The regulation of and disciplinary procedures for all health professionals covered under the Michigan Occupational Health Code are the same (see chapter 1.1).

---

11. R 338.2371.

1.3

Licensure and Regulation of Psychiatric Nurses

The licensure and regulation of psychiatric nurses is governed by statutory law[1] that establishes a State Board of Nursing, defines the practice of nursing, establishes qualifications and procedures for the licensure of registered professional nurses and nurse practitioners, establishes exceptions to licensure, and regulates the conduct of licensed nurses. In addition, the Board promulgates rules and regulations to carry out the provisions of the law.[2] Nurses are also regulated by the general licensing law that governs all boards and professions (see chapter 1.1). There is no separate licensure pertaining to the practice of psychiatric nursing; the law is a generic one that regulates the practice of nursing without regard to specialty.[3]

A) Board of Nursing

The State Board of Nursing is a part of the Department of Consumer and Industry Services and exists under its auspices. The Board is composed of 23 members: 9 registered nurses, 1 nurse midwife, 1 nurse anesthetist, 1 nurse practitioner, 3 licensed practical nurses, and 8 public members.[4]

---

1. M.C.L. § 333.17201 et seq.
2. R 338.10101 et seq.
3. This law also pertains to licensed practical nursing, but this discussion is limited to professional nursing because psychiatric nurses will have the additional education required by the latter category.
4. M.C.L. § 333.17221.

(B) Licensure

In addition to the requirements of the general licensing law (see chapter 1.1), to qualify for a license as a registered professional nurse, an applicant must file an application, establish that he or she has completed a registered nurse program acceptable to the Board and pass the National Council of State Boards of Nursing (NCLEX-RN) examination with a converted score of not less than 75.[5]

To qualify for a specialty certification as a nurse practitioner, the person must be a registered nurse who[6]

1. holds a current valid Michigan license;

2. has a B.A. or higher degree in nursing;

3. submits an application and required fee;

4. successfully completes a formal advanced program for nurse practitioners. The program must consist of at least 120 hours or 30% didactic training and 360 hours or 30% supervised clinical experience and must last a minimum of 1 academic year or 9 months.

5. meet the advanced practice certification standards of the American Nurses Credentialing Center, plus other relevant advanced certification requirements of the various nursing subspecialties.

(B)(1) Continuing Education Requirements

Registered nurses must complete at least 25 hours of continuing education in the 2 years prior to renewing their licenses. The requirement may be completed by attending, reading, or listening to educational programs, publishing articles or chapters in nursing or health care journals, and completing a national nursing specialty examination.[7]

(B)(2) Exceptions to Licensing

Nurses who are licensed in another state or country can be licensed by endorsement in Michigan as long as they have completed an educational program acceptable to the Board and can establish that they achieved an appropriate passing score on the

---

5. R 338.10204.
6. R 338.10404.
7. R 338.1405.

NCLEX-RN or, in the case of a practical nurse, the NCLEX-PN examination.[8]

(C) Regulation

The regulation of and disciplinary procedures for all health professionals covered under the Michigan Occupational Health Code are the same (see chapter 1.1).

---

8. R 338.10206. Passing scores are: NCLEX-RN—1600 if exam taken between 7/13/82 and 2/14/89; 75 if exam taken after 2/14/89. NCLEX-PN—350 if exam taken between 10/19/82 and 10/18/88; 75 if taken after 10/18/88. Those licensed before 1982 do not have to provide exam scores.

1.4

Licensure and Regulation of Psychologists

The licensure and regulation of psychologists is governed by statutory law[1] that establishes a State Board of Psychology, defines the practice of psychology, establishes qualifications and procedures for the licensure of psychologists, establishes exceptions to licensure, regulates the conduct of licensed psychologists, and provides for administrative hearings. In addition, the Board promulgates rules and regulations to carry out the provisions of the statute.[2] Psychologists are also regulated by the general licensing law that governs all boards and professions (see chapter 1.1).

(A) Board of Psychology

The state Board of Psychology is a part of the Department of Consumer and Industry Services. The Board is composed of 9 members: 5 psychologists, at least 1 of whom must be a nondoctoral psychologist, and 4 public members.[3]

(B) Licensure

In addition to the general requirements for the licensure of professionals (see chapter 1.1), applicants for a full license as a psychologist must have received a doctoral degree in psychology or a

1. M.C.L. § 333.18201 et seq.
2. R 338.2501 et seq.
3. M.C.L. § 333.18221.

closely related field, from an institution approved by the Board, and must have not less than 2 years postdoctoral experience in the practice of psychology in an organized health care setting.[4] In addition, the administrative rules require that applicants must[5]

1. file an application with the Department and pay a fee;

2. demonstrate a working knowledge of the English language;

3. pass a written examination;[6]

4. complete an internship of at least 2000 hours in an organized health care setting[7] which is supervised by a psychologist licensed at the independent practice level; and

5. complete at least 2 years (not less than 4000 hours) of postdoctoral experience in an organized health care setting.

The doctoral degree must be a result of an integrated, organized sequence of study that includes instruction in research design and methodology, statistics, psychometrics, and scientific and professional ethics and standards. Seventy-five percent of the hours must be psychological in content.[8]

Though the law allows the Board to require continuing education for license renewal, and mandates courses in pain and symptom management, there are no administrative rules specifying such requirements.[9] Thus, psychologists currently have no continuing education requirement in Michigan.

(B)(1) Exceptions to Licensing

The law does not restrict the activities and services of all persons who call themselves psychologists. Nothing in the law may be interpreted to affect or prevent[10]

1. the use of the title *psychologist* by a person who holds a doctoral degree in psychology from a regionally accredited college or university;

---

4. M.C.L. § 333.18223.
5. R 338.2504.
6. Currently, the Board requires a score of at least 70% on the Examination for Professional Practice in Psychology (EPPP) in order to receive a passing grade.
7. This is defined by R 338.2501 as an organized governmental entity, nonprofit organization, or private agency engaged in the delivery of health care services. It must provide an opportunity for continuous professional interaction and collaboration with other disciplines, for the use of a variety of theories, and for working with a broad range of populations and techniques.
8. R 338.2506.
9. M.C.L. § 333.18233.
10. M.C.L. § 333.18214.

2. the use of the title *school psychologist* by a person approved by the state Department of Education who is employed as such in an elementary or secondary school;

3. a person employed by a college or university from doing research in or teaching psychology;

4. a person who is certified, licensed, registered, or otherwise statutorially recognized (e.g., lawyers, social workers, school counselors) from practicing his or her profession; and

5. persons such as the clergy, educators, or professional counselors whose practice may include preventative, counseling, or behavior modification techniques from practicing their profession consistent with the training and code of ethics for the respective profession.

(C) Regulation

The regulation of and disciplinary procedures for all health professionals covered under the Michigan Occupational Health Code are the same (see chapter 1.1).

(D) Advertising

Licensed psychologists are permitted to advertise unless the advertising is false and misleading.[11] False and misleading advertising is defined as advertising that is inaccurate, exaggerated, deceptive, unfair, fails to reveal a material fact that tends to mislead the public, intended or likely to create unjustified expectations, or likely to cause confusion or misunderstanding by the public. Licensees are responsible for ensuring that their advertising is not in conflict with these rules.

---

11. R 338.2514.

1.5

Subdoctoral Psychologists

In Michigan, certain persons who do not hold the doctorate may receive limited licenses, and typically are referred to as *limited license psychologists*. These persons are regulated by the state Board of Psychology,[1] which is a part of the Department of Consumer and Industry Services. The Board establishes qualifications and procedures for limited licensure, establishes exceptions to licensure, and regulates the conduct of limited license psychologists. In addition, the Board promulgates administrative rules and regulations to carry out the provisions of the statute.[2] Limited license psychologists are also regulated by the general licensing law that governs all boards and professionals (see chapter 1.1). Their licenses are limited because they may practice only under the supervision of a fully licensed psychologist and may not advertise their services in such a manner as to lead the public to believe that they are engaging in the practice of psychology.[3] There is, however, an exception to this in that persons who hold a limited license and are employed by governmental entities or nonprofit agencies are not required to be supervised by a licensed psychologist.[4] There are several types of limited licenses granted by the Board.

---

1. M.C.L. § 333.18201.
2. R 338.2501 et seq.
3. M.C.L. § 333.18223.
4. 5550 Op. Att'y. Gen. 400 (1979).

(A) Limited License Psychologist

Applicants for this license must have a master's degree in psychology from a regionally accredited institution approved by the Board and 1 year of supervised post-master's experience in an organized health care setting or other setting approved by the Board.[5] The administrative rules add that the applicant must have at least one course in assessment and one course in treatment and 75% of the course work must be primarily psychological in content. He or she must also have completed a practicum of not less than 500 hours of psychological work and have had one year (2000 hours) of post-master's experience, accumulated at not less than 16, or more than 40, hours per week. The applicant must demonstrate that he or she is supervised by a psychologist licensed at the independent practice level. If a fully licensed psychologist is not available, the applicant may petition the Board to accept supervision by a limited license psychologist with not less than 3 years (6000 hours) of post-master's experience, or another individual approved by the Board.[6]

(B) Temporary Limited License for Post-Master's Degree Experience

The Board may issue a 2-year temporary limited license to an applicant who has completed the educational and training requirements for the master's degree and has made appropriate arrangements for supervision by a psychologist.[7]

(C) Limited License for Postdoctoral Training

This limited license, also known as the *Rule 10* license, can be granted for those persons who have received the doctoral degree and are pursuing postdoctoral training and experience to fulfill the requirements of full licensure.[8] They must be supervised on a regular, weekly, face-to face basis, reviewing all active work functions and records.

---

5. M.C.L. § 333.18223.
6. R 338.2507.
7. R 338.2507a.
8. R 338.2510.

1.6

Certification and Regulation of Social Workers

In Michigan, social workers are not licensed, but are certified to practice at several levels.

(A) Board of Examiners for Social Workers

Social workers are regulated by statutory law that establishes a Board of Examiners for Social Workers, located within the Department of Consumer and Industry Service and are regulated by the Public Health Code. The law defines terms contained within the act, and establishes qualifications and procedures for certification[1] and is itself further defined by administrative rules.[2] Social workers are also regulated by the general licensing law (see chapter 1.1)

(B) Certification

There are three levels of certification for social workers. Each level requires experience that must be supervised by a certified social worker.[3]

---

1. M.C.L. § 339.1601 et seq.
2. R 338.2901-338.2915.
3. R 338.2906a.

(B)(1) Social Work Technician

A person can be registered as a social work technician if he or she[4]

1. has had 1 year of acceptable social work experience, or has successfully completed 2 years of college;
2. is employed in the practice of social work (waived if the person has 2000 hours of service with a recognized agency or has an associate degree in social work from an approved college that includes supervised fieldwork); and
3. is of good moral character.

Qualifying experience includes any of the following:[5]

1. interviewing clients to obtain data and provide information about available services and providing specific assistance to help people use community resources; and
2. conducting case finding activities in the community and encouraging and providing linkages to available services.

(B)(2) Social Worker

A person can be registered as a social worker if he or she[6]

1. has a baccalaureate degree;
2. has 2 or more years of acceptable social work experience under the supervision of a certified social worker, or is enrolled in social work graduate school, or has a master's degree from an accredited school of social work, or has 4000 hours of service with a recognized agency;
3. is employed in the practice of social work or enrolled in a social work graduate school (waived if the person has a bachelor's or master's degree from an accredited social work school); and
4. is of good moral character.

Qualifying experience includes any of the following:

1. social casework, assessment, planning, and intervention with individuals, couples, families, or groups to enhance or restore the capacity for social functioning;
2. case management of health and human services;
3. providing information and referring people to resources and monitoring the results; and

---

4. M.C.L. § 339.1604.
5. R 338.2906a.
6. M.C.L. § 339.1605.

4. planning and collaborating with communities, organizations, or groups to improve their social or health services.

(B)(3) Certified Social Worker

A person can be registered as a certified social worker[7] if he or she has met the requirements for social worker, has 2 or more years of acceptable social work experience under the supervision of a certified social worker, and has a master's degree from an accredited school of social work.

Qualifying experience means either of the following:

1. psychosocial assessment, diagnosis, or treatment of mental, emotional, and behavioral disorders or planning and intervention with individuals, couples, families, or groups by providing counseling, psychotherapy, social casework, or social group work; or
2. helping communities, organizations, or groups improve their social or health services by using community organization techniques.

(C) Regulation

(C)(1) Unlawful or Prohibited Practices

There are a number of actions that may subject a social worker to disciplinary action. These include[8]

1. violating the privileged communication part of the social work regulation law;[9]
2. paying a gratuity to anyone in return for recommending a client;
3. splitting a fee;
4. immoral conduct;
5. willful or negligent failure to provide or arrange for continuity of necessary service;
6. being convicted of a sexual offense;
7. refusing to provide professional services based on the person's race, creed, color, national origin, age, or sex;
8. practicing while registration is suspended; and
9. misleading advertising.

---

7. M.C.L. § 339.1606.
8. R 338.2909.
9. M.C.L. § 339.1610.

Certification and Regulation of School Psychologists

The Michigan Department of Education certifies persons in school psychology who are employed in primary and secondary school settings.[1] The Department also promulgates rules and regulations to carry out the provisions of the statute.[2] The certification is entirely independent of the Board of Psychology (see chapter 1.4). Only a person holding certification may call him- or herself a school psychologist.

(A) Certification

To receive a preliminary certificate, an applicant must have completed a minimum of 45 graduate semester hours in an approved program and completed at least a 600 hour supervised internship with school-age pupils, 300 of which must be in a school setting under the supervision of a certified school psychologist. This certificate is valid for 3 years during which the person must be supervised by a fully certified school psychologist.[3]

To be fully certified, an applicant must[4]

1. hold a valid preliminary certificate;

2. have a specialist's degree or its equivalent from an approved program;

---

1. M.C.L. § 380.1251.
2. R 380.201.
3. R 380.204.
4. R 380.206.

3. have completed a minimum of 15 graduate hours, including an internship, over and above the 45 hours required for preliminary certification;

4. have completed 1 year of successful employment as a school psychologist supervised by a certified school psychologist; and

5. be recommended by one's educational program as meeting the competencies required for a school psychologist.[5]

B) Responsibilities

The role of a school psychologist includes[6]

1. providing school psychological services to any pupil;

2. collaborating with staff in planning education interventions, curriculum, behavioral management, and teaching strategies;

3. consulting, counseling, and collaborating with pupils, parents, school personnel, and appropriate outside personnel regarding mental health, behavioral, and educational concerns using psychological principle;

4. providing psychological evaluations and reports for pupils referred for special education programs;

5. performing systematic direct observations of pupils;

6. administering tests that may include intelligence, achievement, personality, adaptive behavior, and perceptual-motor tests;

7. interpreting psychological and other diagnostic data for professionals, parents, pupils, and appropriate others; and

8. collaborating in program planning and evaluation services for decision-making purposes.

---

5. R 380.208.
6. R 380.203.

1.8

Certification of School Social Workers and School Counselors

The Department of Education certifies school social workers.[1] Their practice is limited to the school setting. The Department also promulgates administrative rules and regulations to carry out the provisions of the statute.[2]

(A) School Social Workers

(A)(1) Certification

In order to be certified as a school social worker, a person must have completed a master's degree in social work from a program approved by the Board and completed 1 year of employment as a school social worker supervised by a fully certified school social worker. The MSW program must be at least 2 years and include at least a 500-hour supervised practicum.[3]

(A)(2) Responsibilities

The role of a school social worker includes[4]

1. identifying problems and situations interfering with the ability of children to make optimal use of the educational experience;

---

1. M.C.L. § 380.6.
2. R 340.1011 et seq.
3. R 340.1012.
4. R 340.1011.

2. providing a problem-solving service to children and their families through individual, group, and community social work methods;

3. serving as a liaison between the school, home, and community to build and maintain positive relationships;

4. coordinating and developing resources within and outside the school for children, families, and school personnel;

5. collaborating with principals, teachers, and other school personnel to improve the use of existing programs and procedures, as well as developing new ones;

6. coordinating or serving as a member of diagnostic and educational planning and placement committees and providing biological, psychological, and sociological assessment information relating to planning for children with adjustment problems;

7. providing comprehensive diagnostic evaluations of children suspected of being emotionally impaired;

8. serving as a consultant to teachers;

9. providing therapy and intervention services for emotionally impaired children;

10. participating with staff in altering situations adversely affecting the personal, social-emotional, and academic development of children; and

11. conducting in-service education for staff.

B) School Counselors

)(1) Certification

Teachers with a current valid Michigan teaching certificate can be endorsed as school counselors at either the elementary or secondary level. They must have successfully completed a Board approved counselor education program of not less than 18 semester hours which must include the areas of guidance services, individual and group analysis, guidance information, counseling theory and practice, evaluation, and also must include a supervised experience.[5]

)(2) Responsibilities

The role of school counselor means that the counselor performs specialized activities when (a) assisting students to identify, plan, and attain those goals consistent with their aptitudes, needs,

---

5. R 390.1303.

abilities, and interests; (b) coordinating and integrating services directly related to the mental, physical, social, and emotional well-being of students; and (c) consulting with parents, teachers, and other specialists regarding pupil growth, learning, and development.[6]

---

6. R 390.1301.

1.9

Licensure and Regulation of Marriage and Family Therapists

The state Board of Marriage and Family Therapy regulates the practice and use of the professional title *marriage and family therapist* by prescribing education, experience, and skills.[1] MHPs must obtain licensure to use the titles of *marriage and family therapist, licensed marriage counselor,* or *L.M.F.T.* In addition, the Board promulgates rules and regulations to carry out the provisions of the statute. Marriage and family therapists are also regulated by the general licensing law that governs all boards and professions (see chapter 1.1).

A) Board of Marriage and Family Therapy

The Board is a part of the Department of Consumer and Industry Services and consists of 9 members: 6 licensed marriage and family therapists and 3 public members.[2]

B) Licensure

To be licensed as a professional marriage and family therapist, a person must either have a master's degree or higher from an accredited training program in marriage and family therapy approved by the Board or have a master's degree or higher from an

---

1. M.C.L. § 333.16901 et seq.
2. M.C.L. § 333.16907.

approved institution and have completed at least 6 semester hours or 9 quarter hours each in family studies, family therapy methodology, and human development, personality theory, or psychopathology; 2 semester hours or 3 quarter hours in ethics, law, and standard of professional practice, and 2 semester hours or 3 quarter hours in research.[3] He or she must also meet Board criteria for supervised client contact hours, as well as supervision time.

(B)(1) Exceptions to Licensure

Nothing in the law may be interpreted to limit or prevent people engaged in social work, those employed as members of the clergy who charge no fee, those fully licensed in the practice of psychology or psychiatry, or any other statutorily regulated profession or occupation to provide services to families or couples, as long as they do not hold themselves out to be licensed marriage and family therapists and are practicing consistent with the requirements of their profession or occupation.[4]

(C) Regulation

The regulation of and disciplinary procedures for all health professionals covered under the Michigan Occupational Health Code are the same (see chapter 1.1).

---

3. M.C.L. § 333.16909.
4. M.C.L. § 333.16905.

1.10

Licensure and Regulation of Professional Counselors

The licensure and regulation of professional counselors is governed by statutory law[1] that establishes a state Board of Counseling, defines the practice of counseling, establishes qualifications and procedures for licensing, and regulates the conduct of licensed counselors. In addition, the Board promulgates administrative rules and regulations to carry out the provisions of the statute.[2] Professional counselors are also regulated by the general licensing law that governs all boards and professions (see chapter 1.1).

A) Board of Counseling

The state Board of Counseling is a part of the Department of Consumer and Industry Services. The Board consists of 11 members: 6 members who are practicing counselors, 3 of whom are engaged primarily in practice, 2 of whom are primarily teachers or researchers, and 1 of whom is primarily an administrator, 4 public members, and 1 member who must be a statutorily regulated mental health professional such as a psychologist, social worker, or psychiatrist.[3]

---

1. M.C.L. § 333.18101 et seq.
2. R 338.1751 et seq.
3. M.C.L. § 333.18103.

(B) Licensure

To be licensed as a professional counselor, a person must be at least 21 years old, have a master's or doctoral degree in counseling or student personnel work from a Board approved program, and have at least 2 years experience under the supervision of a licensed professional counselor (unless they have completed 30 hours beyond the master's degree, in which case the supervised experience may be reduced to 1 year.)[4] A person may receive a limited license if he or she has graduated from a master's or doctoral program and practices only under the supervision of a fully licensed professional counselor. Administrative rules also require that if an applicant for full licensure has not been licensed in another state before October 1, 1994, he or she must pass either the National Counselor Examination or the Rehabilitation Counselor Examination with a fine converted score of at least 75%.[5] Counselor training programs must consist of at least 48 semester hours or 72 quarter hours and include an internship of at least 600 hours.

By law, licensees must provide a professional disclosure statement to all prospective clients before beginning counseling services.[6] The statement must include the licensee's name, address, and phone number, a description of his or her practice, a description of his or her education and experience, a fee schedule and the address and telephone number of the Department of Consumer and Industry Services.

(B)(1) Exceptions to Licensing

Nothing in the law may be interpreted to limit or prevent a person from practicing a statutorily regulated profession that includes counseling as part of the services provided by that profession.[7] Also, the law does not apply to

1. ordained clergy if counseling is incidental to his or her religious duties and he or she does not hold him- or herself out to be a counselor;

2. people who volunteer for public or private nonprofit organizations if they are approved by that organization;

3. people who are employed by or volunteer at programs licensed by the Office of Substance Abuse Services; and

---

4. M.C.L. § 333.18107.
5. R 338.1752.
6. M.C.L. § 333.18113.
7. M.C.L. § 333.18155.

4. people in fields such as human resource or organizational development whose practice may include counseling procedures.

The law also allows the use of the word *counselor* by unlicensed people, as long as they do not hold themselves out as licensed or professional counselors.

(C) Regulation

The regulation of and disciplinary procedures for all health professionals covered under the Michigan Occupational Health Code are the same (see chapter 1.1).

1.11

Licensure and Regulation of Hypnotists

In some states, the law regulates hypnosis and the professional title *hypnotist* by prescribing education, experience, and skills. In these states, MHPs would have to obtain certification to use the title *hypnotist*. Michigan does not license or certify hypnotists. However the use of hypnotically induced testimony in the court-room is regulated (see chapter 6.8).

1.12

Licensure and Regulation of Polygraph Examiners

The Forensic Polygraph Examiners Act and its administrative rules regulate polygraph examinations and the professional title *polygraph examiner* by prescribing education, experience, and skills. MHPs must obtain licensure to use the title *polygraph examiner*. An examiner is any person, other than an intern, who purports to or represents that he or she can or does offer the services of detecting deception, verifying truthfulness, or providing a diagnostic opinion of such matters by using an instrument or mechanical device to measure or record a person's bodily responses or psychophysiological activities.[1] The use of polygraph evidence in court, however, is strictly limited by case law (see chapter 6.3).

No one who uses polygraph equipment or holds themselves out to be a polygraph examiner may do so without a license.[2]

(A) Board of Forensic Polygraph Examiners

A state Board of Forensic Polygraph Examiners is appointed by the governor with the advice and consent of the senate. The Board is located within the Department of State Police. It consists of five members, at least two of whom are public examiners who are licensed and employed in a governmental law enforcement

---

1. M.C.L. § 338.1703.
2. M.C.L. § 338.1708.

agency, two of whom are licensed private examiners, and one of whom is a member of the public at large.[3]

(B) Licensure

There are two types of licenses that can be obtained.[4] A public examiner performs polygraph examinations in his or her official capacity as a salaried employee of a state, county, or local agency. A private examiner performs polygraph examinations in any capacity other than a public examiner. To qualify for either license as a forensic polygraph examiner, an applicant must[5]

1. file an application and pay a fee of $100 if filing for a private license or $25 if filing for a public license;[6]
2. be at least 18 years of age;
3. be a United States citizen;
4. not have been sentenced for the commission of a felony within 5 years before the application;
5. provide a complete set of fingerprints in duplicate, and any verification of their authenticity that the Board may require;
6. not have had a previous license refused, revoked, suspended, or otherwise invalidated;
7. satisfy the Board that no substantial derogatory information exists regarding his or her loyalty, honesty, or integrity that would justify denying a license;
8. have lived in Michigan for at least 6 months immediately prior to the date of application, or been eligible to apply for an absentee ballot during those 6 months;
9. have passed a written and oral qualifying examination;[7] and
10. have either satisfactorily completed an internship program approved by the Board or satisfied the Board that they have suitable equivalent experience.

In meeting the professional education requirement, a licensed forensic polygraph examiner must have graduated with at least a baccalaureate degree from an accredited college or university and have an academic major or two minors that are suitable for and related to specialization as an examiner. This includes not less than 15 hours of social or behavioral sciences.[8]

---

3. M.C.L. § 338.1705.
4. M.C.L. § 338.1703.
5. M.C.L. § 338.1710.
6. M.C.L. § 338.1715. Renewal fees are $50 for private examiners and $25 for public examiners.
7. R 338.9013.
8. R 338.9012.

A person who fulfills the basic requirements for licensure and is engaged in an approved internship program that provides academic and practical training may qualify for an intern's license.[9] To qualify to sit for the examiner's licensing examination, the intern must personally administer at least 200 polygraph examinations (50 of which must be specific issue examinations) that must be supervised by an approved supervisor, and maintain a record of each examination.[10] If not engaged in an internship, the applicant must satisfy the Board that he or she has training or experience equivalent to an internship by showing that he or she has at least 1 year experience conducting examinations after completing an accredited program, has completed school, and has performed at least 200 polygraph examinations, 50 of which must be about a specific issue or question.[11]

(C) Regulation

(C)(1) Unlawful or Prohibited Practices

There are a number of actions that may subject a forensic polygraph examiner to disciplinary action. These include[12]

1. misstating application information;
2. being convicted of a felony, or a misdemeanor punishable by more than 1 year of incarceration or involving moral turpitude;
3. making a false promise or falsely advertising for the purpose of obtaining business;
4. showing unworthiness or incompetency in a manner so as to affect the public interest;
5. allowing his or her license to be used by an unlicensed person;
6. aiding or abetting someone in violating the licensing law;
7. being judged mentally ill, mentally deficient, or in need of mental treatment;
8. failing to provide information requested for adjudication to the Board;
9. asking test questions about the examinee's sexual practices, union, political, or religious affiliations, or marital relationship unless the questions bear on the examination;

---

9. M.C.L. § 338.1711.
10. R 338.9006.
11. R 338.9009.
12. M.C.L. § 388.1719.

10. failing to inform the examinee of all of the specific question areas to be explored prior to actually exploring them;

11. conducting an examination without telling the examinee all of the following:

    a. they have the right to refuse or accept the examination;

    b. they cannot be discharged from or denied employment solely because they refuse or accept the examination;

    c. they have the right to stop the examination at any time;

    d. they are not required to answer any questions or give any information; and

    e. that the information they give could be used against them, or made available to the party requesting the examination, unless otherwise specified and agreed to in writing; and

12. conducting an examination that he or she knew violated the Polygraph Protection Act of 1981 (see chapter 6.3).

(C)(2) Investigations by the Board

The Board must investigate any written complaint that sets forth facts which if proven would constitute grounds for denial, suspension, or revocation of a license.[13] If it is determined that the complaint has merit, a hearing for the purpose of determining whether the licensee may hold the license is held. The Board must notify the licensee in writing of the nature of the charges and the date of the hearing at least 20 days before the hearing. The licensee and/or his or her counsel may testify and present evidence at the hearing, which is closed to the public unless the licensee requests otherwise. If action is taken, the licensee must be notified and may move for a rehearing within 20 days of notification.[14]

(C)(3) Penalties for Violations

Violation of the Polygraph Protection Act is a misdemeanor punishable by a fine of not more than $1000 or 90 days in jail, or both. Falsely holding oneself out as being or ever having been a forensic polygraph examiner is also a misdemeanor.[15] Penalties for violating the Forensic Polygraph Examiners Act include suspension, revocation, or denial of a license.

---

13. M.C.L. § 338.1720.
14. M.C.L. § 338.1723.
15. M.C.L. § 338.1729.

1.13

Regulation of Unlicensed Mental Health Professionals

The Public Health Code,[1] while prohibiting an unlicensed person from engaging in activities that are part of the practice of a profession, does not appear "to be a prohibition against the unlicensed use of counseling methods, principles or procedures *per se*." Instead, the law appears to prohibit the use of counseling methods only if the person holds him- or herself out to be *licensed* or *professional*.[2] It also makes some specific exceptions, allowing several parties to use the word *counselor*. These include clergy, volunteers for non-profit organizations, providers of substance abuse services, and people who use counseling methods and principles, such as human resources or organizational development professionals.[3] However, the unlicensed practice of mental health services is clearly not encouraged.

---

1. M.C.L. § 333.18101 et seq.
2. 6677 Op. Att'y. Gen. 18 (1991).
3. M.C.L. § 333.18115.

1.14

Sunset of Credentialing Agencies

A sunset law is the means by which a legislature reviews and revises most facets of state government from entire departments to small commissions. Such laws work by automatically terminating the authority of an agency to continue to operate unless the legislature, after a mandatory review of the entity's past work, extends the termination date. Michigan does not have such a law.

Business Matters

2.1

Sole Proprietorships

Mental health professionals who practice alone and without any formal organization are *sole proprietors*. Unlike partnerships and professional corporations (see chapters 2.2 and 2.3), there is no law directly regulating this type of business entity. Rather, sole proprietors must abide only by the laws regulating businesses in general. The sole proprietor is personally liable for any torts he or she commits in the course of business.

Professional Corporations

Mental health professionals who do not work for an employer typically organize their business in one of three forms: sole proprietorship (see chapter 2.1), partnership (see chapter 2.3), or professional corporation (PC).[1] The value of the professional corporation is that it offers many of the tax, legal, and practice benefits of regular incorporation.[2] Note that if MHPs wish to incorporate, they must do so under the PC law because professionals are not permitted to incorporate their practice under regular incorporation laws.

(A) Benefits of Incorporation

There are three main benefits to MHPs incorporating their practices. First, there are certain tax deductions available only to a PC (e.g., for the purchase of health insurance, death benefits, and certain retirement plans). Second, while MHPs are usually considered fully liable for their and their direct employees' negligence or malpractice, where there is more than one shareholder (MHP) in the corporation they are typically protected against all other corporate liabilities. Third, meeting the requisites of corporation law, such as holding shareholder meetings and issuing

---

1. Because the law discussed in this chapter applies to many types of professionals, this section can only serve as an introduction rather than a comprehensive analysis.
2. Michael L. Stefani, *Incorporating Professionals*, 58 MICH. B.J. 168 (1979).

regular reports, forces professionals to become more sensitive to the business aspects of their practice.[3]

B) Incorporation and Operation Procedures

A professional corporation provides one or more professional services to the public. As such, the services, with the exception of secretaries, bookkeepers, technicians, and assistants,[4] must be performed by professionals who are duly licensed or otherwise legally authorized to perform them.[5] Corporate shareholders must be licensed to render the same professional services that the PC provides.[6]

PC's are under the supervision of the Department of Commerce.[7] The general incorporation law controls where there is no contrary provision in the PC law.[8] In order to incorporate, the shareholders must file articles of incorporation with the Department of Commerce, which provides a certificate of incorporation.[9] The corporation must establish a board of directors, elect officers, and adopt bylaws.[10] A corporation must file an annual financial report within 4 months of the end of its fiscal year.[11] After the first year of incorporation, the corporation must also file an annual report no later than May 15 of each year.[12]

C) Liability and Accountability

A professional corporation in Michigan differs from a regular corporation in one critical way: each shareholder, employee, or agent is personally and fully liable and accountable, as is any person under his or her direct supervision. This means that individual shareholders are liable for their own acts, and acts of their subordinates, to the same degree as if engaged in an individual

---

3. For more information on whether to incorporate and the particular benefits and liabilities involved, MHPs should seek the advice of a tax consultant and a business planning attorney.
4. M.C.L. § 450.225.
5. There does not appear to be any restriction as to whether or not multidisciplinary group practices can be PCs.
6. M.C.L. § 450.222.
7. M.C.L. § 450.1105.
8. M.C.L. § 450.223.
9. M.C.L. § 450.1201.
10. M.C.L. § 450.1011 et seq.
11. M.C.L. § 450.1901.
12. M.C.L. § 450.1911.

practice. The corporation is also liable for any negligent or wrongful acts or misconduct committed by any of its shareholders, employees, or agents while they are engaging in rendering professional services on behalf of the corporation. Secretaries, bookkeepers, technicians and other assistants who are not usually considered to be rendering professional services for which a license is required are not considered employees in this sense.[13] If any member of the PC becomes legally disqualified to render services, they must sever their employment and financial interests with the PC within a reasonable period, under penalty of possible dissolution of the corporation if this is not done.[14]

(D) Termination of the Professional Corporation

The PC continues perpetually until voluntary or involuntary dissolution occurs pursuant to the laws governing dissolution of regular corporations.[15] Corporations are dissolved by filing a certificate of dissolution with the Department of Commerce, which states the name of the corporation and that it is dissolved. Dissolution may occur by action of the board and shareholders, by judgment of the court if an action has been brought against the corporation, or for failure to file an annual report.

---

13. M.C.L. § 450.225.
14. M.C.L. § 450.229.
15. M.C.L. § 450.1801 et seq.

2.3

Partnerships

A partnership[1] is formed when two or more persons, each of whom is a co-owner, enter into a for-profit agreement. It allows the partners to pool their resources to undertake projects that would be financially difficult for one person. However, the law may find that any joint endeavor is a partnership whether or not the persons label it as such. Such a finding could result in a forced sharing of profits and debts or unexpected liability for another's tortious actions. Thus, MHPs should be aware of this form of business whether they form a partnership or merely work in a close business relationship with other persons that could be construed as a partnership.

(A) Formation of a Partnership

A partnership is formed when two or more persons agree to carry on as co-owners of a business for profit.[2] The intent to share profits is the most important factor in determining whether a partnership exists.[3] For example, MHPs who work out of a co-owned building under a common name will not have partnership status forced upon them unless there also is an intent to share the profits of their services. A mere sharing of rental income does not invoke partnership status. The sharing of profits where the payment was for the purpose of repaying a debt, paying wages,

---

1. Because the law discussed in this chapter applies to many types of businesses, an attempt is made only to introduce the reader to it rather than present a comprehensive analysis.
2. M.C.L. § 449.6.
3. M.C.L. § 449.7.

paying an annuity to a representative or spouse of a deceased partner, or payment of interest on a loan or related transaction does not invoke partner status. Rather, any agreement between the parties that meets the above definition, even an oral one, suffices to initiate a partnership. Profits are generally split equally in the absence of an express agreement that distributes them in another fashion. Partnerships are required to file a declaration at the county level.

(B) Rights and Duties Between Partners

Partners have a fiduciary responsibility to the partnership. This means that each partner must act in good faith for the benefit of the partnership at all times.[4] Partners have equal rights in the management and conduct of the business.[5] In addition, each partner has the right to inspect the partnership books,[6] receive all information that may affect the partnership,[7] and demand a formal accounting.[8]

In fact, the law views each partner as an agent of the partnership and every act of an individual partner is seen as an act of the partnership, unless it can be seen as not carrying on business in the usual way. A partner cannot individually assign the partnership property in trust for creditors, dispose of the goodwill of the business, do any other act that makes it impossible to carry on the ordinary business of the partnership, acknowledge responsibility in any suit against the partnership, or submit a partnership claim or liability to arbitration or reference.[9]

Perhaps most important, any wrongful act or omission of any partner acting in the ordinary course of the business of the partnership that results in a loss, injury, or penalty becomes the responsibility of all of the partners.[10] Therefore, if any partner misapplies money or property of a third party, the partnership is financially responsible.[11] The partners are jointly and severally liable for the above, which means that a wronged person may sue one, several, or all of the partners. In fact, the injured person could

---

4. M.C.L. § 449.21.
5. M.C.L. § 449.18.
6. M.C.L. § 449.19.
7. M.C.L. § 449.20.
8. M.C.L. § 449.22.
9. M.C.L. § 449.9.
10. M.C.L. § 449.13.
11. M.C.L. § 449.14.

sue only the noninjuring partners if desired.[12] A person joining an existing general partnership is liable for all of the prior obligations of the partnership as though he or she had been a partner when they occurred.[13]

(C) Dissolution of a Partnership

A partnership is dissolved by[14]

1. the terms of the partnership agreement;
2. a situation where the partners have not agreed to carry out a particular business activity for a specified length of time and one of the partners wishes to dissolve the partnership, that person may do so;
3. the expulsion of any partner from the business in accordance with such power conferred by the partnership agreement;
4. a violation of the agreement between the partners, where one of them expressly intends for the partnership to dissolve;
5. any event which makes it unlawful for the business of the partnership to be carried on or for the members to carry on;
6. the death of any partner;
7. the bankruptcy of any partner or the partnership; or
8. the decree of the court when[15]

   a. a partner has been declared a lunatic[16] in any judicial proceeding or is shown to be of unsound mind;

   b. a partner becomes in any other way incapable of performing his or her part of the partnership contract;

   c. a partner has been guilty of such conduct as tends to affect prejudicially the carrying on of the business;

   d. a partner willfully or persistently commits a breach of the partnership agreement, or otherwise so conducts him- or herself in matters relating to the partnership that it is not reasonably practicable to carry on the business of the partnership with that partner;

   e. the business of the partnership can only be carried on at a loss; or

   f. other circumstances render a dissolution equitable.

---

12. M.C.L. § 449.15.
13. M.C.L. § 449.17.
14. M.C.L. § 449.31.
15. M.C.L. § 449.32.
16. This term is contained in the law and would now apply to guardianship and/or conservatorship proceedings (see chapters 4.2 and 4.3).

Generally, the dissolution of a partnership terminates the authority of the partners except to wind up the partnership affairs.[17] This does not absolve the partners of whatever liability may have accrued to the partnership prior to dissolution, however.

---

17. M.C.L. § 449.33.

2.4

Health Maintenance Organizations

A health maintenance organization (HMO) is a health care program whereby an individual or a group pays a single fee, usually annually, to receive health care services at little or no additional cost. The services are provided by HMO employees or by professionals who contract with the organization on a fee-for-service or capitated basis. The overall costs are kept lower by limiting the organization's expenses to the prepaid amount and by centralized administration. Most Michigan employers with 25 or more employees are required to offer HMO plans.[1]

(A) Benefits for Mental Health Services

Every HMO must offer at least primary health maintenance services to qualify for an initial license. In order to renew the license, it must offer at least basic health services,[2] including home health services, outpatient mental health services, not fewer than 20 visits per year, and intermediate and outpatient substance abuse services.[3]

The administrative rules for HMOs state that information in a clinical patient record must be treated as confidential and may be disclosed only to authorized persons. However, the information

---

1. M.C.L. § 333.21091.
2. M.C.L. § 333.21034.
3. M.C.L. § 333.21003.

must be made available to the state regulatory agency (the Medical Services Administration of the Department of Community Health) for examination and review.[4]

---

4. R 325.6810.

2.5

Preferred Provider Organizations

A preferred provider organization (PPO) is a group of health care providers and/or hospitals that contracts with employers, unions, or third-party payers (such as Blue Cross/Blue Shield) to provide services to the employees, members, and insured for a discounted fee in return for an exclusive service arrangement. The service providers are members of a provider panel, and see the patients in their own offices. In Michigan, these contracts are called *prudent purchaser contracts*.[1] Any health facility or persons licensed, certified, or registered as health care providers can apply to be on a provider panel. Panels must open for new applications for 60 days every 4 years. A provider who is terminated from a panel must be provided a written explanation for the reason upon request.[2]

---

1. M.C.L. § 333.21007.
2. M.C.L. § 333.2105c for HMOs and M.C.L. § 550.51 et seq. for insurance companies.

2.6

Individual Practice Associations

An individual practice association (IPA) is a group of health care providers that contracts to provide services for an organization that provides a prepaid health plan, frequently an HMO. The members of the IPA practice in their own offices but are compensated by the organization on a fee-for-service or fee-per-patient basis. While there is no law regulating the formation or operation of IPAs in Michigan, such organizations may be covered under the term *affiliated provider*.[1] Any health facility or persons licensed, certified, or registered as health care providers can apply to be on a provider panel. Panels must open for new applications for 60 days every 4 years. A provider who is terminated from a panel must be provided a written explanation for the reason upon request.[2]

---

1. M.C.L. § 333.21002.
2. M.C.L. § 333.2105c for HMOs and M.C.L. § 550.53 for insurance companies.

2.7

Hospital, Administrative, and Staff Privileges

The law in many states governs which classes of MHPs are eligible for agency and hospital staff and administrative privileges. With few exceptions, Michigan law does not directly differentiate among classes of MHPs either in agency privileges or in hospital administrative positions. However, the law does require that the medical director of community mental health agencies must be a psychiatrist.[1] It also requires that the executive director of a community mental health center select a physician, psychiatric nurse specialist, or licensed psychologist to advise on treatment issues.[2] Both private and public hospitals seeking approval by such organizations as the Joint Commission on the Accreditation of Health Organizations (JCAHO), may be required to have certain professionals in particular administrative positions. By law, every hospital must have a board, which makes policy regarding the eligibility and qualifications of its medical staff.[3]

---

1. M.C.L. § 3300.1231.
2. M.C.L. § 330.1226.
3. M.C.L. § 331.6.

2.8

Zoning for Community Homes

Zoning regulations are the laws by which state and local governments guide the rate and type of growth of communities, including their residential and commercial buildings. These laws can be, and have been, used to exclude certain classes of people thought to be undesirable from particular communities or areas within communities in some states. For example, some zoning boards have prohibited community homes for people with mental disorders from locating in single-family residential neighborhoods even though such a placement would be in the best interests of the community home residents.

Michigan has a detailed statute regulating procedures for the establishment of state licensed residential facilities in neighborhoods.[1] These homes must provide services or care for 6 or fewer persons[2] and must provide 24-hour supervision for those residents that need it. They include child and adult foster care facilities and group homes, but do not include residences for persons released from adult correctional facilities. Licensed residential facilities of this size are considered by law to be single-family dwellings and cannot be subject to special use or conditional use permits, nor can deed restrictions interfere with their establishment.[3]

When a state licensing agency has decided to establish a residential facility in a community, it must notify the city council at least 45 days beforehand in order to give the council an opportunity to review whether there are any other facilities within a

---

1. M.C.L. § 125.583b.
2. 5365 Op. Att'y. Gen. 594 (1978).
3. City of Livonia v. Dep't of Social Serv., 333 N.W.2d 151, 123 Mich.App. 1, aff'd, 378 N.W.2d 402, 423 Mich. 466 (1983).

1500 foot radius and to notify neighbors within the 1500 foot radius. To avoid undue concentration of facilities in a particular neighborhood or city, residential facilities must be outside a 1500 foot radius from each other, outside a 3000 foot radius in a city with a population of one million or more. The exception to this notification regulation is that it does not apply to homes caring for four or fewer minors. Courts have ruled that homeowners living near proposed adult foster care small group homes were not entitled to a hearing prior to the home being licensed.[4] A recent appeals court opinion found that the part of the statute requiring notifications discriminated against disabled persons and was preempted by the Fair Housing Amendments Act (FHAA).[5] Clarification awaits the result of the appeals process.

---

4. *City of Livonia*, 378 N.W.2d 402, 423 Mich. 466 (1985).
5. Larkin v. Mich. Dep't of Social Serv., 6 Mich. 89 (1996).

Insurance Reimbursement for Services

Health insurance carriers (insurers) typically have provisions providing reimbursement for mental health services. The policies sometimes limit reimbursement to certain classes of health care providers, usually physicians, and to particular types of services. In Michigan, insurers are regulated by the state Department of Insurance.[1] However, the Insurance Code does not specifically address coverage for mental health services, nor does it address which mental health care providers can be reimbursed.[2]

Federal law now requires that group insurance plans offering coverage for both medical/surgical and mental health benefits must not apply differential annual or lifetime dollar limits to mental health reimbursement.[3] Small employers, that is those who have 50 or less employees, are exempted from this requirement. Also, employers who can prove a greater than 1% cost in total benefit costs as a result of the implementation of this law can apply for exemption. The law does not require health plans to offer mental health benefits.

---

1. M.C.L. § 500.200.
2. MHPs who see elderly or disabled patients may be subject to federal Medicare regulations, which are beyond the scope of this book but may be found in the *Code of Federal Regulations* (C.F.R.).
3. 110 Stat. 2874 (Mental Health Parity Act of 1996).

2.10

Mental Health Benefits in State Insurance Plans

In some states, the law mandates that any health insurance plan provided for state government employees must include certain mental health benefits. Michigan law, however, does not specify which health benefits must be offered to state employees.

2.11

Tax Deductions for Professional Services and Education

Payments for mental health services may be deductible as either an individual medical deduction or a business expense, depending on the nature of the service and the use by the recipient taxpayer.

(A) Mental Health Services as a Medical Deduction

Professional services relating to the diagnosis or treatment of mental or emotional disorders are allowable as medical deductions under both federal and state law. Expenses incurred for the medical care of the taxpayer, spouse, or dependent (minus what is reimbursed through insurance) may be deducted if they total greater than 7.5% of the taxpayer's federal adjusted gross income.[1]

The law obviously allows for a deduction for services performed by a psychiatrist. It also provides that[2] amounts paid to psychologists who are qualified and authorized under state law to practice psychology for services rendered by them in connection with the diagnosis, cure, mitigation, treatment, or prevention of disease, or for the purpose of affecting any structure or function of the body, constitute expenses paid for medical care within the meaning of section 23(x) of the Internal Revenue Code and may

---

1. I.R.C. Reg. 1.213-2.
2. Rev. Rul. 143, 1953-2 C.B. 129.

be deducted in computing net income for federal income tax purposes, to the extent provided therein.

The Internal Revenue Service also allows deductions for payments made to other types of mental health providers:[3] Accordingly it is held that amounts paid for medical services rendered by practitioners, such as chiropractors, psychotherapists, and others rendering similar type services, constitute expenses for "medical care" within the provisions of section 213 of the Code, even though the practitioners who perform the services are not required by law to be, or are not (even though required by law) licensed, certified, or otherwise qualified to perform such services.

B) Mental Health Services as a Business Deduction

The use of mental health services by a business can be deductible as a trade or business expense. Federal law provides that "there shall be allowed as a deduction all the ordinary and necessary expenses paid or incurred during the taxable year in carrying on any trade or business."[4]

C) Mental Health Services Received by MHPs

Mental health professionals may not deduct the cost of their basic professional education as a business expense. However, they may deduct education courses if (a) they are employed or self-employed, (b) they meet the minimum requirements of the job or profession, and (c) the course maintains or improves job skills, or the person is required by the employer or by law to take the course to keep the present salary or position.[5]

The expenses cannot be deducted if they are part of a program of study that will lead to a new trade or business.[6] Under this rule, licensed psychiatrists are permitted to deduct expenses associated with training at a psychoanalytic institute, including personal psychoanalysis. In a tax court decision, a clinical social worker was also permitted a deduction for her own psychoanaly-

---

3. Rev. Rul. 91, 1963-1 C.B. 54.
4. 26 U.S.C. § 162(a).
5. I.R.C. Reg 1.162-5(a).
6. I.R.C. Reg.1.162-5(b)(3).

sis,[7] and a psychiatrist was allow to deduct his own psychother-apy.[8] Thus, the trend appears to be to permit educational business deductions for personal psychotherapy if the expense improves the MHP's job skills.

---

7. Voigt v. Commissioner, 74 T.C. 82, *nonacq.*, 1981-33 (1980).
8. Porter v. Commissioner, T.C. Memo 1986-70.

Limitations on and Liability for Practice

3.1

Informed Consent for Services

Informed consent should be obtained before administering services, disclosing information concerning the client to a third party, or taking any other action that has an impact on the client. The failure of MHPs to obtain consent may be considered professional misconduct by a licensing board (see Section 1), and it renders MHPs liable to a malpractice suit (see chapter 3.10).

(A) Requirement of Informed Consent

The basis of informed consent is that in order to agree to an action taken in connection with their care, patients or clients must understand the nature of the action, possible alternatives to it, and the risks and benefits attached to each. With the exception of a few cases such as emergency treatment, the person must be competent to understand the information being provided and must voluntarily consent to the action being taken. The general requirement for medical procedures is that the physician make a reasonable disclosure, which in Michigan is defined by the customary practice of other physicians in the community.[1] However, in Michigan there are no statutes or case law specifically regarding consent to receive psychotherapy. Consent is required in certain other cases, such as electroshock therapy, and information pertinent to this can be found elsewhere in this volume (see chapters 4.21, 4.22, 8.3, and 8.4).

---

1. Marchiewicz v. Stanton, 50 Mich.App. 344, 213 N.W.2d 317 (1973); McPhee v. Bay City Samaritan Hosp., 10 Mich.App. 567, 159 N.W.2d 880 (1968).

3.2

Extensiveness, Ownership, Maintenance, and Access to Records

An MHP's records are an important, required part of a practice. They are the primary means to document diagnoses and treatment plans, as well as to detail how such plans are carried out. Records may be essential for obtaining reimbursement for treatment and are a central means of demonstrating accountability in practice. While there is no statute regarding the ownership of clinical records, the Michigan Attorney General, in a formal opinion, has stated that the actual record belongs to the provider while the information in the records belongs to the patient.[1]

(A) Extensiveness of Records

The Mental Health Code, which applies to the care of patients by state licensed or contracted facilities, requires that any licensed health professional maintain a complete record for each patient. This means, at minimum, that it must contain a written assessment, an individual treatment plan, a statement of the purpose of hospitalization or treatment, a statement of any tests and examinations performed, and a description of any observations made and treatments provided.[2] While the licensing laws do not specifically address record-keeping, it is presumed that good professional practice would require similar record content for those in private or other agency practice. The administrative rules for HMOs include a detailed listing of what must be included in the medical records of contracting facilities and groups. In addition to

1. 5125 Op. Att'y. Gen. (1978).
2. M.C.L. § 330.1141.

demographic data, these include an initial medical evaluation, including history, reports from other providers or consultants, and clinical treatment or progress notes.[3]

In addition, health facilities must keep and maintain a record for each patient including a full and complete record of tests and examinations performed, observations made, treatments provided, and in the case of a hospital, the purpose of hospitalization. The facilities must take precautions to assure that the records are not altered or destroyed.[4] Anyone licensed to prescribe or dispense controlled substances must keep all invoices and a log of prescriptions for at least 5 years.[5]

(B) Maintenance of Records

Michigan has no requirement for the length of time patient records must be retained. However, it would be reasonably expected that MHPs would want to follow the guidelines of their respective professions, if any. Most, if not all, health care professions underscore the importance of keeping records for a reasonable length of time in order to be able to document and justify the care and services rendered, and to be able to provide information about that care to other professionals, as requested by the client.

(C) Client Access

Since March 28, 1996, a recipient of mental health services from the Department of Community Health or its contractees has a right to access to information in his or her record upon request, if he or she does not have a guardian, and has not been declared legally incompetent. A request must be complied with no later than 30 days after the receipt of the request by the holder of the record, or if the person is receiving treatment, before he or she is released.[6] If a decision is made to withhold information from the client because it may be detrimental to him or her or to others, an appeal can be made to the director of the Department, whose decision can be subject to judicial review.[7]

There is no law pertaining to access to records for clients of other types of mental health services, however customary prac-

---

3. R 325.6805.
4. M.C.L. § 333.20175.
5. M.C.L. § 333.7303a.
6. M.C.L. § 330.1748.
7. 6764 Op. Att'y. Gen. (1993).

tice is typically to allow client access providing it would not be detrimental.

(D) Access by Regulatory Departments and Boards

Patient records can be subpoenaed during the investigation of a licensing complaint, and, unless privileged, must be provided by the licensee. The subpoena may require a person to submit all records of patients seen on a given day if the allegation made pertains to or was made by one or more of those patients.[8] Information about patients, including their identity, obtained during an investigation or compliance conference (see chapter 1.1) is considered confidential and must not be disclosed outside of these proceedings (see chapters 3.3, 3.4, and 8.4).[9]

(E) Hospital Utilization Review

Information about the physical or psychological condition of a person, the necessity, appropriateness, or quality of health care given to a person, or the qualifications, competence, or performance of a health care provider can be provided to organizations providing peer or utilization review.[10] However, the identity of the client is confidential and must be removed from any published report or record. Information obtained by such entities is not part of the public record and therefore generally cannot be used as evidence in state legal proceedings.[11]

(F) Disposition of Records on Termination or Relocation of Practice

There is no Michigan law pertaining to the disposition of records in such cases, nor does the law provide guidance regarding record disposition after the death of an MHP. MHPs may find guidelines regarding these issues are available from their respec-

---

8. M.C.L. § 333.16235.
9. M.C.L. § 333.16238.
10. M.C.L. § 331.531.
11. M.C.L. § 333.533.

tive professional associations. However, willful destruction of a patient's record may be a felony.

(G) Liability for Violation

Violation of these laws may result in an action against an MHP's license. Furthermore, because these laws set the standard for MHPs in Michigan, failure to abide by them may result in civil liability (see section 1.0, and chapters 3.10 and 3.11).

3.3

Confidential Relations and Communications

Generally, a confidential communication is written or verbal information conveyed by the client to an MHP in the course of a professional relationship. Confidentiality originated in professional ethics codes from a belief that effective psychotherapy required a guarantee from the therapist that no information obtained in the course of evaluation or treatment would be given to others. In this sense, the therapist owes a duty to the patient to keep his or her records confidential. MHPs may be liable in civil suits or licensing actions initiated by clients who have been harmed by breaches of confidentiality. However, statute and case law cite circumstances where confidential information may be disclosed. Confidentiality is distinguished from privilege, which governs the type and breadth of information that must be divulged in the course of legal proceedings (see chapter 3.4).

(A) Overview of Confidentiality in Michigan

Michigan law regarding confidentiality is somewhat complicated since references to confidentiality are found in case law and in state statutes regulating the practice of various professions,[1]

---

1. *See* Occupational Regulation Sections of the Michigan Public Health Code, M.C.L. § 333.16101 et seq.

abuse reporting (see chapters 4.7 and 4.8), and the provision of mental health services.[2]

B) Confidentiality as Related to Treatment in Mental Health Treatment Facilities

Recipients of services provided by or contracted with the state Department of Community Health are entitled to the confidentiality of their records.[3] Records may be released without the consent of the person only

1. if subpoenaed by the court or legislature, providing the information is not privileged (see also chapter 3.4);
2. to a prosecutor as necessary for a commitment proceeding;
3. to the person's guardian, or parent, in the case of a minor;
4. to the Department or auditor general if necessary for it to comply with a law; and
5. in the case of the death of the patient, to a surviving spouse or close relative, for the purpose of applying for and receiving benefits.

Records may be released to treating mental health professionals and the client's attorney with the client's consent. The holder of the record may disclose information in the record at his or her discretion without patient consent

1. in order for the person to apply for or receive benefits;
2. for research purposes only if identification is essential to achieve the purpose of the research and only if no harm will come to the person from the information release; and
3. to providers of mental health or other health services or to a public agency if there is a compelling need for disclosure based on a substantial probability of harm to the person.

---

2. M.C.L. § 330.1748 for psychologists, M.C.L. § 333.18117 for licensed professional counselors, M.C.L. § 333.16911 for marriage and family therapists, and M.C.L. § 339.1610 for social workers.
3. *Id.*

(C) Confidentiality as Related to Mental Health Professionals

Statutes governing the professional practice of psychologists, counselors, marriage and family counselors, and social workers each include a section addressing confidentiality (see chapters 1.1–1.13). These statutes all indicate that these professionals may release confidential information obtained in the course of rendering services to a patient only with the consent or waiver of the individual or his or her guardian.[4] MHPs are subject to legal penalties if they violate confidentiality (see section (D) below). There are several instances when the law requires an MHP to break confidentiality, including when there is possible danger to a third party (see section (E) below), and in cases of abuse and neglect (see chapters 4.7 and 4.8).

(D) Penalties for Violation of Confidentiality

Betrayal of a professional confidence is considered unprofessional conduct and is grounds for investigation by a licensing board.[5] In addition, the Michigan Criminal Code states that any person, firm, or corporation who furnishes, receives, buys, offers to buy, sells, or offers to sell the identity of a patient or any information concerning his or her treatment, without his or her prior written permission is guilty of a misdemeanor punishable by 6 months in prison or a fine of not more than $500 or both.[6] While this is connected with laws prohibiting attorneys from soliciting personal injury claims, it may also apply to MHPs.

(E) Confidentiality and the Duty to Protect or Warn: *Tarasoff* Issues

Based on a California state court decision, *Tarasoff v. Regents of University of California*,[7] regarding the duty of a mental health professional to protect third parties from the dangerous acts of their clients, many states have developed laws that require the

---

4. M.C.L. § 333.18237.
5. M.C.L. § 333.16221.
6. M.C.L. § 750.410.
7. 551 P.2d 334 (1976).

MHP to breach confidentiality in such situations. Michigan has such a law.[8] It states that if a patient communicates a threat of physical violence against a reasonably identifiable third person to a mental health practitioner who is treating the patient, the MHP has a duty to take certain action. The MHP can discharge his or her duty to act by doing one or more of the following in a timely manner:

1. hospitalize the patient or initiate proceedings to involuntarily hospitalize the patient;

2. make a reasonable attempt to communicate the threat to the third person and communicate the threat to the local police department or county sheriff in the area where the third person resides or in the area where the patient resides, or the state police; and

3. if the MHP has reason to believe that the third party is a minor or is incompetent, he or she must also communicate the threat to the Family Independence Agency in the county where the minor lives, and to the minor's custodial parent, noncustodial parent, or legal guardian, whoever is appropriate to the best interest of the minor.

If a threat is made in a hospital setting where the patient is being treated by a team of MHPs, a particular person must be designated to discharge the duty to warn. This does not have to be the person who actually hears the threat. A psychiatrist or psychologist who determines in good faith that a particular situation presents a duty to warn or protect does not violate the privilege statute.

E) Notification of Partner of HIV + / AIDS Status

Michigan law requires that a person or governmental entity that administers a test for HIV must refer a person found to be HIV infected to the appropriate local health department if it is determined that the person needs assistance in notifying partners.[9] The person or entity must inform the individual that he or she has a legal obligation to inform each sexual partner about being HIV positive before engaging in sexual relations, and that failure to do so can be a criminal offense. Physicians who have knowledge of a

---

8. M.C.L. § 300.1946.
9. M.C.L. § 333.5114a.

person who has contact with an HIV positive person and who thus may be at foreseeable risk for HIV infection have an affirmative duty to disclose such information to the potential partner.[10] The duty can be discharged by referring the infected person to the local health authority for assistance in partner notification, providing the name of the person with HIV or AIDS, and the name of the partner at risk.[11] This law has not been applied to other MHPs.

---

10. M.C.L. § 333.5131.
11. For a thorough discussion of the law pertaining to HIV, *see* S.P. Clifton, W.S. Wheeler, & S.H. Patton, *HIV-Related Laws in Michigan Public Health Code: A Primer for the General Practitioner*, 73 MICH. B.J. 156 (1994).

3.4

Privileged Communication

Two primary areas of law exist that attempt to protect the client's communications from disclosure. The most well known is confidentiality law, whose principles originated in professional ethics codes and have now been incorporated in legislation and court rulings (see chapter 3.3). It is designed to encourage frank discussion and the exchange of reliable information and protects the client from improper disclosure of information by the MHP in most situations. It does not, however, protect the client from court orders requiring the MHP to disclose information. MHPs disclosing information under court order are generally protected from litigation regarding the disclosure.

For production in a court proceeding, the communications must not be covered under a privileged communication statute. MHPS must have knowledge of these laws so that they can advise their clients of the limits of confidential information and respond appropriately when contacted by the court. Unlike confidentiality, which is a duty of an MHP to a client, privilege resides with the client and can only be waived under certain circumstances.

In Michigan, information provided to a physician in the course of treatment is privileged and may not be revealed in a legal proceeding without the patient's consent.[1] The state Mental Health Code, which applies to recipients of state mental health services, further defines privileged communication as "a communication made to a psychiatrist or psychologist in connection with the examination, diagnosis, or treatment of a patient, or to another person while the other person is participating in the exami-

---

1. M.C.L. § 600.2157, M.C.L. § 767.5.

nation, diagnosis, or treatment."[2] Though it is unclear whether this law extends the definition to MHPs practicing outside the state system, a recent Supreme Court decision has extended privilege to communications between psychotherapists and patients.[3] It is thus assumed that communications between most MHPs and their patients are privileged in Michigan. In addition, laws regulating the practice of psychology, social work, counseling, and marriage and family therapy address privilege; these will be discussed individually below.

Privilege is waived when a person brings a civil suit or malpractice action in which he or she claims injury or damage and produces a witness who will testify regarding this damage.[4] At this point the patient essentially opens his or her past medical or psychiatric treatment to discovery by the opposing side. The Mental Health Code also holds that privilege can be waived[5]

1. if the communication is relevant to a matter under consideration in a mental health proceeding, but only if the patient was informed that any communication could be used;

2. if the communication is relevant to a proceeding to determine legal competence or the need for a guardian, but only if the patient was informed that any communication could be used;

3. in a civil or criminal malpractice action against an MHP;

4. if the communication was made during an examination ordered by the court, but only if the patient was told that it would not be privileged;

5. if the communication was made during treatment the patient was ordered to undergo to render him or her competent to stand trial.

Since the physician–patient privilege does not apply in an investigation or proceedings conducted regarding the licensing and regulation of professionals, unless otherwise waived, MHPs should refer to their own licensing law in dealing with their own profession.[6]

---

2. M.C.L. § 330.1750.
3. Jaffee v. Redmond, 116 S.Ct. 1923, 518 U.S. 1 (1996).
4. M.C.L. § 600.2157, M.C.L. § 767.5; Landelius v. Sackelares, 556 N.W.2d 472, 453 Mich. 470 (1996); M.C.L. § 600.2912f.
5. M.C.L. § 330.1750.
6. M.C.L. § 333.16244.

MHPs may sometimes feel caught between the requirements of the court to disclose information and the ethical standards of their profession. There is some case law that speaks to this issue.[7]

(A) Psychologists

Psychologists cannot be compelled to disclose confidential information received from a person consulting them in their professional capacity. The information is privileged unless consent is given by the person, or a minor person's guardian.[8]

(B) Social Workers

Communications between a certified social worker, social worker, or social work technician and a person counseled are privileged and cannot be waived except by consent of the client or during the course of the social worker's supervision within the agency in which they are employed.[9]

(C) Licensed Professional Counselors (LPC)

The confidential relations and communications between an LPC and a client are considered privileged and can be disclosed only by consent of the client unless otherwise provided by law.[10]

(D) Marriage and Family Therapists

Information regarding a person to whom a licensed marriage and family therapist provided therapy is privileged regardless of[11]

---

7. In one case involving an optometrist, a court ruled that the fact that disclosing information regarding a patient is unethical does not mean that the testimony is privileged, and that the ethical standard could not be invoked over the need for the court to hear evidence. People v. Baker, 288 N.W.2d 430, 94 Mich.App. 365 (1979).
8. M.C.L. § 333.18237.
9. M.C.L. § 339.1610.
10. M.C.L. § 333.18117.
11. M.C.L. § 333.16911.

1. whether the information was obtained from the individual, from another person involved in the therapy, from a test or other evaluation mechanism, or from other sources;
2. whether the information was obtained before, during, or after therapy; and
3. whether the person is a present or a former client.

Privilege is waived only

1. if disclosure is required by law or is necessary to protect the health or safety of a person;
2. in the case of a licensing proceeding; and
3. if a waiver is obtained in writing from each person over age 18 involved in the marriage and family therapy.

(E) Privilege in Cases of Sexual Assault

A confidential communication, or any report or working paper connected with a consultation between a victim and a sexual assault or domestic violence counselor, is privileged and is not admissible in any civil or criminal proceeding without the written consent of the victim.[12] However, where the defendant can establish reasonable probability that privileged records of a psychologist, sexual assault counselor, social worker, or juvenile diversion officer are likely to contain information specifically necessary to the defense, they must be reviewed by the judge, who must provide any necessary information he or she discovers to the defense.[13]

---

12. M.C.L. § 600.2157a.
13. People v. Stanaway, 521 N.W.2d 557, 446 Mich. 643 (1994), *cert. denied by* Michigan v. Caruso, 115 S. Ct. 923, 513 U.S. 1121 (1995).

3.5

Search, Seizure, and Subpoena of Records

The search of an MHP's office and seizure of any records may occur within the context of a criminal investigation of the MHP or a client. Our discussion in this chapter is limited to the latter situation. If a court, during a civil or criminal action, demands information from an MHP that was obtained during the course of a professional relationship with the client, the request will usually come via subpoena. Both types of request, search and subpoena, are important to MHPs because they provide major exceptions to confidentiality (see chapter 3.3) and privileged communication law (see chapter 3.4). Note, however, that the seizure of records does not necessarily mean that they will ultimately be admissible in court. That determination will be made separately by the court.[1]

(A) Search and Seizure

The Michigan Constitution protects the houses, papers, and possessions of every person from unreasonable searches and seizures.[2] A search warrant may be issued if an affidavit by a law enforcement officer is made under oath to a magistrate and the magistrate decides that probable cause exists for a search.[3] The warrant may be issued to search for and seize any property which

---

1. Note that substance abuse treatment records are also subject to special federal protection.
2. MICH. CONST. art. 1, § 11.
3. M.C.L. § 780.651.

is stolen or embezzled, intended to be used or used in a criminal offense, owned or used in violation of the law, evidence of a crime, or contraband.[4] The warrant must be directed to the sheriff or any peace officer and must designate and describe the location to be searched and the property or thing to be seized. It must also state the grounds or reasonable cause for its issuance.[5] The person whose property is searched must be provided a copy of the warrant and a list of anything seized.[6]

(B) Subpoena

A subpoena is a command by the court at the behest of a party in a legal proceeding to appear at a specified time and place and to give testimony. A subpoena may also command that books, papers, documents, or other designated objects be produced; this type is typically referred to as a subpoena *duces tecum*.[7] MHPs may be subpoenaed to testify at a trial, a hearing, or a deposition. A witness must be given at least a 2-day notice of the need to appear and must be kept informed of any adjournments of the hearing or trial. Subpoenas can be served by personal delivery to the witness, or by mail, and must tender a small fee for 1 day's attendance and travel expenses allowed by law.[8] Expert witnesses can be paid higher fees if authorized by the court.[9]

Compliance with a subpoena is mandatory unless excused by the court or the person issuing the subpoena. Failing or refusing to comply is considered contempt of court and is punishable by fine, imprisonment, or both.[10] It should be noted that the mere issuance of a subpoena does not indicate that a privileged communication with an MHP must be revealed (see chapter 3.4). Rather, the MHP must assert the privilege until the client expressly waives it or the court orders the privilege waived as a matter of law. Failure by the MHP to initially assert a statutory privilege may result in a licensure hearing and/or civil liability.[11] A person served with a subpoena who believes its requirements

---

4. M.C.L. § 780.652.
5. M.C.L. § 780.654.
6. M.C.L. § 780.655.
7. M.C.R. § 2.506, M.C.L. § 600.1455.
8. M.C.L. § 600.2552.
9. M.C.L. § 600.2164.
10. M.C.L. § 600.1701.
11. For an excellent article about how to deal with subpoenas, *see* American Psychological Association Committee on Legal Issues. (1996). Strategies for Private Practitioners Coping With Subpoenas or Compelled Testimony for Client Records or Test Data. *Professional Psychology, 27*, 245–251.

are burdensome, or that he or she should not be compelled to comply with it can file a motion to quash the subpoena.[12] The court may excuse a witness from compliance for good cause with or without a hearing.

---

12. M.C.R. § 2.506, 2.302.

State Freedom of Information Act

Michigan's Freedom of Information Law regulates the extent to which government agencies may withhold information from public access. It states that all persons, except those who are incarcerated, are entitled to full and complete information regarding the affairs of the government and the official acts of those people who represent them as public officials and public employees, unless they are specifically exempted from disclosure.[1] The law requires all government agencies to promulgate regulations providing for the availability of records. Records and reports of MHPs, insofar as they are part of such governmental agency records, may be subject to this law.

Any request for records must be responded to within 5 business days. Denials must be accompanied by an explanation, and can be appealed to the head of the agency from whom the information was requested.[2]

The law clearly states which items are exempt from disclosure under the act.[3] Those items relevant to MHPs are

1. information of a personal nature[4] where the public disclosure of the information would constitute a clearly unwarranted invasion of an individual's privacy;

2. a public record that if disclosed would prejudice an agency's ability to maintain the physical security of anyone admitted

---

1. M.C.L. § 15.231.
2. M.C.L. § 15.235.
3. M.C.L. § 15.243.
4. "Information of a personal nature" has been defined as information that reveals intimate or embarrassing details of an individual's private life. Bradley v. Saranac Community Schs. Bd. of Educ., 565 N.W.2d 650, 455 Mich. 285 (1997).

because of a mental disability, unless the public interest in disclosing the information outweighs the public interest in not disclosing it;

3. any records or information specifically exempted from disclosure by statute;[5]

4. records or information subject to the physician–patient privilege, the psychologist–patient privilege, the minister or priest privilege, or any other privilege recognized by statute or court rule;

5. test questions and answers, scoring keys, and other examination instruments or data used to administer a license, public employment or academic examination, unless the public interest in disclosure outweighs the public interest in nondisclosure;

6. medical, counseling, or psychological facts or evaluations concerning an individual if the individual's identity would be revealed by a disclosure of those facts or evaluation; and

7. records or information pertaining to an investigation or compliance conference conducted by the Department of Consumer and Industry Services, except for the fact that an allegation was received and an investigation is being conducted, or that an allegation has been received and was dismissed.

---

5. *See* chapter 3.4 regarding privileged communication.

3.7

Right to Refuse Treatment

People who have the capacity to seek voluntary treatment have, by definition, the capacity to refuse such treatment. However, the right of involuntarily committed patients to refuse treatment has not always been recognized. The extent to which civilly committed mentally ill and developmentally disabled individuals have the right to refuse treatment is discussed in chapters 8.4 and 8.7.

3.8

Regulation of Aversive and Avoidance Conditioning

Behavioral therapies using aversive stimuli are carefully regulated or prohibited in some states when they are intended for use with developmentally disabled or mentally ill individuals. Michigan has no laws specifically addressing this issue. Appropriate care is addressed in the Recipients Rights section of the Mental Health Code.[1]

---

1. M.C.L. § 330.1700 et seq.

3.9

Quality Assurance for Hospital Care

In order to meet standards for accreditation and licensing, hospitals are required to review their professional practices and procedures to assure that their quality provides for adequate patient care.

(A) Peer Review

Michigan law allows information and data relating to the physical or psychological condition of a person, the necessity, appropriateness, or quality of health care rendered, or the qualifications, competence, or performance of a health care provider to be provided if requested to a "review entity." Review entities include[1]

1. a duly appointed peer review committee of: the state, state or county association of health care professionals, a licensed health facility, health care association, health care network, or a health plan;

2. a professional standards review organization qualified under federal or state law;

3. a foundation or organization acting with the approval of a state or county association of health care professionals;

4. a state department or agency whose jurisdiction includes the type of information listed above; and

---

1. M.C.L. § 331.531.

5. an organization established by a state association of hospitals or physicians whose purpose is to collect data regarding the competence or performance of licensed health care professionals.

(B) Privilege, Confidentiality, and Immunity

Persons and organizations are not civilly or criminally liable for providing information under this law unless they act with malice. The data obtained and any reports, findings, and conclusions of a review entity are confidential, are not public records, and cannot be used as evidence in a civil lawsuit. The identity of any person studied by a review entity is also confidential and their names must be removed before any findings are released.[2] Releasing or publishing the findings and conclusions of review entities may only be done[3]

1. to advance health care research or health care education;

2. to maintain the standards of the health care profession;

3. to protect the financial integrity of any government funded program;

4. to review the qualifications, competence, and performance of a health care professional with respect to his or her selection and appointment to the medical staff of a health care facility; and

5. to comply with record-keeping requirements.

The identity of any person studied is confidential.

---

2. M.C.L. § 331.533.
3. M.C.L. § 331.532.

3.10
Malpractice Liability

A malpractice suit is a civil action in which the plaintiff alleges that he or she suffered damages as the consequence of an act or omission by a professional who did not exercise the level of ordinary and reasonable care possessed by the average member of that discipline. Plaintiffs can claim compensation for damages suffered. In Michigan, licensed professionals can be sued for malpractice. MHPs can also testify as expert witnesses in malpractice actions regarding the appropriate standard of care, the presence and extent of mental or emotional damages suffered, the relationship of the damages to the alleged malpractice by the professional, and appropriate treatment.

(A) Malpractice Law
(A)(1) Who May Be Sued

In Michigan, anyone holding themselves out to be a member of a state licensed profession can be sued for malpractice.[1] A person cannot begin a malpractice action against a health professional unless he or she notifies the professional in writing at least 182 days before filing a complaint. After receiving such a notice, the MHP must respond within 154 days with a written response that states the factual basis for the defense of the claim, the standard of practice he or she claims to be applicable, the manner in which he or she claims there has been compliance with the standard of care, and why his or her actions were not the proximate cause of the

---

1. M.C.L. § 600.2912.

alleged damage.[2] When a complaint is made, the plaintiff must include an affidavit of merit signed by a professional who is reasonably believed to meet the requirements of an expert witness (see chapter 6.2). The affidavit of merit must list the records reviewed and must contain a statement about each of the following:[3]

1. the applicable standard of care;
2. an opinion that the standard of care was breached by the defendant;
3. the actions that should have been taken or omitted by the defendant in order to have complied with the standard of care; and
4. how the breach of the standard of care was the proximate cause of the injury.

The defendant must then file an affidavit of meritorious defense, countering each of the plaintiff's claims. Plaintiffs who claim damages in malpractice action automatically waive their rights of privilege (see chapter 3.4) regarding professional relationships that have a bearing on their lawsuit.[4]

In Michigan, hospitals can also be sued for malpractice if a physician they employ or whom a person has reason to believe they employ is negligent.[5] In another case, a physician who had supervisory responsibility for health care workers could be sued for their negligence.[6]

Malpractice suits can be resolved through out-of-court settlements, arbitration, or at trial. If arbitration is chosen, the plaintiff and the defendant agree to have the suit heard by a mutually chosen neutral third party, known as the arbitrator. A hearing is held and the parties must agree in advance to abide by the decision of the arbitrator. If an out-of-court settlement is reached by any method, a complete copy of the settlement agreement must be filed with the Department of Consumer and Industry Services within 30 days.[7]

)(2) Standard of Care

Michigan law provides that the plaintiff must prove that, in light of the state of the art existing at the time of the alleged malpractice, the professional failed to provide the recognized standard of

2. M.C.L. § 600.2912b.
3. M.C.L. § 600.2912d.
4. M.C.L. § 600.2912f.
5. Grewe v. Mt. Clemens Gen. Hosp., 273 N.W.2d 429, 404 Mich. 240 (1978).
6. McCullough v. Hutzel Hosp., 276 N.W.2d 569, 88 Mich.App. 235 (1979).
7. M.C.L. § 600.2912h.

acceptable professional practice or care in the community in which the professional practices, or in a similar community. If the professional is a specialist, he or she must have failed to provide the recognized standard of practice or care within that specialty as reasonably available in facilities in the community or in other facilities reasonably available under the circumstances.[8] This standard of proof is called *preponderance of the evidence* and means that the judge or jury (depending on who is deciding the outcome of the case) is convinced that the claim or complaint is more true than false.

Case law has defined medical malpractice as the failure of a member of the medical profession, who is employed to treat a case professionally, to fulfill their "duty to exercise that degree of skill, care, and diligence exercised by members of same profession, practicing in same or similar locality, in light of the present state of medical science."[9] There is no indication that this standard would not apply to other professions as well.

In most medical malpractice, the plaintiff is required to use expert testimony to establish the standard of care and the breach of the standard.[10] If an expert is not used, the plaintiff must prove that negligence can simply be inferred from the fact that the injury happened and that what caused the injury was under the exclusive control of the professional.[11] An important limitation on the qualifications of expert witnesses in medical malpractice actions was enacted as a reform measure.[12] The statute requires that in the year preceding the event in question, an expert must have devoted the majority of his or her professional time to either active clinical practice in the same profession, and if applicable specialty as the person being sued, or in teaching that profession or specialty in an accredited institution or program. The statute also prohibits testimony provided by experts on a contingent fee basis.

It has been held that being of a different school of thought than the defendant does not disqualify an expert from testifying as long as the expert is familiar with the applicable standard of care.[13]

---

8. M.C.L. § 600.2912a.
9. McLeod v. Plymouth Court Nursing Home, 957 F. Supp. 113 (1997). This is a case where Michigan law was interpreted by a federal court.
10. Wallace v. Garden City Osteopathic Hosp., 314 N.W.2d 557, 111 Mich.App. 212 (1981).
11. Wischmeyer v. Schanz, 536 N.W.2d 760, 449 Mich. 469 (1995).
12. M.C.L. § 600.129.
13. Haisenleder v. Reeder, 318 N.W.2d 634, 114 Mich.App. 258 (1982).

(3) Proximate Cause

In a malpractice suit, the plaintiff must prove that a professional's failure to provide the standard of care was the proximate cause of their injury. This means that the injury would not have occurred but for the negligent acts of the professional. A plaintiff must prove this by a preponderance of the evidence (see section above). In appropriate cases, the law allows a plaintiff to sue for the loss of the opportunity to survive, or to have had the opportunity to obtain a better result from treatment.[14]

(4) Statute of Limitations

A medical malpractice claim must be begun within 2 years of the negligent action[15] or within 6 months after the plaintiff discovered or should have discovered the existence of the claim, whichever is later.[16] However, the suit cannot begin later than 6 years after the date of the alleged negligent act or omission, unless its discovery was prevented by fraudulent conduct on the part of the MHP.

If a plaintiff was insane at the time of the claim, the statute of limitations is delayed until 1 year after the disability is removed or the plaintiff dies. The statute of limitations is also delayed in the case of children under age 18, as claims for malpractice occurring during childhood can be brought until 1 year after the child's 18th birthday.[17] Adults who claim that they have recovered forgotten memories of sexual abuse (not necessarily induced by an MHP) cannot apply either the insanity or childhood delay, suggesting that lawsuits by adults recovering memories of events occurring as children are outside the boundaries of the statute.[18]

3) Avoiding Malpractice

MHPs who wish to minimize the likelihood of becoming the target of a malpractice suit should adhere to the following principles:

1. abide by the rules and regulations of their applicable state licensing board;
2. abide by the ethical principles of any relevant national or state professional associations;

---

14. M.C.L. § 600.2912d.
15. M.C.L. § 600.5805.
16. M.C.L. § 600.5838a.
17. M.C.L. § 600.5851.
18. Lemmerman v. Fealk, 534 N.W. 2d 695, 449 Mich. 56, *reh'g denied*, 539 N.W.2d 504, 450 Mich. 1211 (1995).

3. adhere to any practice guidelines or parameters published by relevant professional associations;

4. keep abreast of new developments in their profession with respect to diagnosis and treatment;

5. maintain appropriate boundaries with clients; and

6. seek consultation with more experienced members of the profession when faced with difficult professional or ethical issues

MHPs who adhere to all of these principles may nevertheless be sued by a dissatisfied client who assumes, wrongly, that an unsatisfactory result of treatment necessarily implies negligence. The MHP's best defense to a nonmeritorious claim will be a complete and accurate set of patient records that indicate consideration of and adherence to professional standards throughout the course of the patient's treatment.

(C) Malpractice Review Committees

Some states have committees that screen malpractice suits prior to adjudication. Michigan has no such committee.

3.11

Other Forms of Professional Liability

In general, when clients sue MHPs it is for malpractice (see chapter 3.10), which covers suits alleging that a standard of care was violated in treating a patient. Much more rarely, other legal causes of action may also be brought against MHPs. Although malpractice law will provide sufficient grounds for most lawsuits against MHPs, several alternative legal grounds for lawsuits will be briefly described below. Criminal-related actions are discussed in chapter 3.12.

A) Intentional Torts

A *tort* is a private legal wrong committed against a person or property. A tort may be *intentional*, that is done on purpose to cause a wrong, or *negligent*, where there is a failure to exercise the appropriate care. Malpractice is an example of a negligent tort. Lawsuits for most torts (malpractice is an exception, see chapter 3.10) have a statute of limitations of 2 years. Criminal-related actions are discussed in chapter 3.12.

A)(1) Slander and Libel

Slander is a false statement made orally to a third party that would tend to injure a person's reputation. To libel someone the statement must be published or in writing. A patient could bring a lawsuit against an MHP if he or she made a false statement about the patient's mental condition or behavior to a third party. Such a lawsuit can always be successfully defended by proof that

the supposedly defamatory statement is in fact true.[1] The exis
tence of a privilege may prevent liability for a statement tha
might otherwise be considered defamatory. Thus statement
made in reports ordered by a court or in testimony before a cour
would enjoy a judicial privilege.

(A)(2) Malicious Prosecution, False Imprisonment, and Abuse of Process

Persons who arrest or sue someone in a civil action withou
probable cause in order to vex, trouble, or maliciously harm tha
person are liable and can in turn be sued by the person arrested o
maliciously sued. A person who initiates a vexatious lawsuit ma
be held liable for twice the amount of damages and expense
caused by the suit and are also guilty of a misdemeanor.[2] Thi
type of action could be brought by an MHP against a party if ther
was reason to believe that the party had filed a malpractice sui
against the MHP for which there was no basis in fact. Howeve
the allegedly vexatious malpractice suit must have terminated i
favor of the defendants.[3]

A person who has been confined wrongfully and against hi
or her will may bring a lawsuit for *false imprisonment*. In th
context of mental health treatment, Michigan case law has estab
lished that if a patient has been confined in a private hospita
(rather than a state hospital) on a proper petition pending
commitment hearing (see chapter 8.4), that patient can bring sui
for false imprisonment if he or she can show that his or he
detention at the hospital would have ended sooner if the respon
sible psychiatrist had acted differently.[4] In this case a woman wa
committed on a petition filed by her husband. She refused t
consent to treatment and the psychiatrist did not allow her t
contact anyone outside the hospital, resulting in her suit for fals
imprisonment because the psychiatrist's action deprived her o
her legal right to contact someone who could represent her rights
The courts have also ruled that statements made by MHPs i
clinical certificates filed in commitment proceedings are privi
leged and may not be used as evidence in lawsuits by patient
alleging false imprisonment. Thus the patient in this case coul
not recover damages for false imprisonment for being confined t
a hospital under an emergency order, even though the order wa
later rescinded.[5]

---

1. MICH. CONST. art. 1, § 19.
2. M.C.L. § 600.2907.
3. Gasis v. Schwartz, 264 N.W.2d 76, 80 Mich.App.600 (1978).
4. Stowers v. Ardmore Acres Hosp., 172 N.W.2d 497, 19 Mich.App. 115 (1971
5. Dabkowski v. Davis, 111 N.W.2d 68, 364 Mich. 429 (1961).

The tort of *abuse of process* involves misuse of the legal process to accomplish an unlawful ulterior purpose.[6] No reported cases involving MHPs suing or being sued for abuse of process were found in Michigan. MHPs might use this tort if they were wrongfully sued for malpractice, because they need not prove that the malpractice suit was brought maliciously or without probable cause.

B) Other Types of Civil Liability

Three other kinds of civil claims that may be brought against MHPs, in addition to claims based on malpractice and intentional torts, are described below.

(1) Breach of Fiduciary Duty

In law, a professional is often said to be in a fiduciary relationship to his or her client. This means a person has placed trust in the MHP by entering into a professional relationship with him or her and the MHP thus has a duty to act for the person's benefit. When an MHP acts in a manner that is detrimental to a client's interests, he or she may be accused of breaching fiduciary duty. The term is usually applied to ethical breaches rather than to malpractice.

(2) Breach of Contract

A person can sue for breach of contract if they have not lived up to their part of an express agreement. Many MHPs have their patients sign agreements regarding treatment that can be construed as contracts. Although the therapist–patient relationship can be seen as creating an implied contract that imposes certain obligations on both parties that could be breached, the typical lawsuit would be in the form of malpractice.

(3) Ordinary Negligence

Where an MHP is sued because of an act or omission that did not relate to his or her professional expertise, for example in a case where a patient was injured from a fall in the MHP's office, the lawsuit may be one of ordinary negligence. The distinction between the two is that ordinary negligence is judged according to the standard of behavior of a reasonably prudent person under the facts and circumstances of the particular case, whereas professional malpractice is judged according to a professional standard of care (see chapter 3.10). Unlike professional malpractice, which usually must be proven by expert testimony, the jury is deemed capable of deciding how a reasonably prudent person should have acted under the circumstances.

---

6. Black v. Spears, 180 N.W. 593, 213 Mich. 29 (1921).

Criminal Liability

Among the criminal laws that may be relevant to MHPs are th laws regarding sexual offenses, assault, and manslaughter.

(A) Sexual Offenses

Some states have criminal statutes specifically prohibiting MHP from engaging in certain behaviors (e.g., sexual relations with client). At this time, Michigan does not have such a law, thoug one is being considered in the legislature.

There are four degrees of criminal sexual conduct in Mich gan; the first three are felonies and the fourth is a misdemeanor. person is guilty of criminal sexual conduct in the first degree[1] if h or she engages in sexual penetration of another person and any c the following circumstances exist:

1. the other person is under the age of 13;
2. the other person is at least 13 but less than 16 years old and th perpetrator is a member of the same household;
3. the perpetrator is related to the victim by blood or affinit (such as a spouse or stepparent);
4. the perpetrator is in a position of authority over the victim an used the authority to coerce the victim to submit;

---

1. M.C.L. § 750.520b.

5. the perpetrator either knows or has reason to know that the victim is mentally incapable, mentally incapacitated, or physically helpless;[2]

6. the perpetrator uses force or coercion; or

7. a perpetrator engages in the medical treatment or examination of the victim in a manner or for purposes that are medically recognized as unethical or unacceptable.

Sexual penetration is defined as sexual intercourse, cunnilingus, fellatio, anal intercourse or any other intrusion, however slight, of any part of a person's body or of any object into the genital or anal openings of another person's body. Emission of semen is not required.

A person is guilty of criminal sexual conduct in the second degree if he or she engages in sexual contact with another person and any of the same circumstances listed above exist except for the last one.[3] Sexual contact is defined as the intentional touching of the victim's or perpetrator's intimate parts (genital area, groin, inner thigh, buttock, or breast) or the immediate area of the victim's or perpetrator's clothing covering the intimate parts, if that touching can reasonably be construed as being for the purpose of sexual arousal or gratification.[4] Criminal sexual conduct in the third degree is charged if the person engages in sexual penetration with another person and at least one of the following exists:[5]

1. the other person is at least 13 but less than 16 years old;

2. force or coercion is used;

3. the actor knows or has reason to know that the victim was mentally incapable, mentally incapacitated, or physically helpless; or

4. the other person is related to the perpetrator by blood or affinity and the penetration occurs under circumstances not otherwise covered by the criminal sexual conduct law.

---

2. *Mentally incapable* means that a person has a mental disease or defect that renders that person temporarily or permanently incapable of appraising the nature of his or her conduct. *Mentally incapacitated* means that a person is rendered temporarily incapable of appraising or controlling his or her conduct due to the influence of a narcotic, anesthetic, or other substance administered to that person without his or her consent, or due to any other act committed upon that person without his or her consent. M.C.L. § 750.520a.
3. M.C.L. § 750.520c.
4. M.C.L. § 600.2907.
5. M.C.L. § 750.520d.

A person is guilty of criminal sexual conduct in the fourth degree if he or she engages in sexual contact with another person and any of the following circumstances exist:[6]

1. the victim is at least 13 and under 16 years of age and the perpetrator is 5 or more years older than the victim;

2. force or coercion is used;

3. the perpetrator knows or has reason to know that the victim is mentally incapable, mentally incapacitated, or physically helpless;

4. the victim is under the jurisdiction of the Department of Corrections and the perpetrator is an employee or volunteer with the Department and knows that the victim is under the Department's jurisdiction;

5. the victim is a prisoner or probationer in a county jail or work program and the perpetrator is a county employee or volunteer who knows the victim is under the county's jurisdiction;

6. the victim is in a juvenile facility and the perpetrator is an employee or volunteer with the facility; and

7. the victim is related to the perpetrator by blood or affinity (other than marriage) and the sexual contact occurs under circumstances not otherwise prohibited by the criminal sexual conduct law.

(B) Assault

In Michigan, assault can be a misdemeanor or a felony and is categorized by the manner in which it is done, if a weapon is used, any injury inflicted, and the intention of the perpetrator.[7] To assault someone means to willfully attempt to inflict an injury on another person, coupled with an apparent ability to do so, which gives the person reason to fear bodily harm.

There may be circumstances in which an MHP is justified in touching a client, for example, if the client has become agitated and appears to present a threat of harm to self or others. In such a case, the force that may be used is only that degree necessary to prevent the potential danger. However, the MHP should be wary of touching a client in any but the most socially permissible manner (for example, a handshake at the beginning or end of a session.)

---

6. M.C.L. § 750.520e.
7. M.C.L. § 750.81 et seq.

(C) Manslaughter

Manslaughter is a homicide, that is, an illegal killing, that is not a murder. In Michigan manslaughter is a felony.[8] An MHP could conceivably be charged with manslaughter or criminally negligent homicide if he or she causes the death of a patient through the reckless or grossly negligent use of drugs or other modes of therapy.

---

8. M.C.L. § 750.321.

3.13

Liability of Credentialing Boards

Certain branches of government, such as the legislature and judiciary, are immune from lawsuits. This originated from the maxim that "the king can do no wrong," but is now premised on the theory that it cannot be tortious (i.e., injurious) conduct for a government to govern. This absolute immunity does not extend to all aspects of government, however. This issue is important to MHPs because they may be sued for their actions as members of a credentialing board.

Michigan has waived immunity from liability for many actions of its agencies and employees.[1] A federal court in Michigan has established that members of credentialing boards possess quasi-judicial immunity and may not be sued. Quasi-judicial immunity means that the person or entity who would be sued in a civil case operated with the independence and discretion similar to that of a judge or a court and therefore may not be held liable for actions taken in the course of their role.

A former physician brought a civil rights suit in federal district court seeking damages against the Michigan State Board of Medicine challenging the revocation and denial of reinstatement of his license.[2] The physician had been convicted in federal court on charges of conspiracy and intent to distribute controlled substances. The court ruled the State Board of Medicine was entitled to quasi-judicial absolute immunity because it performs a judicial function. The court referred to a previous federal case[3] where a physician sued individual members of the Tennessee Board of

---

1. M.C.L. § 691.1407.
2. Alexander v. Margolis, 921 F.Supp. 492 (1995).
3. Watts v. Burkhart, 978 F.2d 269 (1992).

Medicine for damages for giving him a choice of voluntarily surrendering his license or having it suspended by the Board. In this case the court also held that members of a state board have quasi-judicial immunity.

The peer review statute[4] creates an immunity from civil liability for damages for any person who provides information to a medical review committee for the purpose of assisting in evaluating qualifications, fitness, or character of a health care provider (see also chapter 3.9).

---

4. M.C.L. § 331.532.

3.14

Antitrust Limitations to Practice

Antitrust laws were enacted to prevent the formation of monopolies and prevent the abuses of economic power. In recent years, health care providers and their organizations have increasingly become defendants in antitrust litigation. Scrutinized activities include price fixing (an agreement among competitors to establish a common price or a system for setting prices), the division of markets (an agreement among competitors to allocate certain markets to certain participants), a group boycott (an agreement among competitors to patronize only certain businesses), and tying arrangements (where a party agrees to sell a certain product or service only on the condition that the buyer also purchases a different product). All of these fall under the general prohibition of *restraint of trade*.

Most enforcement is through federal law in federal court. However, state law also applies. This chapter is limited to Michigan antitrust law. It applies to any MHP or organization.

(A) Prohibited Activities

Any agreement between two or more persons to restrain or monopolize trade or commerce,[1] or to set or fix prices[2] is unlawful in Michigan. A professional association (such as a bar association or state psychiatric association) may not suppress the lawful advertising of its members.[3] The antitrust law generally does not apply

---

1. M.C.L. § 445.772.
2. M.C.L. § 445.773.
3. 5024 Op. Att'y. Gen. 299 (1978).

to actions of health maintenance corporations, health insurers, or health care corporations when the intent is to reduce the cost of health care and is permitted by the insurance commission.[4] In addition, in Michigan case law, participation agreements between health insurers and outpatient psychotherapy clinics which set fees for service were not to be considered in violation of antitrust laws.[5] In this case, a clinic sued Michigan Blue Cross/Blue Shield because it wanted to give different reimbursements to those services provided by therapists depending on their educational qualifications. The court ruled that this policy is reasonable and does not constitute a restraint of trade or price-fixing. It ruled that fixing a set fee Blue Cross will pay did not prevent the clinic from charging either over or under the set fee or from charging whatever they wanted.

4. M.C.L. § 445.774.
5. Michigan Ass'n of Psychotherapy Clinics v. Blue Cross & Blue Shield of Mich., 325 N.W.2d 471, 118 Mich.App. 505 (1982).

Families and Juveniles

4.1

Competency to Marry

To marry, many states require a minimum mental status. In Michigan, each party must be competent to contract and a marriage is voidable if a party was incapable of consenting to the marriage for "want of understanding." The marriage can be annulled (see chapter 4.4) if a party, because of illness or retardation, was not able, at the time of the marriage, to comprehend the significance of the decision to marry. It must be proven that the party was mentally incapable of understanding the nature, effects, and consequences of the marriage. MHPs may be called to evaluate a party in question and testify in court.

(A) Standard for Voiding a Marriage

Although there is no statutory definition of civil competency, the lack of competency has been defined in case law as "one who is so affected mentally as to be deprived of sane and normal action or who lacks sufficient capacity to understand in a reasonable manner the nature and effect of the act he is performing."[1] Marriages made when either party was "insane or an idiot" are void (that is they do not have legal force), but children of such a marriage are legitimate.[2] If a person has been committed to a public institution or judged by a court to be insane or so severely developmentally disabled as to be incompetent, then he or she is determined to be unable to contract in marriage. This can be waived by the person filing certificates from at least two licensed physicians indicating

1. May v. Leneair, 297 N.W.2d 882, 99 Mich.App. 209 (1980).
2. M.C.L. § 552.1

that he or she has been cured of the insanity or developmental disability and that there is no likelihood that any defects can be transmitted to possible children.[3] It is a felony to knowingly enter into a marriage with such a person without submitting the appropriate certificates.[4]

---

3. M.C.L. § 551.6.
4. M.C.L. § 552.1.

4.2

Guardianship for Adults

Individuals who are legally incapacitated, that is, unable to conduct their day-to-day affairs because of an emotional or cognitive disability, may be appointed a guardian who will control their lives much as parents oversee the lives of their children. There are two classes of persons for whom guardianship is generally obtained: minors and adults incapacitated because of mental impairment, retardation, old age, or disease. This chapter is limited to a discussion of guardianship for incapacitated and similar persons. Guardianship for minors is discussed in chapter 4.11. An MHP may become involved in this process by being asked to evaluate the person and testify as to whether the person meets the test for a guardianship, and/or by providing therapeutic services to the person after a guardianship has been imposed.

(A) Application for Guardianship

The legally incapacitated person or any person interested in the person's welfare may petition the court for a finding of incapacity and appointment of a guardian.[1] The petition must contain specific facts about the person's condition and specific examples of the person's recent conduct that demonstrate that he or she needs a guardian. On the filing of a petition, the probate court in the county where the person resides or is found must appoint a guardian ad litem, usually an attorney, unless the person has legal counsel of his or her own. A guardian ad litem is an individual who can represent the person's interest in the proceedings.

---

1. M.C.L. § 700.443.

The court may also order that the person be examined by a court-appointed physician or mental health professional who must submit a written report to the court at least 5 days before the hearing. This report is not made a part of the public record of the hearing. The allegedly incapacitated person has the right to obtain an independent evaluation in addition to the court-ordered one. The report must be signed and contain (a) a detailed description of the physical or psychological infirmities of the person, if any, (b) an explanation of how and to what extent any infirmities interfere with the ability of the person to receive or evaluate information in making decisions, (c) a listing of all medications, their dosage, and any effects each medication has on the person's behavior, and (d) a prognosis for improvement and a recommendation for the most appropriate rehabilitation plan.[2]

(B) Guardianship Hearing

At the guardianship hearing the person alleged to be incapacitated has the right to be present and see and hear all evidence, to be represented by counsel, to present evidence, and to cross-examine all witnesses including the court-appointed physician or mental health professional, have a trial by jury, and have the matter decided at a closed hearing.[3] There is no statutory definition of civil incapacity in Michigan. Definitions have generally been determined by case law. The person must be so mentally impaired that he or she is incapable of understanding and acting with discretion in the ordinary affairs of life.[4] If elderly, a person's debility must be such that they cannot intelligently direct the management of their affairs as a result of which their estate might suffer loss or waste.[5]

---

2. *Id.*
3. *Id.*
4. *In re* Johnson's Estate, 281 N.W. 598, 286 Mich. 213 (1921). Case law has established that a person may be deemed mentally competent but still may be incapable of managing his or her affairs (*In re* Swisher's Estate, 37 N.W.2d 657, 324 Mich. 643 (1949)).
5. *In re* Swisher's Estate, 37 N.W.2d 657, 325 Mich. 643 (1949). Showing that an elderly person is unwise, lacks judgment, indulges in folly, or squanders his or her property is not sufficient grounds for appointing a guardian. (*In re* Johnson's Estate, 281 N.W. 597, 286 Mich. 213 (1921)).

(C) Appointment, Duties, and Power of the Guardian

While any competent person may be appointed as guardian, the law indicates that if a suitable and willing person is specified by the incapacitated person, that person will be so appointed. If this is not possible, the choice of guardian is made according to the following priorities:[6]

1. the spouse of the incapacitated person;
2. an adult child of the incapacitated person;
3. a parent of the incapacitated person;
4. a relative with whom the legally incapacitated person has resided for more than 6 months prior to the filing of the petition; and
5. the nominee of a person who is caring for or paying benefits to the person.

Guardians are appointed for the person in question only if there is clear and convincing evidence that the person is incapacitated.[7] If the legally incapacitated person lacks the capacity to do some, but not all self-care tasks, a limited guardian may be appointed.[8]

Guardians of incapacitated persons are responsible for the care, custody, and control of their wards, but are not liable for the acts of a ward.[9] The law further specifies the following powers and duties:[10]

1. to have custody of the ward and establish the ward's residence in or out of the state;
2. to provide for the welfare and training of the ward, and to secure services designed to enable the ward to return to self-management at the earliest possible time;
3. to consent to or approve medical or other professional care;
4. if no conservator has been appointed (see chapter 4.3), to receive money and tangible property deliverable to the ward; and
5. to report on the condition of the ward, as required by the court.

---

6. M.C.L. § 700.45.
7. M.C.L. § 700.444(1).
8. M.C.L. § 700.444(3).
9. M.C.L. § 700.455(1).
10. *Id.*

(D) Termination of the Guardianship

The authority and responsibility of a guardian terminates if the ward or guardian dies, a court determines that the guardian is incapacitated, the court removes the guardian; or the guardian resigns.[11] Before the court approves any changes in guardianship, it must follow the same procedures and respect the rights of the person as described previously in sections (A) and (B) of this chapter.[12]

---

11. M.C.L. § 700.446.
12. M.C.L. § 700.447(2).

4.3

Conservatorship for Adults

In addition to appointing a guardian, the law authorizes the court to appoint a person to manage the estate (e.g., property, financial resources, and business enterprises) of an incompetent ward. This chapter focuses on adult wards. Conservatorship for minors is discussed in chapter 5.13. MHPs may become involved in this process by being asked to evaluate the person and to testify as to the person's capacity to manage his or her estate, and/or by providing therapeutic services to the person after a conservatorship has been imposed.

(A) Application for Conservatorship

Conservatorship may be obtained by filing a petition with the probate court. The person to be protected, or anyone who is interested in that person's estate, affairs, or welfare or who might be adversely affected by poor management of the person's affairs may petition.[1] The petition must describe[2]

1. the interest of the petitioner;
2. the name, age, residence, and address of the person to be protected; the name and address of the guardian, if any, of the person to be protected;
3. the name and address of the nearest relative of the person to be protected known to the petitioner;

---

1. M.C.L. § 700.464(1).
2. M.C.L. § 700.464(2).

4. a general statement of the property of the person to be protected with an estimate of its value, including any compensation, insurance, pension, or allowance to which the person is entitled;

5. reasons why appointment of a conservator is necessary; and

6. the name and address of the person to be appointed and the reasons for appointing that person.

(B) Conservatorship Hearing

After receiving a petition, the court will set a date for the hearing. If the person does not have an attorney, the court must appoint one who will act as guardian ad litem. A guardian ad litem is a person who is empowered to represent the person's interests in the hearing. The court may also order that the person to be protected be examined by a physician, and/or may send a visitor to interview the person. This visitor may be the guardian ad litem or an officer or employee of the court.[3]

In order to appoint a conservator, the court must determine that there is an underlying basis for the person's inability to manage his or her estate (i.e., mental illness, mental incompetency, physical illness or disability, chronic use of drugs, chronic intoxication, confinement, detention by a foreign power, or disappearance) and that either the person has property that will be wasted unless proper management is provided or that funds are needed for the support and care of the person. A conservator can be appointed for a person who is mentally competent, but due to age or physical infirmity is unable to manage his or her property and affairs and who, recognizing the disability, asks for a conservator to be appointed.[4]

(C) Appointment, Duties, and Power of the Conservator

A conservator is appointed by the court. The powers and duties of the conservator are very broad. For instance, title to all the person's property and assets passes to the conservator, who can sell, transfer, divide, or otherwise manage it in the same manner as any person would handle his or her own financial affairs. Thus the conservator can sell or lease property, invest assets, hold a

---

3. M.C.L. § 700.467.
4. M.C.L. § 700.461.

security in the name of the person, obtain insurance for property, borrow money to be repaid from the person's assets, pay taxes, and pay others to assist the conservator in carrying out these duties.[5] The conservator can pay out money to those responsible for the education or care of the protected person and that person's dependents.[6] The law does not require any special reports to be made to the court regarding the conservator's activities. Within 60 days of appointment, the conservator is required to compile and submit to the court a complete inventory of the estate of the protected person. The conservator must keep suitable records of the administration of the estate and provide them upon request to the court or any other interested party.[7]

(D) Termination of the Conservatorship

Any interested person, including the protected person, may petition the court to terminate the conservatorship. Protected persons seeking termination are entitled to the same rights and procedures as are followed during the application process(see Section (B) above). Thus, a hearing is held and evidence is heard regarding the capacity of the person to manage his or her affairs. If the court decides that the person's disability has ceased it can order the conservatorship terminated. Upon termination, title of all property passes back to the protected person.[8]

---

5. M.C.L. § 700.484.
6. M.C.L. § 700.485.
7. M.C.L. § 700.477.
8. M.C.L. § 700.490.

Annulment

Whereas a divorce dissolves what was once a valid, functioning marriage, annulment is the process whereby a marriage is declared void and is legally held never to have existed. This result can have legal significance. For instance, a widowed spouse of a worker receives compensation benefits until the widow remarries, and if the second marriage ceases by virtue of an annulment rather than divorce, the person regains the benefits. MHPs may be involved in an annulment proceeding directly through evaluation and testimony, or indirectly when they are working with persons who are contemplating the dissolution of their marriage.

(A) Grounds for Annulment

A marriage may be annulled in cases where the consent of one of the parties is obtained by force or fraud and there is no subsequent voluntary cohabitation of the parties.[1] For example, where a man enters into a marriage with the sole intent of defrauding the woman out of her property, the marriage can be annulled. However, if she voluntarily lived with him knowing that this was his intent, it could not.[2] Marriages also can be annulled if the parties are illegally related to each other, if either of the parties have a wife or husband then living, or where either of the parties is insane or incompetent because of retardation (see also chapter

---

1. Voluntary cohabitation means that the spouse would have knowledge of all the essential facts relied on as grounds for annulment.
2. M.C.L. § 552.3.

4.1).[3] Illegal relationships include consanguinity, which are blood relationships, or affinity, which is the connection that people have with each other through marriage (e.g., stepfather and step-daughter).

In order to annul a marriage, a petition must be filed in the circuit court of the county in which one party resides. The procedures are then similar to those pursuant to filing a divorce (see chapter 4.5).[4]

---

3. M.C.L. § 552.1.
4. M.C.L. § 552.3.

4.5

Divorce

Prior to 1972, divorce law in Michigan (and in many states today) required the petitioning party to allege fault by the other spouse. This changed when Michigan included a no-fault divorce provision in the divorce law, which eliminated all prior statutory ground for divorce and substituted the single requirement that there has been a breakdown in the marriage such that the objects of matrimony have been destroyed and there remains no reasonable likelihood that the marriage can be preserved.[1] Now, so long as one spouse alleges such a breakdown, litigation will typically center around property division, child support, alimony, or child custody (see chapter 4.6). Aside from custody assessments, MHPs become involved in divorce issues by providing counseling and psychotherapy to individuals, couples, and families who are contemplating, participating in, or recovering from a divorce. In addition, many MHPs participate as trained mediators, helping divorcing families to resolve problems in divorce through negotiation rather than litigation. Also, some MHPs participate as parenting coordinators, assisting parents with custody and visitation disputes, often with the authority to arbitrate the issue, if necessary.

(A) Divorce Procedure

The dissolution of a marriage is initiated by a complaint filed in the Circuit Court. A complaint cannot be filed unless one of the parties has resided in Michigan for at least 180 days immediately

---

1. M.C.L. § 552.6(1).

preceding the filing. One of the parties must also have lived in the county in which the complaint is filed for at least 10 days immediately prior to the filing.[2] The complaint may not state any explanation of the grounds for the divorce other than that the objects of matrimony have been destroyed and there is no reasonable likelihood that the marriage can be preserved.[3] The person who files the complaint is considered the plaintiff and the subject of the complaint is considered the defendant. After the complaint has been filed, the defendant must be served with notice as to its existence.[4] The defendant may either admit or deny the grounds for divorce alleged by the plaintiff without further explanation.[5] The court then decides whether or not to grant the divorce based on evidence presented in open court as to whether the two statutory requirements have been met.[6]

There is no statutory definition of what is meant by the "objects of matrimony," but it has been interpreted to include the bearing and rearing of children, economic goals, the status attached to being a spouse, acceptance within the section of society within which one functions, sexual fulfillment, mutual kindness, affection, respect, and emotional support.[7] As established by case law, the objects of matrimony are seen as destroyed when either party in a marriage relationship is unwilling to live together with the other.[8] In the case of a contested divorce, where the defendant objects to the dissolution of the marriage, each party would present evidence to the court as to whether or not these objects have been destroyed.

In some counties, divorcing parties have access to a Marriage Counseling Service, available under the auspices of the Circuit Court, which may help in determining the sources and causes of their dispute and may assist the parties in resolving them.[9]

Upon a finding that the marriage should be dissolved, the court will make provisions for division of property, support payments, and child custody. These matters are incorporated into a judgment of divorce that is final when entered.

---

2. M.C.L. § 552.9.
3. M.C.L. § 552.6(1).
4. M.C.L. § 552.9a.
5. M.C.L. § 552.6(2).
6. M.C.L. § 552.6(3).
7. 50 MICH. B.J. 740 (1971).
8. Grotelueschen v. Grotelueschen, 113 Mich.App. 395 (1982).
9. Marriage Counseling Certification Act, M.C.L. § 551.331 et seq.

4.6

Child Custody After Marital Dissolution

Child custody determinations can result from four types of changes in the legal status of the marriage: annulment, legal separation, divorce, and modification of a divorce decree. The Child Custody Act of 1970 (since amended twice) governs the process of determining child custody and visitation, now defined as *parenting time*.[1] Unlike some states, there is no presumption of a particular type of custody arrangement. However, the parents are to be advised of joint custody and joint custody may be considered by the court.[2]

MHPs may become involved in this determination in one of two ways. First, the judge, the Friend of the Court,[3] or any other party may request an evaluation of the child and his or her parents and/or proposed stepparents for the purpose of assisting the court in determining what custody and visitation arrangement is in the best interest of the child. This process frequently culminates in an MHP's court appearance as an expert witness. Second, an MHP who has provided services to the family unit, whether diagnostic or therapeutic, may be subpoenaed by either party to present evidence as a witness. A subpoena from one parent may not be sufficient to release the confidential rights of

---

1. M.C.L. § 722.21 et seq.
2. M.C.L. § 722.26a.
3. Each jurisdiction has a Friend of the Court, whose duty it is to assist the court in family law matters. When parents cannot agree or when ordered by the judge, the Friend of the Court conducts investigations and makes recommendations to the court regarding custody, parenting time, and child support. It may also offer mediation and family education services. It is responsible for collecting and distributing child support payments. It also provides enforcement services on court orders. M.C.L. § 552.503.

other family members, however (see chapter 3.5 and this chapter, section (C)(1)).

A) Criteria to Establish Court Jurisdiction

The authority of the court to assume jurisdiction over the child is generally a factual determination based upon the domicile of the child and parents. In the absence of a statute providing otherwise, and as established by precedent, the court which has jurisdiction in the original suit for divorce assumes jurisdiction over custody of the children.[4] If, however, the child and the parent have relocated out of state after the divorce and a new custody action is filed in Michigan, the court will consider the ties of the parents and children to the state of Michigan in determining whether to continue to assume jurisdiction.[5]

When there is a preliminary finding in Circuit Court that a child under the age of 17 is dependent and neglected, the court may waive jurisdiction of custody to the Family Court Division of the Circuit Court, which is charged with adjudicating these issues.[6]

B) Legal Standards in Custody Determinations

The court determines custody in accordance with the welfare and best interests of the child.[7] Michigan's best interest statute requires the court to consider the sum total of and make specific findings on,[8] the following factors, which define best interests:[9]

1. the love, affection, and other emotional ties existing between the parties involved and the child;

---

4. *E.g.*, Lehman v. Lehman, 342 Mich. 708 (1956); Rex v. Rex, 331 Mich. 399 (1951).
5. Bigelow v. Bigelow, 119 Mich.App. 784 (1983).
6. Matter of Robey, 136 Mich.App. 566 (1984).
7. There is a presumption that when there is a dispute between the parent(s) and an agency or third party, the best interests of the child are served by giving custody to the parent(s), unless clear and convincing evidence is presented otherwise. M.C.L. § 722.25.
8. Troxler v. Troxler, 61 Mich.App. 1 (1978).
9. M.C.L. § 722.23.

2. the capacity and disposition of the parties involved to give the child love, affection, and guidance and to continue the education and raising of the child in his or her religion or creed, if any;

3. the capacity and disposition of the parties involved to provide the child with food, clothing, medical care, or other remedial care recognized and permitted under the laws of the state in place of medical care, and other material needs;

4. the length of time the child has lived in a stable, satisfactory environment, and the desirability of maintaining continuity;

5. the permanence, as a family unit, of the existing or proposed custodial home or homes;

6. the moral fitness of the parties involved;

7. the mental and physical health of the parties involved;

8. the home, school, and community record of the child;

9. the reasonable preference of the child, if the court considers the child to be of sufficient age to express preference;

10. the willingness and ability of each of the parties to facilitate and encourage a close and continuing parent–child relationship between the child and the other parent or the child and the parents;

11. domestic violence, regardless of whether the violence was directed against or witnessed by the child; and

12. any other factor considered by the court to be relevant to a particular child custody dispute.

The court may recommend and provide for reasonable visitation with the child by the parties involved or by others. There is a presumption that it is in the child's best interest to have a strong relationship with each parent and visitation is to be granted in a frequency, duration, and type reasonably calculated to promote this relationship.[10]

Grandparents can seek a court order allowing them visitation with their minor grandchildren if a child custody dispute is pending before the court.[11] Grandparents, however, lack legal standing to initiate a petition for visitation or custody in the absence of a parental custody dispute. The court may modify its order of judgment on custody and/or visitation upon the petition of either of the parents. The petitioning party must show that there has

---

10. M.C.L. § 722.27a. This section also contains specific factors for the court to consider in determining the frequency, duration, and type of visitation to be granted.
11. M.C.L. § 722.27b.

been a change of circumstances and must meet a standard of clear and convincing evidence in order to support a modification.[12]

C) Mental Health Evaluations

In all situations in which a dispute over custody arises, there must be an investigation by the Friend of the Court[13] of the home environment and surroundings of the parties and any other person in whose home the children are to be kept.[14] The Friend of the Court then submits a report to the court regarding the home conditions, moral surroundings, and the care given to the children.[15] An MHP employee of the Friend of the Court participates in these investigations. In investigating and studying a custody dispute or modification of custody or visitation, the Friend of the Court or the judge may use community resources in the behavioral sciences and other professions and consider their recommendations for the resolution of the dispute.[16] MHPs customarily perform such evaluations by order of the court. However, evaluations may also be requested by an individual party or his or her attorney.

(1) Confidentiality and Privileged Communications

In the majority of examinations, the information obtained by an MHP is confidential (see chapter 3.3) and privileged (see chapter 3.4) even though it is undertaken by order of the court. In some cases an MHP who is a treating therapist of one or both of the parties or the children may be subpoenaed by one of the parties to provide testimony in a custody proceeding. Unless written consent is obtained from the concerned parties, an MHP is required to provide information only as directed by the court and after consideration of the effects of such testimony on the MHP–patient relationship.

---

12. M.C.L. § 552.17.
13. *Supra* note 3.
14. M.C.L. § 552.505.
15. M.C.L. § 552.501 et seq. This report is not generally admissible as evidence unless the parties agree. Dempsey v. Dempsey, 96 Mich.App. 276 (1980); Mann v. Mann, 190 Mich.App. 526, 476 N.W.2d 439 (1991).
16. M.C.L. § 722.27.

4.7

Reporting of Adult Abuse

The law requires certain individuals who suspect or have reasonable cause to believe that a vulnerable person 18 or over is being abused, neglected, exploited, or is endangered to make a report. MHPs may become involved either because of a duty to report or by being requested to evaluate the adult as part of an ensuing investigation.

(A) Who Must Report

The requirement to report is based on a person's profession and employment and not on any relationship to or responsibility for the adult. There are a broad number of categories of people who have a duty to report adult abuse. Any person, except for a physician, who is employed, licensed, registered, or certified to provide health care, educational, social welfare, mental health, or other human services is required to report. Law enforcement officers and employees of the county medical examiner's office must also report. There is a different standard for physicians, who must make a report only if in the physician's professional judgment it is in the best interest of the adult to make such a report.

---

1. M.C.L. § 400.11.
2. *Id.*

B) When Must a Report Be Made?

The duty to report adult abuse or neglect applies when the person is deemed vulnerable. This means that the person is unable to protect himself or herself because of a mental or physical impairment or because of the frailties of advanced age. An MHP must report when there is reason to suspect or reasonable cause to believe that abuse, neglect, endangerment, or exploitation is occurring. Abuse means harm or threatened harm to the person's health or welfare by another person such as nonaccidental physical or mental injury, sexual abuse, or maltreatment. Neglect includes such harm to a person's welfare as failure to provide adequate food, clothing, shelter, or medical care. Endangerment means placing or allowing a person to be in a situation that is life-threatening to which that person is unable to respond in order to protect themselves. Exploitation means the misuse of the person's funds, property, or personal dignity.

C) How a Report Must Be Made

The duty to report is fulfilled by reporting to an Adult Protective Services worker at the Family Independence Agency[3] of the county in which the abuse is suspected to have occurred.[4] An oral report must be made immediately by telephone or otherwise. The reporting person may, but is not required to file a written report. The report must contain the name of the adult and a description of the suspected abuse. If possible, the adult's age, and information about the person's next of kin, guardian, or caretaker should be included.

D) Immunity From Liability

Any person reporting under this law is immune from civil liability arising out of the report and is assumed to be acting in good faith.[5]

---

3. Formerly known as the Department of Social Services.
4. M.C.L. § 400.11a.
5. M.C.L. § 400.11c.

(E) Confidentiality and Privilege

Most services provided by an MHP are confidential, eith
through law or the ethics of the profession (see chapter 3.3). Whi
the law keeps the identity of the reporter of abuse confidenti
unless judicial process requires that it be made known, it abr
gates the MHP–client privilege and requires the MHP to brea
confidentiality in order to report.[6]

(F) Failure to Report

A person who fails to make a report when required to do so
civilly liable for any damage proximately caused by the failure
report and can be subject to a civil fine of not more than $500 fe
each failure.[7]

---

6. *Id.*
7. M.C.L. § 400.11e.

4.8

Reporting of Child Abuse

The law requires MHPs to report known or suspected incidents of child abuse. Although the initial duty to report is discharged once the report is properly filed, the MHP may also have to appear in court proceedings as a witness on this issue (see chapter 4.10).

A) Who Must Report

The law applies to psychologists, physicians, coroners, dentists, registered dental hygienists, medical examiners, nurses, persons licensed to provide emergency medical care, audiologists, marriage and family therapists, licensed professional counselors, certified social workers, social workers, social work technicians, school administrators, school counselors or teachers, law enforcement officers and regulated child care providers.[1] Government employees do not have immunity from reporting child abuse and neglect.[2]

B) When Must a Report Be Made?

When a person listed above has "reasonable cause to suspect child abuse or neglect," he or she must report it. The law defines abuse as harm or threatened harm to a child's health or welfare caused by nonaccidental physical or mental injury, sexual abuse, sexual exploitation, or maltreatment. Neglect is defined as any

---

1. M.C.L. § 722.623(3).
2. Williams v. Coleman, 488 N.W.2d 464, 194 Mich.App.606 (1992).

negligent treatment of the child, such as failing to provide ade
quate food, clothing, shelter, or medical care or as placing a chil
in a situation of unreasonable risk.[3] In addition, the pregnancy c
a child under age 12 or the presence of venereal disease in a chil
under 12 years old and over 1 month of age is deemed reasonabl
cause to suspect abuse. While the term *reasonable cause to suspect* i
not further defined in the law and therefore gives MHPs littl
guidance in terms of how broadly to apply the standard, th
Michigan Court of Appeals has held that the term provides fai
notice of the conduct expected and is neither vague nor overl
broad.[4]

The reporting requirement includes harm caused by paren
and by guardians, teachers, teacher's aides, or any other perso
responsible for the child's health or welfare. The fact that a parer
is seeking treatment for the child does not absolve the profes
sional of the duty to report. The law does not speak to whether c
not a person required to report must have actually seen or exam
ined the child.

(C) How a Report Must Be Made

The duty to report is fulfilled by making an immediate ora
report, by telephone or otherwise, to a Child Protective Service
worker at the Family Independence Agency.[5] A written repo
must follow within 72 hours and be sent to the agency in th
county where the child resides. In addition, if the reporter is
staff member at a hospital, school, or agency, he or she mus
notify the person in charge that a report has been made and mak
a copy of the written report available to that person. The writte
report should contain the name of the child, a description of th
abuse or neglect, and any information that might help establis
the cause of the abuse or neglect. If known, it should also includ
the age of the child and the names and addresses of the child'
parents, legal guardian, or caretaker.

---

3. M.C.L. § 722.622; M.C.L. § 722.623.
4. People v. Cavaiani, 423 N.W.2d 409, 172 Mich.App. 706 (1988). This is a cas
   in which a limited license psychologist and family therapist did not repo
   possible abuse by the father that was suspected by the mother, alleged b
   the child, and not acknowledged by the father. The therapist appeale
   maintaining that the statute was overbroad and vague and that it interfere
   with therapist–patient privilege. The appeal was upheld in Circuit Cou
   but reversed by the Court of Appeals. Cavaiani was acquitted at trial.
5. Formerly known as the Department of Social Services.

(D) Immunity From Liability

A person who acts in good faith when making a report of child abuse and neglect is immune from civil or criminal liability arising out of making the report.[6] However, a person is guilty of a misdemeanor if he or she knowingly and maliciously makes a false report.[7]

(E) Confidentiality and Privilege

Most services provided by an MHP are confidential, either through law or the ethics of the profession (see chapter 3.3). The identity of the reporter of abuse or neglect is kept confidential unless judicial process requires that it be disclosed.[8] There is no confidentiality if the MHP is required to report suspected child abuse under this law. While MHP–client privilege is generally held on a par with attorney–client privilege, the child protection law abrogates this privilege in cases of child abuse and neglect and requires reporting.[9]

(F) Failure to Report

A person who fails to report under this statute is guilty of a misdemeanor and is also civilly liable for any damages proximately caused by failing to report.[10]

---

6. M.C.L. § 722.625.
7. M.C.L. § 722.633.
8. The law also requires that the Family Independence Agency keep a registry with information on substantiated cases of child abuse. Access to the registry is regulated, but available to a broad range of interested parties. M.C.L. § 722.627.
9. M.C.L. § 722.631.
10. M.C.L. § 722.633.

4.9

Abused and Neglected Children

Procedures for handling child abuse and neglect cases typically involve three stages: a) taking the child into protective custody, b) holding a fact-finding hearing, and c) holding a dispositional hearing. It is generally a hierarchical process that may stop at any point if the allegations are unfounded or on a showing that the parents are currently capable of raising their children in a responsible manner. Each stage may involve a mental health evaluation of the child and/or parent. In addition, the MHP may be called to testify as an expert witness (see chapter 4.10).

(A) Temporary Custody

A law enforcement officer may take a child into temporary custody if the child is found in a situation that endangers "his or her health, morals, or welfare."[1] If appropriate, the child's parents or guardian are then immediately contacted and, if appropriate, a hearing date is set and the child is released to their custody. If it is not appropriate for the child to be released, a preliminary hearing on the status of the child is immediately held. At this point, a complaint may be filed and a time for an adjudicatory hearing is set. The child may then be placed in the custody of the parents or guardian, or placed elsewhere, such as with relatives or in foster care.

If a physician at a hospital, upon examining a child, suspects that the child has been abused and determines that releasing the child would endanger his or her health or welfare, the person in

---

1. M.C.L. § 712a.14.

charge can place the child in temporary protective custody until the next business day of the court. The court then determines action as delineated above.[2]

The state Family Independence Agency (FIA) has the primary responsibility for the investigation, within 24 hours, of all complaints of alleged child abuse and neglect.[3]

(B) Adjudication of Alleged Child Abuse or Neglect

An adjudicatory hearing must be held after the filing of a petition (often by a child protective services worker or law enforcement officer).[4] After the petition has been filed, the court may order the child to be evaluated by a physician, dentist, psychologist, or psychiatrist.[5] Every child in an abuse and neglect proceeding is represented by a guardian ad litem, usually an attorney, who is charged with representing the child's best interest.[6] Children who may be required to testify at a hearing are provided by law with a number of supports. They are permitted to be assisted by using dolls (including anatomically correct dolls), having a support person sit close by, being allowed to testify out of the view of the alleged abuser, and, if it is determined that psychological harm would occur if testifying in person, testifying via videotape.[7]

At the hearing, the state must prove by a preponderance of the evidence,[8] that the parent or other legally responsible person refuses or neglects to provide the child with "necessary support, education, medical, surgical, or other care necessary for his or her health or morals," has abandoned the child, or has subjected the child to a "substantial risk of harm to his or her mental well-being."[9] MHPs may participate as expert witnesses at this and subsequent hearings.

---

2. M.C.L. § 722.626.
3. M.C.L. § 722.628.
4. *In re* Nelson, 475 N.W.2d 448, 190 Mich.App. 237 (1991).
5. M.C.L. § 712a.12.
6. M.C.L. § 722.630.
7. M.C.L. § 712a.17b. *In re* Brock, 485 N.W.2d 110, 193 Mich.App. 652 (1992).
8. Matter of Campbell, 342 N.W.2d 607, 129 Mich.App. 780 (1983).
9. M.C.L. § 712a.2.

(C) Dispositional Alternatives

The court has a number of alternatives if it finds that the allegations in the petition are true. It may return the child to the home under supervision or

1. order the abuser to leave the home if it is in the best interest of the child to remain in the home; the abuser presents a substantial risk to the child and removal is necessary to safeguard the child;[10]
2. place the child in a foster home;
3. place the child in a state licensed private institution or agency;
4. place the child in a public institution; or
5. place the child with a guardian.[11]

In addition, for a child placed outside the home, a petition for termination of the parent–child relationship may be filed (see chapter 4.10).

---

10. M.C.L. § 712.13a.
11. M.C.L. § 712.18.

4.10

Termination of Parental Rights

After child abuse, neglect, or maltreatment has been reported and a finding is made (see chapters 4.8 and 4.9), the question will sometimes arise as to whether parental rights should be terminated. This is an extreme and infrequent measure, particularly if it involves a first allegation of abuse. If a determination is made to petition for termination of parental rights, the parent is afforded the range of procedural due process rights, with which the parent must strictly comply. Because such a decision inevitably involves consideration of the child's emotional well-being and of the parent–child relationship, MHPs are frequently called on to undertake individual and family evaluations to assist the court in the decision.

A) Filing the Termination Petition

A petition for termination of rights can be filed if a child remains in foster care after a review hearing or permanency planning hearing (see chapter 4.13). It can be filed by the prosecutor, the child, a guardian, a custodian, a relevant agency, or an ombudsman for the child.[1] If a foster parent has specific knowledge of parental behavior that is grounds for termination, has contacted either FIA, the prosecutor, the child's attorney or the guardian ad litem and finds that none of them intends to file a petition, he or

---

1. M.C.L. § 712A.196, (1). M.C.L. § 722.927 created the role of ombudsman, which is a state-sponsored but independent watchdog office that oversees the care and treatment of abused and neglected children.

she may file as a *concerned person*.[2] There is no stipulation as to what the petition must contain.

(A)(1) Pre-Hearing Requirements

Written notice of the termination of rights hearing must be served on the following parties not less than 14 days before the hearing takes place: the agency, the parents, the guardian, the guardian ad litem, the tribal leader (if the child has a tribal affiliation), the attorneys for all parties, and the prosecutor and the child, if he or she is 11 years of age or older.[3]

(B) Grounds for Termination

In order to terminate parental rights, the court must find by clear and convincing evidence that one of the following exists:[4]

1. parental desertion: that the child has been deserted by the parent for 91 or more days and the parent has not sought custody of the child during this time. Desertion is also determined if the parent of a child is not able to be identified and has not sought custody for 28 or more days;

2. physical injury of the child or sibling or physical or sexual abuse of the child or sibling by the parent if the court finds that there is a reasonable likelihood that such abuse will reoccur in the foreseeable future if the child is placed with the parent. These grounds also apply if the parent had an opportunity to prevent the abuse and did not and there is a reasonable likelihood this could reoccur.

3. parental failure to rectify conditions: this applies when the court has made a previous disposition, usually giving the parent a chance to comply with necessary conditions for protecting or caring for the child. Rights may be terminated if the conditions at the previous disposition have not changed within 182 or more days and the parent, given a reasonable opportunity, has not and cannot be counted on to change within a reasonable time given the child's age;

4. the parent has placed the child in a limited guardianship[5] and has failed to comply with the plan to the point where it has disrupted the parent–child relationship;

---

2. M.C.L. § 712A.196, (6).
3. M.C.L. § 712A.19b, (2).
4. M.C.L. § 712A.19b, (3).
5. *See* M.C.L. § 700.242a.

5. the parent of the child who has a guardian and who can regularly support and assist his or her child, has failed to do so for 2 years or more. Also, a parent who is able to contact, visit, or communicate with his or her child and does not do so for 2 years or more falls under this category;

6. failure of the parent, whether intentionally or not, to provide proper care and custody of the child with no expectation that he or she will be able to within a reasonable time;

7. imprisonment of the parent for more than 2 years where the parent has not provided proper care and custody and will not be able to within a reasonable time;

8. termination of the parental rights to siblings due to serious and chronic abuse or neglect and where prior efforts to rehabilitate the parent have been unsuccessful; and

9. there is a reasonable likelihood based on the parent's conduct or capacity that the child will be harmed if returned to the parent.

C) The Termination Hearing and Decision

Written notice of a hearing must be given no less than 14 days before the hearing to: the agency caring for the child, the child if he or she is 11 years of age or older, the foster parent or custodian of the child, the parents, the guardian and/or guardian ad litem, if one exists, the child's attorney and the attorneys for all parties, and the prosecutor. Parents can be represented by counsel if they so desire. If the court determines at the hearing that there are grounds for termination, it may so rule and further order that there be no reunification attempts made. However, the court may choose not to terminate rights if it believes this would not be in the child's best interest.[6] The court must state its findings of fact and conclusions of law with respect to whether or not rights should be terminated either in writing or on the record (recorded as part of the proceedings of the hearing.)

D) Effects of Termination

If a child is still in foster care after parental rights are terminated, the court must hold a hearing not more than 182 days after termination, and at least every 182 days thereafter to review the

---

6. M.C.L. § 712A.19b, (5).

progress being made toward adoption or other permanent placement.[7] Parents whose rights have been terminated are not entitled
to visitation privileges.

(E) Emancipation of Minors

A minor may petition the court to be emancipated, which means
that the rights of the minor's parents to his or her custody, control,
services, and earnings are terminated.[8] A minor can be emancipated if they are married and at least age 16, have reached the
age of 18, or are on active duty in the armed services. The petition
for emancipation must declare that the minor has demonstrated
an ability to manage his or her financial, personal, and social
affairs, and must include an affidavit from any one of a number of
medical, mental health, or educational professionals indicating
that the professional believes that emancipation is in the best
interest of the child. A hearing is held and if the court orders
emancipation, the minor is considered to have all the rights and
responsibilities of an adult.[9]

---

7. M.C.L. § 712a.19c.
8. M.C.L. § 722.1.
9. M.C.L. § 722.4.

4.11

Guardianship for Minors

A guardian may be appointed for a minor in situations where the custodial parent(s) is unable to care for the child because of death, legal termination of parental rights, or other circumstances. In Michigan, guardians are appointed to undertake parental responsibilities, whereas conservators (see chapter 4.12) are appointed to manage the estate (e.g., money, property, and business enterprises). MHPs are likely to become involved in a guardian selection process and follow-up treatment, if any, for the children.

(A) Application for Guardianship

There are two methods of appointing a guardian of a minor. The first is by testamentary appointment in which the parents indicate in their will whom they wish to be guardian of their children.[1] This method takes effect only if both parents are dead or if the surviving parent is legally incapacitated.[2] Children ages 14 or older may object to a testamentary appointment by filing a written objection in the court before the estate is settled or within 30 days of the court's acceptance of the guardian.[3] Absent an objection, a testamentary appointment becomes effective when the guardian files an acceptance in the court in which the will is probated.

The second method of appointment is by a formal court hearing convened because a person interested in the child's wel-

---

1. M.C.L. § 700.422.
2. *Id.*
3. M.C.L. § 700.423.

fare, or the child him- or herself if over the age of 14, has petitioned the court requesting that it appoint a guardian. In these situations, the court may order an agency or MHP to investigate the proposed guardianship and to file a written report of the investigation.[4]

(B) The Guardianship Hearing

The petitioner must give notice to minors if they are over age 14; to the person who has had the principal care and custody of the minors during the 60 days preceding the filing of the petition; and to each living parent, or if neither parent is living, to the adult next of kin to the minor.[5] At the hearing the court first determines whether it has authority to appoint a guardian. A guardian may be appointed if (a) the parental rights of the parents have been terminated because of prior court order, judgment of divorce, death, mental incompetency, disappearance, or incarceration, (b) if the parents have allowed the child to live with another person and have not given that person legal authority to care for the child, and (c) if all of the following have occurred: the biological parents have never been married, the parent with custody dies or is missing and the other parent has not been granted legal custody and the person whom the petition cites for guardianship is related by blood, marriage, or adoption in at least the fifth degree.[6]

Michigan law allows for the appointment of a second type of guardian, known as a limited guardian. The limited guardian may be appointed by the court after petition of the parents if the parents consent to the appointment and voluntarily consent to the suspension of their parental rights. In addition, a limited guardianship placement plan must be developed and consented to by both the parents and the anticipated guardian.[7] The plan must include the reason for the request for a limited guardian, a parenting time schedule, the planned duration of the limited guardianship, provisions for financial support and any other provisions agreed to by the parties. The court upon review may approve, disapprove, or modify the proposed plan. In considering who should be appointed as a child's guardian, the court will usually consider close relatives first,[8] and, when differentiating between those relatives so entitled to guardianship, will consider the

---

4. M.C.L. § 700.424.
5. M.C.L. § 700.427(1).
6. M.C.L. § 700.427(2).
7. M.C.L. § 700.424a(1).
8. *In re* Stockman, 38 N.W. 876, 71 Mich. 180 (1888).

child's best interest of paramount importance.[9] However, all that the court is required by statute to consider is that the appointment serve the welfare of the minor.[10] Unlike custody determinations following marital dissolution that have a defined best interest standard, there is no statutory law defining what the welfare of the minor is as it pertains to guardianship. Similarly, if it serves the welfare of the child, the court may also order reasonable support by the parents and reasonable parenting time and contact between the child and the parents.[11]

C) Duties of the Guardian

Guardians of minors have the same powers and responsibilities as parents, except that guardians are not legally obligated to provide their own funds for the children and are not liable to third persons for acts of the children.[12] The law further specifies that the guardian

1. must take reasonable care of the children's personal effects;

2. may receive money payable for the support of the children;

3. shall facilitate the children's education and social and other activities; authorize medical or other professional care, treatment, or advice; and consent to marriage or adoption of the children; and

4. shall report on the condition of the children as specified by court order.

D) Termination of the Guardianship

A guardian's authority and responsibility terminates upon the death, resignation, or removal of the guardian; upon the child's death, adoption, or marriage, or when the child reaches the age of majority (18 years old).[13] Parents may petition for removal of the guardian.[14] If such a petition has been filed, the court may order an investigation, written report, and/or testimony by the Family Independence Agency or an MHP regarding the best interest of the child.[15] If the guardianship is a limited one, the court will terminate it if the parents have substantially complied with the

---

9. *In re* Greene, 60 N.W.2d 425, 337 Mich. 448 (1953).
10. M.C.L. § 700.426.
11. M.C.L. § 700.424(5).
12. M.C.L. § 700.431(1).
13. M.C.L. § 700.433.
14. M.C.L. § 700.424c(1).
15. M.C.L. § 700.424c(2).

limited guardianship placement plan. The court may terminate other guardianships if it determines that this is in the best interest of the child. In the case of termination, best interest is defined similarly to factors enumerated in the Child Custody Act (see chapter 4.6). The court may also decide based on the child's best interest, to continue the guardianship for not more than 1 year and order the parents to comply with a court-structured plan that is designed to enable the child to return home at the end of that year. Finally, if the child has lived with the guardian for at least a year and it has been established by clear and convincing evidence that the parents have failed to provide care, love, guidance, and attention appropriate to the age and individual needs of the child and that this has resulted in a substantial disruption of the parent–child relationship, the court may order that the guardianship be continued.[16]

---

16. M.C.L. § 700.424c(3-6).

4.12

Conservatorship for Minors

A conservator may be appointed to manage the estate (e.g., money, property, and business enterprises) of a minor. There is no requirement that the minor also have a guardian appointed. While this is principally a financial determination, MHPs may be asked to determine whether minors are capable of handling their estates.

(A) Application for Conservatorship

Any person, including the one to be protected, may petition the court for the appointment of a conservator. This includes those who would be adversely affected by the lack of effective management of the property and affairs, as well as those interested in the person's well-being.[1] The petition must describe[2]

1. the interest of the petitioner;
2. the name, age, residence, and address of the person to be protected;
3. the name and address of his or her guardian, if any;
4. the name and address of the nearest relative of the person to be protected known to the petitioner;
5. a general statement of the property of the person to be protected with an estimate of the value, including any compensation, insurance, pension, or allowance which is due to the person;

---

1. M.C.L. § 700.464(1).
2. M.C.L. § 700.464(2).

6. reasons why appointment of a conservator is necessary; and

7. reasons for the appointment of a particular person as conservator.

If a particular person is being proposed to be the conservator, that person's name and the reasons he or she is being proposed should be included in the petition.

(B) The Conservatorship Hearing

After receiving the petition, the court will set a date for the hearing. The minor's parents must be personally served with notice at least 10 days before the hearing.[3] If, at any time in the proceeding the court determines that the interests of the minor may be inadequately represented, it may appoint an attorney to represent the minor; it must give consideration to the minor's preference for a particular attorney if the child is over age 14.[4]

The court may appoint a conservator if it determines that the minor owns money or property that requires management or protection that cannot otherwise be provided; that the minor may have business affairs that may be jeopardized or prevented by the person's minority; or that funds are needed for support and education and that protection is desirable to provide the funds.[5] Note that these circumstances are broad enough to include situations where a conservator may be appointed even though the parents are present and fulfilling the usual parental duties.

(C) Duties of the Conservator

The authority of the conservator is very broad. A conservator of the estate of a minor to whom no person has parental rights has the duties and powers of a guardian. However, this does not preclude the appointment of a guardian (see chapter 4.10).[6] For instance, title to all the person's property and assets passes to the conservator, who can sell, transfer, divide, or otherwise manage it in the same manner as any person would handle his or her own financial affairs.[7] The law does not mention any duty of the conservator to submit reports to the court.

---

3. M.C.L. § 700.465.
4. M.C.L. § 700.467(1).
5. M.C.L. § 700.461(a).
6. M.C.L. § 700.484(1).
7. M.C.L. § 700.484(3).

(D) Termination of the Conservatorship

Any interested person, including the protected person, may petition the court to terminate the conservatorship. Protected persons seeking termination are entitled to the same rights and procedures as are followed during the application process. Thus, a notice of termination must be made and a hearing must be held (see sections (A) & (B)). Upon termination, title of all property passes back to the protected person.[8]

---

8. M.C.L. § 700.490.

4.13

Foster Care

Foster care provides residential housing and support, under the jurisdiction of the family division of circuit court and the supervision of the Family Independence Agency or private adoption agencies, for children who are not able to live in their own homes. Foster care is defined as a foster family home, foster family group home, licensed juvenile care institution, or care provided by a relative under order of the court.[1] The person may be placed in a foster home for as little as 1 night or as long as several years. MHPs may be involved in the approval of homes and in providing assessment and therapeutic services to those placed in them.

(A) Certification of Foster Parents/ Licensing Requirements

Foster homes must be licensed by the Family Independence Agency (FIA). Potential foster parents must apply for a license and undergo an investigation which includes an onsite visit and assesses the activities and proposed standards of care of the applicants, their financial stability, their moral character, and whether the home is conducive to the welfare of children. A license is not granted until the prospective foster parents have undergone an orientation that includes information about the administrative rules and the needs of children in foster care.[2]

---

1. M.C.L. § 712A.13a.
2. M.C.L. § 722.115.

Licenses must be renewed every 2 years and an onsite visit must be conducted every year.[3] In addition, every county or group of counties must have a foster care review board that reviews each initial placement plan for children in foster care, reviews the progress of any children in foster care, and makes recommendations regarding issues in foster care policies and procedures.[4]

No home can be licensed for more than four children unless it is desirable to keep siblings together or if some other special need exists. Licensed homes may not have more than two children under 1 year of age, including the children of the foster parents.[5] The total number of children under age 17 cannot be more than eight. All members of the household must be in a physical and mental condition such that the child and the quality of his or her care will not be affected adversely. The foster family must be of good character, habits, and reputation and create a wholesome family atmosphere. All must be willing to accept the children into the home. Foster parents must be of suitable temperament to care for children, must be able to understand the needs of children, must be capable of handling emergency situations, and must be willing to cooperate fully with the child's parents or the supervising agency. Severe corporal punishment is grounds for license revocation. The parents must be about the same age as the child's parents and may not be over the age of 65, unless an exception is made. Foster parents must demonstrate they have adequate time to care for the children. Their financial status must be secure.[6]

(B) Placement of Children in Foster Homes and Case Plans

The law provides that if children must be removed from their homes they should be placed in care as equivalent as possible to that given by their parents.[7] Children may come under the jurisdiction of the family division if[8]

1. the parent or other legally responsible person neglects or refuses to provide proper or necessary support, education, medical or other necessary care, subjects the child to substantial risk to his or her mental well-being, or abandons the child;

---

3. M.C.L. § 722.118a.
4. M.C.L. § 722.137.
5. R 400.191.
6. R 400.192.
7. M.C.L. § 712A.1.
8. M.C.L. § 712A.2.

2. the juvenile's environment is unfit because of the behavior of the parent;

3. the parent has failed to comply with a court-ordered plan for the improvement of the family situation or has failed to comply with a limited guardian placement;[9] or

4. the parent has abused or neglected the child (see chapters 4.8 and 4.9).

When the question of foster care arises, a preliminary hearing or inquiry must be held in the Family Division of Circuit Court, after which the court can authorize a petition to be filed.[10] The preliminary hearing is usually requested by the Family Independence Agency, as problems that may require the removal of a child from his or her home are referred to this agency. The petition is filed by the FIA or other agency responsible for the welfare of the child and must list any allegations regarding the child and his or her parents that may fall within the requirements listed above. The petition may also recommend appropriate placements. In addition to placing the child in foster care, the court has an option under certain circumstances to require an abusive parent to leave the home, allowing the child to remain in his or her home environment.[11]

Once a petition is filed, the court must hold a disposition hearing, where it reviews the petition, hears testimony from any interested party, and rules on where and under what circumstances the child should be placed. If making a recommendation to the court that the child be placed outside the home, the petitioner must report to the court what efforts were made to prevent the child from having to be removed and what efforts are being made to rectify the conditions that caused the child to be removed. In addition, a case service plan must be prepared for the court's use at the disposition hearing. This plan must include the type of placement and the reasons it was selected; efforts to be made by the child's parent to enable the child to return home; efforts to be made by the agency to return the child home; what services are to be provided to the child, parent, and foster parent that would facilitate either the child's return home or his or her permanent placement; and a schedule for regular and frequent parenting time that is not less than once per week. The court then holds the disposition hearing, where it considers the service plan and any other relevant information and orders placement if ap-

---

9. *See* M.C.L. § 700.424b and § 700.424c.
10. M.C.L. § 712A.13a(2). Note that the child can be placed in foster care on an emergency basis before a hearing is held.
11. M.C.L. § 712A.13a(4).

propriate. Once a child is placed in foster care, the case service plan must be updated every 90 days.[12]

(C) Placement Review

Once a child is in foster care, a review hearing must be held not more than 182 days after the disposition hearing. Written notice of the hearing must be given to the agency supervising the child, the foster parent, the parents, the guardian or guardian ad litem if either is appointed, any nonparent adult required to comply with the case service plan, all attorneys, and any other persons the court may direct. At this hearing, the court reviews the compliance of all involved parties with recommended service plans and parenting time, and the likely harm to the child if he or she remains in foster care or is returned to the parent. It then evaluates progress made and either continues the disposition order, modifies it, or returns the child to the custody of the parent.[13]

(D) Permanent Placement Plans

If the child remains in foster care, a permanency planning hearing must be held no more than 364 days after the disposition hearing and no more than every 364 days thereafter. This hearing reviews the progress being made toward the child's return home and establishes why the child should not be permanently placed elsewhere. If the court decides that a return to the parent would cause a substantial risk of harm to the child's life, physical health, or mental well-being, or is not in the child's best interest, proceedings to terminate parental rights may be authorized (the court must consider the compliance of the parents with the service plan; see chapter 4.10). If termination is not appropriate, the court can order the child to remain in foster care on a long-term basis.[14]

---

12. M.C.L. § 712A.18f.
13. M.C.L. § 712A.19.
14. M.C.L. § 712A.19a.

4.14

Adoption

Adoption is the legal transfer of responsibility for the care and support of a child from a parent to another person. In Michigan, children may be adopted through direct placement by their birth parents to an adoptive parent the birth parents select, or through an agency or department. The law provides that a person who wishes to adopt a child must meet certain minimum requirements (described in the following sections). So, too, the adopted child and natural parents have rights and responsibilities that must be fulfilled for the adoption to be valid. The Adoption Code[1] was enacted in order to help reduce barriers to adoption and to protect and assist adoptive families as they go through the adoption process. MHPs may contribute to this process by providing evaluations of prospective adoptive parents and children, and treatment to the adopted children if necessary. Adoptions are handled in the Family Division of the Circuit Court.

(A) Adoption Requirements

(A)(1) Adoptive Parents

Any adult who can demonstrate good character and ability is eligible to adopt a child. Married persons may adopt with the consent of their spouses; unmarried persons may also adopt. The best interest of the child or adoptee is the court's main consideration in ordering an adoption to be permanent. The criteria differ slightly from those used in divorce proceedings and include[2]

---

1. M.C.L. § 722.951.
2. M.C.L. § 710.22f.

1. The love, affection, and other emotional ties existing between the adopting individual(s) and the adoptee;
2. The capacity of the adoptive individual(s) to give the child love, affection, and guidance, and to educate and create a milieu that fosters the religion, racial identity, and culture of the adoptee;
3. The capacity of the adopting individual(s) to provide food, clothing, education, permanence, medical care, or other remedial care;
4. The length of time the child has lived in a stable, satisfactory environment, and the desirability of maintaining continuity;
5. The permanence of the family unit of the proposed adoptive home;
6. The moral fitness of the adopting individual(s);
7. The mental and physical health of the adopting individual(s);
8. The home, school, and community record of the adoptee;
9. The reasonable preference of the adoptee, if he or she is age 14 or less and the court considers him or her to be of sufficient age to express a preference;
10. The ability and willingness of the adopting individual(s) to adopt the child's siblings; and
11. Any other factor deemed relevant by the court.

When an adoption petition is filed, a preplacement assessment of the potential adoptive home is conducted by the child placing agency or the FIA. The assessment must include a home visit, and must contain all of the following information:[3]

1. Age, nationality, race or ethnicity, and any religious preference;
2. Marital and family status and history, including the presence of other children or adults in the household;
3. Physical and mental health, including any history of substance abuse;
4. Education and employment history and any special skills and interests;
5. A current financial report;
6. Reason for wanting to adopt;
7. Any previous adoption request and its outcome;

---

3. M.C.L. § 710.23f.

8. Whether the individual has ever been involved in a domestic violence proceeding or a proceeding concerning a child who was allegedly abused, dependent, deprived, neglected, abandoned, or delinquent, and the outcome of the proceeding;

9. Criminal record; and

10. Any fact or circumstance that raises a concern about the suitability of the person as an adoptive parent, including the quality of the home environment, the functioning of any other children in the household and any other aspect of the parent's familial, social, psychological, or financial circumstances.

(A)(2) Birth Parents

Adoption may proceed only after the rights of the birth parent have been terminated by the court. The parent(s) and/or adoption agency must formally release the child for adoption and consent to it.[4] Evidence must be provided that the parents have been given a list of support groups and have either received or waived counseling regarding the adoption. If the child has been born out of wedlock, an attempt must be made to obtain the release of the biological father and his biological rights must be terminated.[5] Out of wedlock fathers who wish to assume custody of their children must convince the court that this is in the child's best interest and must have either established a custodial relationship with the child or have supported the child during the 90 days prior to having received notice of possible termination of rights.[6] If a child to be adopted is over the age of 14, he or she must consent to it.[7]

There are some situations where parents do not voluntarily consent to having their child adopted. These are cases where the parent's rights have been terminated for such things as abuse and neglect (see chapter 4.10) and the child has been placed under the supervision of an agency or when a guardian has been appointed for either the parent or the child.[8]

---

4. M.C.L. § 710.28, 710.44.
5. M.C.L. § 710.31.
6. M.C.L. § 710.39. Note that if the birth mother has concealed her pregnancy or birth from the putative father or has failed to identify him in the adoption process, he may be given additional opportunity to assume responsibility for the child.
7. M.C.L. § 710.43.
8. M.C.L. § 710.28.

(B) Adoption Process

Adoptions can be done by direct placement, in which a parent or guardian selects an adoptive parent for the child and then follows appropriate court procedures,[9] or by formal placement through an adoption agency or the Family Independence Agency.[10] When a direct placement is made the parent is assisted by an adoption attorney or a child placement agency. The parent, guardian, or FIA must release the child for adoption. The release must be given in writing. If it is done by a parent or guardian, it must be accompanied by a statement verifying that the parent or guardian[11]

1. has received a list of support groups;
2. has received counseling regarding the adoption of the child, or has waived counseling;
3. has not unlawfully received or been promised any money or anything of value for releasing the child;
4. has made no separate agreement between the adoptive parent or the child-placing agency;
5. understands that it must keep the child-placing agency informed of any health problems that the parent may develop that could affect the child; and
6. understands the importance of keeping the child-placing agency informed of his or her current address.

The release is not executed by the court until the court has fully explained to the parent or guardian what their legal rights are and that what they are doing is voluntarily relinquishing their rights to their child.

A temporary placement of the child can be made with the prospective adoptive parents. When the child is actually transferred to the prospective adoptive parents, a statement that gives evidence of the physical transfer of the child must be signed in the presence of a witness by the parent, guardian, or child-placing agency. The statement must indicate the date of the transfer, the name and address of both parents, that the transfer is for the purpose of adoption, that unless the parent and the prospective adoptive parent agree otherwise, the adoptive parent has the authority to consent to all medical, psychological, educational and related services, that the birth parent still retains full parental

---

9. M.C.L. § 710.23a.
10. M.C.L. § 710.51.
11. M.C.L. § 710.29.

rights, and that the birth parent can revoke the adoption by filing a petition with the court. It must also indicate that the person making the transfer has had the opportunity to review a preplacement assessment of the adoptive parent. The prospective adoptive parents must sign a statement in the presence of a witness that must state the date of the transfer, and must attest that they understand that the temporary placement will not become a formal placement until the parents release their parental rights and the court terminates parental rights and approves the placement. It must also state that the adoptive parents must give up the child within 24 hours if the birth parent files a petition to revoke the adoption. Finally, the statement must say that the adoptive parents agree to reside in Michigan until a change of residence is approved by the court after the formal placement occurs. A report must be submitted to the Family Division of the Circuit Court by the attorney handling the adoption or the child placement agency within 2 days of the transfer of physical custody of the child. This report must include the date of the transfer, the names and addresses of birth and adoptive parents, and the two signed statements mentioned above.

A petition for adoption must be filed by the prospective adoptive parents.[12] If a temporary placement has been made the petition must be filed within 30 days of the placement.[13] The petition must include

1. the name (including maiden name), date and place of birth, and place of residence of each parent;

2. the name, date and place of birth, and place of residence of the adoptee;

3. any relationship of the adoptee to the petitioner;

4. the full name by which the adoptee will be known after the adoption;

5. a full description of any property of the adoptee;

6. the names and addresses of the birth parents if their rights have not already been terminated; and

7. the name and address of the guardian, if one exists.

A statement indicating that the petitioners have been informed of the availability of counseling and whether counseling was received must be attached to the petition, as must be a copy of the preplacement assessment. Points 6 and 7 above are omitted if it has been agreed that the parties will not exchange identifying

---

12. M.C.L. § 710.24.
13. M.C.L. § 710.23d.

information. This information is then filed separately by the attorney or agency.

Once the parent or guardian has released the child, the court immediately orders parental rights to be terminated (see also chapter 4.10). If after reviewing the required investigation of the potential adoptive home the court is satisfied that the placement is in the best interest of the child, a formal placement is made.[14] A final order of adoption is usually entered 6 months after formal placement, though this may be waived or extended if it is in the best interest of the child.[15]

C) Confidentiality of Adoption Records

Adoptions in Michigan may be either open, where birth and adoptive parents agree to exchange information about the child, or closed, where restrictions are placed on the sharing of such information. Birth parents may file a statement with the central adoption agency either consenting to or denying the release of identifying information.[16] Whichever type is chosen, adoptive parents are entitled to receive an account of the child's genetic history, as well as mental and physical health history, any psychological evaluation done when the child was under the jurisdiction of the court and whether the child suffered physical or sexual abuse or neglect. They also are entitled to receive information about the mental and physical health of members of the birth family, including any known hereditary condition or disease and such information as the birth family's racial, ethnic, or religious background, the age of the parents and how long they had been married at the time of termination of rights, and particular interests and achievements of the family.[17]

Information released to adult adoptees in search of their biological parents or to biological parents seeking information about children released for adoption is carefully regulated by statute.[18] A confidential intermediary can be appointed to search for and contact a former family member, if appropriate.[19] Requests for information must be made in writing on a form to the original child placing agency, the court, or the FIA, who in turn submit the

---

14. M.C.L. § 710.51.
15. M.C.L. § 710.56.
16. M.C.L. § 710.27a.
17. M.C.L. § 710.27.
18. M.C.L. § 710.68.
19. M.C.L. § 710.68a.

request to the central adoption registry. Any adult adoptee adoptive parent, former parent, or adult former sibling is entitled to receive nonidentifying information within 63 days of the request. The nonidentifying information is defined as that listed in the paragraph above. Former parents can receive the most recent name and address of the adoptee if the adoptee has given a written consent to release this information. Former parents, adult adoptees, and adult former siblings can request and be provided the identity of the court that confirmed the adoption and the identity of the agency that handled the adoption.

Adults adopted between May 28, 1945, and September 12 1980, are entitled to receive the names of their biological parents their own name at the time of adoption, the names of any siblings and the most recent address of their biological parents as long as both birth parents have a statement on file at the central registry consenting to release of the information. If only one parent has consented, information can be released about that one parent Information can also be released without prior consent about a parent who has died. Adults who have been adopted can also request and receive the name and address of any former siblings who are now adults. Direct descendants of deceased adoptees can also request and receive information.

A birth parent who discovers information about a medical or genetic condition that poses a serious threat to the adoptee's life must submit this information to the central adoption registry. The registry must then send a written copy of the information to the adoptee within 7 days.

4.15

Delinquency

The Family Division of the Circuit Court has exclusive jurisdiction to hear complaints about juveniles who are alleged to be delinquent.[1] With the important exception of cases that are designated by the prosecutor or the judge as cases in which the juvenile is to be tried as an adult, or in which jurisdiction is waived to the court having general criminal jurisdiction (see chapter 4.18), proceedings under the Family Division are not considered criminal proceedings.[2] There is no separate law concerning delinquency or persons in need of supervision. In fact, the word *delinquency* is not used in the law (though it will be used here). Children who appear before the court may see an MHP as part of the process. Although this generally occurs during the dispositional phase, MHPs may also contribute in other ways, such as evaluations of competency, or by treating the juvenile and his or her family.

A) Juvenile Delinquency

)(1) Definitions

A juvenile is defined as any person under the age of 18 concerning whom proceedings are commenced in the Family Division of the court.

---

1. M.C.L. § 712A.2.
2. M.C.L. § 712A.1.

(A)(2) Jurisdiction

Once the court has taken jurisdiction over a juvenile, it can retain it until the child is 21.[3] Taking jurisdiction means that the juvenile comes under the power and authority of the court to hold hearings and rule on his or her case. The court may take jurisdiction if the juvenile[4]

1. allegedly violated the criminal law that applies to adults;
2. has deserted his or her home without sufficient cause and has refused alternative placement and/or exhausted or refused all efforts at counseling;
3. is repeatedly disobedient; and
4. is willfully and repeatedly truant and the parents and school have met about the juvenile's difficulties.

The juvenile court can also take jurisdiction of 17- and 18-year-old children who are repeated substance abusers, repeatedly associate with criminals, disorderly persons, prostitutes or pimps, or are willfully disobedient.[5]

(A)(3) Petition

Any person can give information to the court about the possible delinquency of a juvenile. A preliminary inquiry may take place to determine whether further action should be taken. If the court determines that it should take formal jurisdiction, it will authorize that a petition be filed. The petition must set forth the facts that bring the juvenile under the court's jurisdiction and must include the names and addresses of the juvenile, his or her parents and/or legal guardian, any person having custody or control over the juvenile, or the nearest known relative. If any facts about the child's action are not known, the petition must state this.[6] During the initial investigation or after the filing of a petition, the court may order the juvenile to be examined by a physician, dentist, psychologist, or psychiatrist.[7]

Under the Juvenile Diversion Act, the court may decide not to authorize a petition and may instead refer the minor and his or her parents to an organization or agency that will help the family resolve the problem that caused the investigation.[8]

---

3. M.C.L. § 712A.2a.
4. *Id.*
5. M.C.L. § 712A.2b.
6. M.C.L. § 712A.11.
7. M.C.L. § 712A.12.
8. M.C.L. §§ 722.821 & 722.823.

(4) Hearing Procedure and the Rights of Children in Delinquency Proceedings

After the petition is filed, the court may issue a summons that requires the persons who have custody or control over the child to bring him or her to a hearing. The court may excuse the child from attending the hearing if it deems this appropriate, but cannot restrict the child from the hearing.[9] The law requires that the parent or guardian of a juvenile must attend all hearings unless excused for good cause. Parents who fail to attend can be found in contempt of court.[10]

Juvenile hearings can be conducted informally and are open to the public. However, any interested person can demand that a 6-person jury try the case. The court can close the hearing if it finds that this is necessary to protect the welfare of the juvenile. In determining whether to close a hearing the court must consider the child's age and psychological maturity, the nature of the proceeding, and the desires of the juvenile, his or her family, or the victim.[11]

(5) Adjudication and Disposition

There are a number of possible outcomes after a hearing. The court may decline to take jurisdiction over the child if the facts alleged are not proved. If it is consistent with the facts of the case, the court may take jurisdiction and then issue a warning to the juvenile and dismiss the petition. The court may place the child on probation or under supervision at his or her own home or the home of a close relative. Michigan law currently has a strong emphasis on keeping children in their homes if possible. Anyone recommending to the court that the child be placed away from the parent or guardian must report what efforts were made to prevent out of home placement.[12] If it is found at the hearing that the juvenile must be detained, the court can order detention in a suitable foster home, a child care institution, or a detention home or require him or her to attend a state-administered boot camp.[13] At this point, the minor cannot be held at any police station, prison, jail, or reformatory unless he or she is age 15 or older and considered dangerous to other juveniles or cannot otherwise be safely detained. Juveniles over the age of 17 may be placed in the county jail separate and apart from adults, if appropriate.[14] A case service plan must be formulated that must provide for placing the

---

9. M.C.L. § 712A.2b.
10. M.C.L. § 712A.6a.
11. M.C.L. § 712A.17.
12. M.C.L. § 712A.18f.
13. M.C.L. § 712A.18.
14. M.C.L. § 712A.16.

juvenile in the most family-like setting available which is close
to the parent's home if this is in the child's best interest. The pla
must include reasons for the selected placement, the services to b
provided to the juvenile and his or her family, and a schedule c
parenting time, and must be updated every 90 days.[15]

The court may order any parent or guardian who contribute
to the minor's delinquency to refrain from this behavior. It ca
also require the parent or guardian to participate in the child'
treatment. It can fine the juvenile, require payment of restitutior
or order community service.[16]

(A)(6) Review Hearing

Review hearings can be conducted at any time if requested by an
interested person.[17] Hearings can also be requested if those treat
ing the juvenile believe he or she has been rehabilitated. ⁄
hearing must be conducted before the juvenile's nineteenth birth
day or if on probation, no less than 3 months before the end of th
probation period.[18] If a juvenile has committed a serious crim
the court must conduct a review hearing to determine whether h
or she has been rehabilitated or presents a serious risk to publi
safety. In making this review, the court considers the juvenile'
willingness to accept responsibility for prior behavior, behavic
in his or her current placement, prior record and character, phys
cal and mental maturity, potential for violent conduct as demor
strated by prior behavior, and the recommendations of th
juvenile's placement. If the juvenile cannot prove by a preponder
ance of the evidence that he or she has been rehabilitated and doe
not pose a risk to public safety, jurisdiction by the court can b
continued until he or she is 21 years old.[19]

---

15. M.C.L. § 712A.6a.
16. M.C.L. § 712A.17.
17. M.C.L. § 712A.21.
18. M.C.L. § 712.18i.
19. M.C.L. § 712A.18d.

4.16

Competency of Juveniles to Stand Trial

As in cases where adults are charged with crimes, juveniles are presumed to be competent to stand trial. Although there is no juvenile competency standard identified in state statute or rules, case law indicates that the rules set forth in the Code of Criminal Procedure apply to juvenile offenders unless they conflict with the Juvenile Code.[1] MHPs may be asked to assist in assessing a juvenile's ability to participate in the delinquency adjudication process.

A) Legal Determination of Competency to Stand Trial

)(1) Test of Competency

A defendant is determined to be incompetent to stand trial if he or she is incapable because of his or her mental condition of[2]

1. understanding the nature and object of the proceedings against him or her; or
2. assisting in his or her defense in a rational manner.

)(2) Raising the Competency Issue

The issue of competency can be raised at any time during the proceedings by the prosecutor, the defense attorney, or the

---

1. Matter of McDaniel, 465 N.W.2d 51, 186 Mich.App. 696 (1991). See chapter 7.5 for a more detailed discussion of the competency of adults to stand trial.
2. M.C.L. § 330.2020.

judge.[3] The juvenile is then ordered to undergo an examination
by a psychiatrist or psychologist at the state Center for Forensic
Psychiatry, or by another professional qualified to perform such
an examination.[4] The state and the child may also call other
expert witnesses to testify.

(B) Disposition of Juveniles Found Incompetent to Stand Trial

If the child is found incompetent to proceed and the court finds
that there is a substantial probability that if treated he or she will
be restored to competency, the court can order him or her to
undergo such treatment. If involuntary hospitalization is necessary, the court may commit the child (see chapter 4.19).[5] If the
court determines that there is not a substantial probability that the
child will become competent in the foreseeable future, it can
direct the prosecutor to file a petition asserting that the child is a
person requiring treatment,[6] or it can dismiss the delinquency
petition.[7]

---

3. M.C.L. § 330.2024.
4. M.C.L. § 330.2026.
5. M.C.L. § 330.2032.
6. M.C.L. § 330.2031.
7. M.C.L. § 330.3044.

4.17

Nonresponsibility Defense

Most defenses available to an adult charged with a crime are also extended by statute to juveniles charged with delinquency. These defenses in various jurisdictions include mental disease or defect (insanity), which is defined by statute, and justification, duress, and entrapment, which are defined by case law. The legal standard for an insanity defense is the same for juveniles as for adults (see chapter 7.9). MHPs may participate in the process by performing evaluations and providing testimony in court.

Michigan law states that a person is legally insane if, at the time of the offense, the person lacked substantial capacity either to appreciate the wrongfulness of his or her conduct or to conform his or her conduct to the requirements of the law.[1] If the insanity defense is raised, the juvenile must undergo an examination by a psychologist or psychiatrist, usually conducted at the Center for Forensic Psychiatry.[2] Although the delinquency finding can be dismissed if the prosecution is unable to prove that the juvenile was not legally insane, the court still can retain jurisdiction over the child. Rehabilitative measures such as hospitalization may be ordered if the legal criteria for insanity and commitment are met (see chapter 4.19).

---

1. M.C.L. § 768.21a.
2. M.C.L. § 768.20a.

4.18

Transfer of Juveniles to Stand Trial as Adults

Under certain circumstances the law allows a minor to be transferred from the Family Division of Circuit Court to the court of general criminal jurisdiction, or permits the minor to be tried as an adult in the Family Division.

(A) Waiver of Jurisdiction

(A)(1) Permissive or Traditional Waiver

If a child 14 years of age or older is accused of a crime which if committed by an adult would be a felony, the judge of the Family Division of the Circuit Court, on the petition of the prosecutor, may waive jurisdiction to adult criminal court.[1] If a waiver is granted by the judge in this manner and the juvenile is later convicted in adult court, adult sentencing would take place. As a preliminary matter, if it is determined in the Family Division that there is probable cause to believe that such an offense has been committed and that the juvenile committed it, the court must conduct a hearing to determine whether the best interests of the juvenile and the public would be served by waiving jurisdiction to the adult Criminal Division of Circuit Court. In making that determination the court must consider

1. the seriousness of the alleged offense, including such aggravating factors as the use of a firearm or the impact of the offense on the victim;

---

1. M.C.L. § 712A.4.

2. the juvenile's culpability, including, e.g., his or her alleged participation in planning and carrying out the offense, and any aggravating or mitigating factors;

3. the juvenile's record of delinquency;

4. the juvenile's treatment and programming history, including willingness to participate meaningfully in such;

5. the adequacy of the punishment or programming available in the juvenile justice system; and

6. the dispositional options, such as specific programs, available for the juvenile.[2]

The court must give greater weight to the seriousness of the offense and the juvenile's record.[3] The juvenile court, the prosecuting attorney, or the defense attorney may request an evaluation by MHPs to provide evidence at the waiver hearing. If the offense for which the court finds probable cause would be a felony if committed by an adult, and if the jurisdiction of the juvenile had previously been waived, the court must waive jurisdiction.[4]

A)(2) Automatic Waiver

Juveniles 14 years of age or older and less than 17 who have committed certain very serious offenses, designated in the law as "specified juvenile violations," automatically come within the jurisdiction of the court of general criminal jurisdiction, or adult court.[5] Specified juvenile violations include a number of offenses which, if committed by an adult, would constitute the most serious crimes, such as murder, first-degree criminal sexual conduct or rape, arson of a dwelling, and armed robbery.[6] Juveniles for whom jurisdiction is automatically transferred in this manner, if convicted of felonies that carry a possible sentence of life in prison, or certain drug crimes carrying a mandatory minimum sentence of 25 years, are subject to the same sentencing procedures as adults; other offenses require a hearing to determine if adult sentencing or juvenile disposition will take place.[7]

---

2. M.C.L. § 712A.4(4).
3. *Id.*
4. M.C.L. § 712A.4(5).
5. M.C.L. § 764.1f.
6. M.C.L. § 712A.2(a)(1).
7. M.C.L. § 769.1(1).

(B) Designation Proceedings

Notwithstanding the provisions for automatic waiver of juveniles 14 years of age or older, if a juvenile of any age is alleged to have committed a "specified juvenile violation" or other serious offense[8] the prosecutor may designate the case as one in which the juvenile is to be tried in the same manner as an adult.[9] If the juvenile has allegedly committed any other violation, the court at its discretion and at the request of the prosecutor may designate the case as one to be tried in the same manner as an adult.[10] In either case, if the matter is one designated for adult trial, the trial is conducted in the Family Division of the Circuit Court. If the juvenile is convicted, the court must consider whether to impose a juvenile sentence or disposition, an adult sentence of imprisonment, or whether to delay imposing a sentence of imprisonment.[11] The court may delay imposing an adult sentence for as long as it has jurisdiction of the juvenile. In determining whether to impose an adult sentence or juvenile disposition, the court must consider a number of factors, giving greater weight to the seriousness of the offense and the juvenile's prior record:

1. the seriousness of the offense in terms of community protection, including any aggravating factors, the use of a firearm or other dangerous weapon, and the impact on any victim;
2. the juvenile's culpability;
3. the juvenile's prior record of delinquency;
4. the record of the juvenile's participation in programming;
5. the adequacy of the punishment or programming available in the juvenile justice system; and
6. the dispositional options available for the juvenile.[12]

If the court chooses to delay the imposition of an adult sentence and has instead placed the convicted juvenile on juvenile probation, it must conduct an annual review of the probation[13] and must determine whether the juvenile has been rehabilitated or whether he or she presents a serious risk to public safety.[14] The court may decide to continue the probation, or to impose an adult sentence, considering

---

8. *Id.*
9. M.C.L. § 712.A.2d(1).
10. M.C.L. § 712.A.2d(2).
11. M.C.L. § 712.A.18(1)(n).
12. *Id.*
13. M.C.L. § 712.A.18i(2).
14. M.C.L. § 712.A.18i(3).

1. the juvenile's participation in programming;
2. the juvenile's willingness to accept responsibility for prior behavior;
3. the juvenile's behavior in the current placement;
4. the juvenile's prior record, character, and maturity;
5. the juvenile's demonstrated potential for violence;
6. agency or institutional recommendations; and
7. any other information the prosecutor or the juvenile may submit.[15]

---

15. *Id.*

4.19

Voluntary Admission and Commitment of Minors

In recent years, Michigan has made a strong effort to reduce the incidence of hospitalization for minors for mental health issues. MHPs may become involved in the process by recommending that a minor be hospitalized, by involvement in the treatment of a hospitalized minor, or by participating in a commitment hearing.

(A) Admission of Minors for Mental Health Treatment

(A)(1) Definitions

A "minor requiring treatment" is defined as either[1]

1. a minor with a substantial disorder of thought or mood that significantly impairs judgment, behavior, capacity to recognize reality, or ability to cope with the ordinary demands of life, or

2. a minor having a severe or persistent emotional condition characterized by seriously impaired personality development, individual adjustment, social adjustment, or emotional growth, which is demonstrated in behavior symptomatic of that impairment.

---

1. M.C.L. § 330.1948b.

The procedure for voluntary admission or an involuntary admission is similar. In order to be suitable for hospitalization, the child must meet all of the following:[2]

1. be a minor requiring treatment;
2. be in need of hospitalization and expected to benefit from it; and
3. a less restrictive alternative is not available.

Minors under the age of 14 may become voluntary patients only upon the application of parents, legal guardians, or persons acting in loco parentis, or through the Family Independence Agency. Minors 14 years of age or older may request hospitalization for themselves.[3] A minor can be admitted on an emergency basis if a parent or guardian, a peace officer, or a hospital director has reason to believe that the child is a minor requiring treatment and that he or she presents a serious danger to self or others.[4]

B) Evaluation to Determine Suitability for Hospitalization

The minor must be evaluated by the children's diagnostic and treatment service of the nearest community mental health center (CMHC). Some CMHCs also have screening units designed to evaluate emergency admissions, or may use the emergency services of a local hospital. The evaluation must be made as soon as possible for a voluntary request[5] and immediately in the case of an emergency.[6] The evaluator must determine whether the child meets the definitional criteria mentioned above, and must consult with appropriate school, hospital, and other public and private agencies. If it is determined that the child does not need hospitalization, then an assessment is made as to whether he or she needs mental health services. If this is the case, then appropriate services are offered to the minor and his or her family. If the child is in need of hospitalization, he or she is referred to an appropriate hospital, which may admit him or her or immediately do its own evaluation. If the hospital denies admission, the child is referred

---

2. M.C.L. § 330.1948c.
3. M.C.L. § 330.1498d.
4. M.C.L. § 330.1498e.
5. *Id.*
6. M.C.L. § 330.1498h.

back to a CMHC, which can refer the child to another hospital or offer other services.[7]

If hospitalization is denied, the parent or guardian may request a second opinion. This must be done by a psychiatrist, other physician, or licensed psychologist within 3 days. If the second opinion recommends that the minor be hospitalized, the executive director and the medical director of the CMHC make the final decision.[8]

(C) Notice Requirements

A review of the suitability for hospitalization must occur no more than 90 days after admission. Further reviews must take place every 60 days thereafter.[9]

A written objection to the hospitalization can be made by the child, if he or she is age 14 or over, the parent or guardian, or any person found suitable by the court. If a child who has been in the hospital less than 7 days tells a hospital employee that they want to object, the employee is required to help the child submit an appropriate objection. Failure to do this is a misdemeanor. Other objections must be made within 30 days after admission or within 30 days of a review.[10] A court hearing must be held within 7 days of receiving an objection. The court may only order that the child remain in the hospital if it finds by clear and convincing evidence that hospitalization is suitable.[11]

The parties listed above can also give written notice that they intend to terminate the minor's hospitalization. If it is determined that the child still needs to be hospitalized, the hospital or CMHC must file a petition within 3 days requesting the court to order continuing hospitalization. A hearing must be held within 7 days, and if the court finds the child suitable for hospitalization, it can order it to be continued for no more than 60 days. The court can also order the minor to be discharged.[12]

---

7. M.C.L. § 330.1498f.
8. M.C.L. § 330.1498e.
9. M.C.L. § 330.1498l.
10. M.C.L. § 330.1498m.
11. M.C.L. § 330.1498n.
12. M.C.L. § 330.1498o.

4.20

Education for Gifted and Handicapped Children

The law provides that any person under 26 years of age who is determined to be handicapped is entitled to special education services provided by the public schools.[1] MHPs may become involved in the special education process through evaluations of the children and consultations with special education personnel.

(A) Terms and Definitions

The following terms and their legal meanings are relevant concerning education for gifted and handicapped children:[2]

1. A *handicapped person* means a person under the age of 26 who is determined by an individualized education planning committee or a hearing officer to have a characteristic or set of characteristics that necessitates special education. Impairment is not based solely on environmental, cultural, or economic differences.

2. *Special education* means specially designed instruction to meet the unique educational needs and develop the maximum potential of the special education student. It includes classroom instruction, physical education, occupational therapy, personal adjustment education, physical therapy, prevocational education, and other ancillary services.

---

1. M.C.L. § 380.1701 & 380.1703; R 340.1701 et seq. of the Michigan Administrative Code.
2. R 340.1701–1715. In this section, the law also defines autism, hearing impaired, visually impaired, physically impaired, speech and language impaired, preprimary impaired, and severely multiply impaired.

3. *Individualized education program* (IEP) means a program developed by an individualized planning committee that specifies the special education programs and services to be provided.

4. *Specific learning disability* means a disorder in one or more of the basic psychological processes involved in understanding or in using language, spoken or written, that manifests itself in an imperfect ability to listen, think, speak, read, write, spell, or do mathematical calculations. The term includes such conditions as perceptual handicaps, brain injury, neurological impairment, minimal brain dysfunction, dyslexia, and developmental aphasia. The term does not include children whose learning problems are primarily the result of visual, hearing, or motor handicaps, of mental retardation, emotional disturbance, autism or environmental, cultural, or economic disadvantage. A child who exhibits a severe discrepancy between achievement and intellectual ability, determined on an individual basis, is deemed to have a learning disability.

5. *Emotionally impaired* means the manifestation of behavioral problems primarily in the affective domain which affect the person's ability to learn without special education support. The person exhibits one or more of the following characteristics over a long period of time and to a marked degree:

   a. an inability to build or maintain satisfactory interpersonal relationships with peers and teachers;

   b. inappropriate types of behavior or feelings under normal circumstances;

   c. a generally pervasive mood of unhappiness or depression; or

   d. a tendency to develop physical symptoms or fears associated with personal or school problems.

6. *Mentally impaired* is the manifestation of lack of development primarily in the cognitive domain and of impairment of adaptive behavior. Impairment is divided into three levels based on intellectual functioning in relation to the general population: *educable mentally impaired* means development at a rate approximately 2 to 3 standard deviations below the mean, *trainable mentally impaired* is 3 to 4½ standard deviations below, and *severely mentally impaired* is defined as 4½ or more standard deviations below.

B) Referral and Special Educational Evaluation

Parents must be notified within 10 days of the receipt of a referral by the school evaluation team for a special education evaluation and be provided information about it. A signed consent form must be obtained from the parents in order to conduct an evaluation; if they refuse to provide consent, a hearing must be conducted.[3] The hearing is convened by the school district and a hearing officer appointed by the superintendent of schools presides.[4] Parents, teachers, administrators, and members of the evaluation team may be present and anyone may be represented by counsel. Evidence is presented at the hearing regarding the appropriateness of a special education evaluation. The hearing officer rules on the basis of the evidence. Results of the hearing can be appealed.[5]

The student is then evaluated by a multidisciplinary team consisting of at least one special education teacher and other personnel qualified in the areas of suspected disability. The team completes a diagnostic evaluation, including a recommendation of eligibility for special education services and prepares a written report. Information must be drawn from a variety of sources, including parent input, aptitude and achievement tests, teacher recommendations, classroom observation, physical condition, social or cultural background, adaptive behavior, and any other pertinent information.[6]

The report is provided to an individualized planning committee (IEPC) appointed by the school superintendent. The committee must include, at minimum, a person, other than the child's teacher, who is qualified to supervise or provide special education and the student's regular teacher. Parents are strongly encouraged to participate in the IEPC meetings.[7] The IEPC must meet within 30 days of the initial referral to determine whether the child is eligible for services and to create an individualized educational program for the student. The program must include[8]

1. a statement of the student's present level of performance;

2. a statement of annual goals, including short-term objectives;

---

3. R 340.1721.
4. R 340.1724a.
5. R 340.1725.
6. R 340.1721a.
7. R 340.1721b.
8. R 340.17213.

3. appropriate objective criteria and evaluation procedures and schedules for determining whether the goals are being achieved;

4. the extent to which the student is able to participate in regular education programs;

5. a statement of the least restrictive environment considered and why it was used or not used;

6. a statement of the specific special education services and ancillary services to be given;

7. beginning at age 12, a statement indicating consideration of the child's prevocational/vocational needs; and

8. the projected dates for beginning service and the anticipated duration of service.

The IEPC must meet at least every 12 months to conduct a comprehensive review of the educational program. A comprehensive evaluation must be conducted at least once every 3 years from the time the person has been declared eligible for services.

(C) Placement in a Special Education Program

The agency involved (usually the local school district) must place students as close as possible to his or her home and in the least restrictive environment. To the extent possible, students are to be mainstreamed. That is, they are to be given as much opportunity as possible to participate with persons who do not have disabilities in academic, nonacademic, and extracurricular activities. Separation of students from the regular educational environment occurs only when the nature or severity of the disability is such that it precludes education in regular classes with supplementary aides and services.[9]

(D) Parental Rights

Parents have a right to receive notice of any evaluation or service planned for their child and of any change in the services provided so that they may give informed consent for the services.[10] Parents have the right to inspect and request a copy of their child's

9. R 340.1722.
10. R 340.1723 et seq.

educational records. Parents may request an impartial due process hearing if they disagree with the district's findings or plans. Parents must be notified that they have the right to obtain an independent educational evaluation at public expense if they disagree with the school district's evaluation, or at their own expense in any instance. However, if an impartial hearing sides with the school's findings, the parents must pay for the independent evaluation. The IEPC must notify parents whenever it plans to continue, modify, or change the educational placement of the child.

E) Gifted Pupils

There is no state statute, rule, or mandate to provide or define services for gifted children. The decision as to whether to provide services for gifted students is thus left up to local districts.

4.21

Consent, Confidentiality, and Services for Minors

Whenever a minor requests or receives services without parental knowledge or consent (see chapter 3.1), legal issues arise concerning the minor's capacity to give informed consent and the scope of the confidential relations between the minor and the MHP. Because failure to obtain consent from the appropriate person before providing services and failure to maintain confidential information are grounds for loss of licensure, a malpractice suit, or other types of civil liability for MHPs (see chapters 3.10 and 3.11), it is important to know who the client is from a legal perspective—the minor or the parent. This chapter discusses those circumstances that the law does address.

(A) Emergency Treatment

There is no statute regarding consent to emergency treatment for minors. However, case law has established that invasive medical services such as surgery can be given without the consent of a parent or guardian if an emergency exists and an attempt to secure consent would result in a delay of treatment that would increase the risk to the child's life.[1] Emancipated minors can consent to medical treatment for themselves.[2]

---

1. Zoski v. Gaines, 260 N.W. 168, 271 Mich. 1 (1935).
2. M.C.L. § 722.1 et seq.

B) Treatment for Substance Abuse

There is no statute regarding consent to substance abuse treatment for minors. Those minors who are determined to be incapacitated in a public place can be taken into custody and transported to a substance abuse program or emergency room under the same conditions as adults (see chapter 8.5), with family members being notified as promptly as possible.[3]

C) Consent for Mental Health Treatment of Minors

Minors 14 years of age or older may request outpatient mental health services from an MHP without the knowledge or consent of their parents. MHPs can provide these services for up to 12 sessions or 4 months without notifying the parents except for prescribing psychotropic drugs or pregnancy termination referrals (see chapter 4.22). Parents cannot be informed without the minor's consent unless there is a compelling need to do so because of the substantial probability that the minor may harm him- or herself or someone else. Even in this situation, the minor must be notified that the MHP is going to breach confidentiality. The law requires that to the extent possible, the treatment should attempt to promote the child's relationship with the parent and not attempt to undermine parental values. After 12 sessions or 4 months, the MHP must either terminate services, or with the minor's consent, get permission from the parent to continue treatment. The minor's parent or guardian is not liable for services provided under this law.[4]

---

3. 6108 Op. Att'y. Gen. 769 (1982).
4. M.C.L. § 330.1707.

4.22

Consent for Abortion

Although it is constitutionally forbidden to give parents complete control over a mature woman's informed consent to abortion, state law requires parental notification. MHPs may become involved in the process by evaluation and testifying as to whether the minor woman is mature enough to make the decision without parental notification. In Michigan, abortions may be performed by licensed physicians with the consent of the woman during the first 2 trimesters of pregnancy. A law limiting termination of a pregnancy during the third trimester was recently declared unconstitutional and it is thus unclear what standards currently apply.

An abortion may not be performed on an unemancipated minor under the age of 18 without the written consent of the minor and one of her parents or her legal guardian.[1] If the parent refuses to give consent, or if the minor decides not to ask for consent, she can petition the probate court for a waiver of consent.[2] A confidential hearing must be held within 72 hours. The court must grant a waiver if it finds that the minor is sufficiently mature and well-enough informed to make an independent decision about abortion or that the waiver would be in the best interest of the minor.[3]

---

1. If permitted by the court, minors over the age of 16 can be legally freed of the supervision of their parents and are thus treated as an adult in the eyes of the law (see chapter 4.10).
2. M.C.L. § 722.903.
3. M.C.L. § 722.904.

4.23

Evaluation and Treatment of Children Whose Parents Are Divorced

MHPs may be asked to provide services to children at the request of noncustodial parents or parents with joint custody. Some state laws provide that where one parent has custody, that person exercises exclusive authority over the care and upbringing of the child; the noncustodial parent does not have the authority to give legal consent to evaluation or treatment decisions concerning the child. MHPs who provide services at the request of a noncustodial parent without first obtaining permission of the custodial parent may be vulnerable to a malpractice claim on the basis that consent to the service was not given.

(A) Joint Custody

When parents have joint legal custody of their children, they share decision-making authority as to the important decisions affecting the welfare of their children.[1] When there is a dispute about an important issue such as the child's education, it has been ruled that the dispute should be remanded to the court.[2] No law directly speaks to whether consent from both parents must be obtained.

---

1. M.C.L. § 722.26a.
2. Lombardo v. Lombardo, 507 N.W.2d 788, 202 Mich.App. 151 (1993).

(B) Sole Custody

For the parent without legal custody, the law indicates that during the time that the child is with the parent having visitation, that parent can decide all routine matters concerning the child.[3] However, *routine matters* is not defined and there is no case law that helps to define the contours of this issue. A noncustodial parent can have access to such things as school, medical, or mental health records unless it is denied by a protective order.[4] It is believed that the presumption would be that consenting to mental health treatment would be beyond the definition of a routine matter and that the courts would rule that the parent without legal custody does not have the authority to consent to such. The parent might circumvent this only by obtaining joint custody; by securing an agreement from the parent with legal custody that the other parent will be allowed to make a decision in this area; or by filing a motion in court alleging that the child's emotional development will be significantly impaired unless the parent without legal custody can have the child treated or evaluated by an MHP.

It is important to note that whatever the custodial arrangement, individual divorce orders may include specific provisions for parental decisions about important issues. Thus, MHPs should ask to see a copy of the divorce order in order to determine whether consent issues are dealt with and, if so, should follow the order. If there is no provision in the order and a divorced parent requests treatment for a child, it is clearly the wisest course to obtain permission of the other parent.

---

3. M.C.L. § 722.27a.
4. M.C.L. § 722.30.

Section 5

Other Civil Matters

5.1

Mental Status of Licensed or Certified Professionals

State laws governing the licensure of professionals increasingly include provisions concerning the mental status of these persons. Such provisions generally pertain to disciplinary procedures rather than license application screening.

The Michigan Department of Consumer and Industry Services regulates the vast majority of professions in the state. Its Office of Health Services regulates the professions of chiropractic, dentistry, marriage and family therapy, medicine, nursing, optometry, osteopathic medicine and surgery, pharmacy practice and drug control, physical therapy, podiatric medicine and surgery, counseling, psychology, occupational therapies, sanitarians, veterinary medicine, and social workers. Polygraph examiners are regulated by the Office of Commercial Services (see Section 1). MHPs may be asked to evaluate and testify before the credentialing board or a court concerning the professional's mental status and its effect on job performance.

(A) Licensed Professionals

It is considered professional misconduct for a professional licensed under the Michigan Public Health Code to practice with a physical or mental condition or a substance abuse problem that impairs or may impair the ability to safely and skillfully practice.[1] Among other penalties, the impaired professional may be required to successfully complete a course of therapy, practice under supervision, or enter the health professional recovery pro-

---

1. M.C.L. § 333.16221.

gram (see Section 1).[2] This program is administered by the health professional recovery committee. The committee refers the professional for specialized treatment for his or her impairment and monitors the professional's progress in meeting treatment goals.

(B) Attorneys

Attorneys are regulated separately through rules of professional conduct established by the Michigan Supreme Court.[3] If there is a substantial question as to the honesty, trustworthiness, or fitness of an attorney, he or she can be referred to the Attorney Grievance Commission, which may limit practice or require therapeutic treatment if necessary.

---

2. M.C.L. § 333.16170 et seq.
3. MRPC 1.0.

5.2

Worker's Compensation

Worker's compensation law provides employees with protection against the treatment costs and income losses resulting from work-related accidents or disease. The employer purchases compensation insurance (or is self-insured) to provide the benefits for its employees. These benefits are awarded regardless of whether the employee or employer is at fault. In return, the employee relinquishes the right to sue the employer for covered injuries and illnesses. The employee may elect to forego benefits and retain the right to sue only if worker's compensation coverage is rejected by the employee prior to an accident. Otherwise, the employee is presumed to have elected the coverage. An injured employee may consult an MHP for diagnosis and treatment, with the costs for these services paid for by worker's compensation insurance. In Michigan fees for such treatment are regulated and there is a fee schedule that establishes payment for each class of providers. Second, an insurance company may request a psychologist or psychiatrist to conduct an independent evaluation to determine the nature and extent of an employee's injury, and to testify about the findings at a hearing.

(A) Scope of the Coverage and Benefits

Worker's compensation benefits are payable for accidents or diseases arising out of and in the course of employment.[1] How-

1. M.C.L. § 418.301.

ever, if the employee is injured as a result of his or her intentional and willful misconduct, he or she will not receive benefits.[2] Compensation is provided without regard to the negligence of the employer, according to a fixed schedule of statutory benefits.[3]

Workers who have been made ill or injured in the course of their employment are entitled to be compensated for the reasonable expenses arising out of their difficulty.[4] They can also receive benefits to replace wages if the disease or injury causes a total or partial disability and are entitled to rehabilitation services designed to return them to the workplace.[5] Disability is defined as a limitation of an employee's wage earning capacity in work suitable to his or her qualifications and training resulting from a personal injury or work-related disease.[6] However, establishing that the person is disabled does not create a presumption of wage loss.

(B) Worker's Compensation and Mental Stress/Disorder

Unlike many other states that will compensate mental injuries only if they are connected with a physical injury, Michigan treats mental disabilities and conditions of the aging process (e.g., heart and cardiovascular conditions) as compensable on their own if contributed to or aggravated by the employment in a significant manner. Mental disabilities are only compensable if they arise out of actual events occurring on the job. A mental disability is not compensable if perceptions of events by the employee are seen to be unfounded; that is, where the employee for some reason misperceives or misconstrues work events as aggravating or contributing to his or her mental disorder. Case law establishes some further parameters. For example, the court has ruled that to establish compensable mental disability the worker must prove that he or she has a mental disability that rises out of actual events of employment, not unfounded perceptions thereof, and that those events contributed to or aggravated the mental disability in a significant manner.[7] In another case the court stated that events must be more than ordinary or relatively innocuous job stresses colored by a claimant's hypersensitive or idiosyncratic reactions

2. M.C.L. § 418.305.
3. M.C.L. § 418.321 et seq.
4. M.C.L. § 418.315.
5. M.C.L. § 418.319.
6. M.C.L. § 418.301.
7. Zgnilec v. General Motors Corp., 568 N.W.2d 690, 224 Mich.App. 392 (1997).

in order to grant benefits. Further, it ruled that benefits are not available just because the employee establishes that an event occurred that was upsetting; the event must rise to the level of a personal injury from an objective person's point of view.[8] Ordinary stresses of employment were ruled not sufficient to sustain a claim of mental disability, even if they result in hypersensitive or idiosyncratic reactions in the employee.[9]

Employees will not be compensated for aggravation of a preexisting condition if they falsely represent in writing that they have not previously suffered from the disease.[10]

C) Processing a Claim

If an employee seeks compensation under the worker's compensation laws, the employee must file a claim with the Bureau of Worker's Compensation, located in the Department of Labor. The claim can be given to the employer or directly to the Bureau. A claim can be filed any time after 1 week of disability.[11] If an injury to an employee results in a disability lasting more than 7 days or causes death, the employer must immediately report it to the Bureau. The employer must also give a copy of the report to the employee or his or her dependent in case of death. The employee must provide the employer with the name of the health professional with whom he or she intends to seek treatment and must obtain and promptly furnish a report from the professional to the employer or insurance agency that is handling the claim. The report must state the history, diagnosis, prognosis, and any other information reasonably necessary to properly evaluate the injury or disability. A current report must be made at least every 60 days and be accompanied by an itemized statement of charges for services rendered. Fees must be usual and reasonable for the services performed.

Employers can reach a voluntary agreement regarding the amount and length of compensation with an employee or, in the case of death, his or her dependents. Disputes are handled by a specialized worker's compensation magistrate who is a member of the Board of Magistrates.[12] The rules governing the conduct of hearings, as well as appeals, are defined by statute and by admin-

---

8. Lombardi v. William Beaumont Hosp., 502 N.W.2d 736, 199 Mich.App.428 (1993).
9. Boyle v. Detroit Bd. of Educ., 494 N.W.2d 818, 197 Mich.App. 255 (1992); Bach v. Flint Bd. of Educ., 494 N.W.2d 870, 443 Mich. 869 (1992).
10. M.C.L. § 418.431.
11. M.C.L. § 418.311.
12. M.C.L. § 418.210.

istrative rules and regulations.[13] Employees disputing a worker'
compensation claim must file an application with the Bureau
who forwards a copy to the employer.[14] The application mus
include any medical records relevant to the claim, and contain th
date and nature of the injury, any witnesses who are not curren
employees of the employer, who treated the injury, the name c
the employer, the dates the employee was unable to work an
whether and with whom the person was employed by at the tim
of the injury. The employer must then make a written response t
the claim that specifies any legal grounds supporting its positior
any factual matters that are disputed, and whether there was
medical evaluation of the employee and who performed it.

Disputes that do not involve stopping or reducing payment
or the termination of payments made through a voluntary agree
ment can be mediated under certain circumstances.[15] These ar
(a) when the claim concerns a definite period of time and th
employee has returned to work, (b) the claim is for medica
benefits only, (c) if the employee is not represented by an attorne
(though they can be represented by a non-attorney at a media
tion), or (d) if the Bureau determines that the claim should b
settled by mediation. The Bureau schedules a mediation confei
ence. Immediately before the conference, the Bureau must reviev
the case with the employee and provide a clear explanation of hi
or her rights and responsibilities, including an estimate of th
maximum amount of benefits that the employee is entitled to i
the claim is approved and the amounts that could be deducted fo
attorney fees if the mediation fails and the claim goes to a forma
hearing. If a mediation conference takes place and the claim is stil
not resolved, the mediator must recommend a hearing in smal
claims court if the dispute is for $2000 or less or a formal hearinç
with a magistrate if it is for more than $2000.

For claims that do not meet the criteria for mediation, withii
30 days of receiving the employee's application, the director o
the Bureau must review and investigate the claim, and eithe
deny it, or if it is found that there may be grounds, must schedul
a hearing.[16] The decision of the Bureau can be appealed within 1!
days to the Board of Magistrates. A formal hearing is then helc
before a magistrate whose ruling is binding on all parties. Th
ruling of the magistrate can be appealed to the Worker's Compen
sation Appellate Commission, which is an independent bod
appointed by the governor with the consent of the senate, anc
which has the power and authority to review the orders of th

---

13. *See* R 408.31 et seq.
14. M.C.L. § 418.222.
15. M.C.L. § 418.223.
16. R 408.35.

director of the Bureau and the opinions of the magistrates. Three members of the Commission review the case and must reach a decision by majority.[17]

D) Worker's Compensation Benefits

The law provides that an employer must provide reasonable medical, surgical, hospital services and medicines, or other treatment to an employee who has received an injury arising out of or in the course of employment.[18] Any appliances or apparatus (such as crutches, artificial limbs, dental service) necessary to cure or reasonably relieve the injury must also be provided. The employee may select a health professional of his or her own choice as long as the employer or its insurance carrier approves. The health professional or health care organization chosen must be willing to submit to a utilization review of their treatment by the employer or insurance carrier and must not charge above the maximum charges set by the Bureau. Employees are also entitled to medical and vocational rehabilitation and placement in another job if they are unable to return to their original work.[19] Independent physical and mental evaluations (IMEs) may be requested by the employee or worker's compensation insurance carrier after an employee has given notice of an injury, and from time to time thereafter in order to determine the current state of the disability and any progress made in treatment.[20]

The amount of benefits paid depends on the degree of disability (partial or total), the length of time the person is disabled (temporary or permanent), and the extent to which the employee has reached medical improvement. In the case of the death of a worker due to a work-related injury, his or her spouse or other eligible dependents may be compensated.[21]

---

17. M.C.L. § 418.274.
18. M.C.L. § 418.315.
19. M.C.L. § 418.319.
20. M.C.L. § 418.385.
21. M.C.L. § 408.301 et seq.

5.3

Vocational Disability Determinations (Vocational Rehabilitation Services)

The state Board of Education administers a vocational disability program. It is funded jointly by the state and federal governments, for persons who have a physical or mental disability that currently prevents them from obtaining employment, but who might be able to engage in a gainful occupation if given vocational rehabilitation services. These services include assessment and psychotherapy from MHPs. Other mental health workers are directly employed by the Office of Vocational Rehabilitation (OVR) as rehabilitation counselors, who provide nonpsychological and nonpsychiatric services in accordance with OVR policies. This counseling is considered to be that service of rehabilitation that provides an appraisal of the disabled person's abilities, limitations, interests, and resources in order to achieve maximum potential.[1]

(A) Definitions

An understanding of the Vocational Rehabilitation law requires a review of key definitions:[2]

1. *Vocational handicap* means any disability except blindness that constitutes, contributes to, or if not corrected will probably result in an obstruction to occupational performance.

---

1. R 395.22.
2. M.C.L. § 395.82.

2. *Disabled individual* means any person other than one who is blind who has a vocational handicap.[3]

3. *Vocational rehabilitation* means any educational or other needed services, including determination of extent of disability, vocational diagnosis, vocational guidance, rehabilitation training, medical services, transportation, maintenance, and training books and materials found to be necessary to compensate a disabled individual for his or her vocational handicap, and to enable him or her to engage in a suitable occupation or to be assisted into independent living.

3) Eligibility Criteria

Any disabled person living in Michigan can be considered for vocational rehabilitation.[4] With the exception of training, diagnostic examinations, and specialized consultation services, all disabled persons are required to pay for services to the best of their ability.[5]

C) Evaluation and Rehabilitation

Background information must be secured from reliable and competent sources. The information must include physical, mental, educational, personality, occupational experience, aptitude, and social factors.[6] Every case must have a medical diagnosis and in doubtful cases, the person must be examined by a recognized specialist in the relevant field. As a result of the diagnostic process, a report is made of any abnormal condition, its prognosis, and its probable response to treatment, as well as recommendations for restoration of the person to fullest functioning. Intelligence, aptitude, and interest tests can be used to determine feasible employment objectives and must be administered by those qualified to do so.[7]

Rehabilitation services are provided in a number of forms. Those can include the provision of prosthetic appliances, physical

---

3. There is a separate law for blind and visually impaired persons. The law establishes a state commission for the blind that is responsible for providing for evaluation, treatment, and rehabilitation services. MHPs may work as educational or clinical consultants to the commission as well as providing mental health services to the blind and visually impaired. M.C.L. § 393.351 et seq.
4. R 395.1.
5. R 395.3.
6. R 395.4.
7. R 395.5.

restoration services when it has been determined that the disabi
ity has become static and may worsen if not treated, and trainir
when the disability, interests, and aptitudes indicate that tl
person may improve his or her level of vocational performance

---

8. *Id.*

5.4

Emotional Distress as a Basis for Civil Liability

Emotional distress, also known as mental suffering or distress, may be the basis for a civil tort suit (i.e., one alleging physical or personal injury) or be part of a larger claim. The cause of the distress, the nature of the injury, and the motivations of the injuring person determine whether a suit must be part of a larger claim or can stand by itself. MHPs may be asked to evaluate the person who claims to have suffered the distress and to testify as to its etiology, severity, and duration, as well as methods of treating it.

A) Intentional Infliction of Emotional Distress

Michigan law provides protection against vexing harassment by allowing a person to sue for intentional infliction of emotional distress and to collect monetary damages in compensation or punishment for the injuries sustained if the suit is won. The court must decide whether as a matter of law such emotional distress can be found, and the jury decides whether it has in fact been proved. In order to support an award of damages, the conduct must be outrageous and regarded as atrocious and utterly intolerable. In one case the court ruled that liability does not include "mere insults, indignities, threats, annoyances, petty oppressions, or other trivialities."[1]

---

1. Roberts v. Auto-Owners Ins. Co., 374 N.W.2d 905, 422 Mich. 594 (1985).

In some states, emotional distress can be claimed only if ther has been an associated physical injury. However, in Michigar this *impact* requirement has been overturned by the Michiga Supreme Court.[2] A woman who was not injured physically bu whose husband was killed and daughter was seriously injured i a car accident was allowed to recover damages from the othe driver because her subsequent mental suffering was caused by h deliberate acts. A plaintiff in this state can recover damages fc emotional distress caused by acts done with the deliberate inter to cause mental suffering. No concomitant physical injury is r quired, although plaintiffs can also sue for emotional damage arising in conjunction with physical injuries.

(B) Negligent Infliction of Emotional Distress

The law also provides for protection against negligent infliction c emotional distress. An individual can establish such a clai where the defendant's negligence resulted in physical injury t another person, was witnessed by the plaintiff, and thereb caused emotional distress. The law limits this action by requirin that the emotional distress be manifested in a definite and obje tive physical injury (here the impact law still stands) and that th injury witnessed must be to an immediate family member.[3] Som states require that the plaintiff must have been in danger c immediate physical injury him- or herself (known as being in th Zone of Danger). However, Michigan does not require this.[4] In case where parents sued to recover damages for emotional di: tress as a consequence of witnessing an injury to their child, th court ruled that the injury must be a serious one and that it mu: be of a nature to cause severe mental disturbance to the paren The shock from witnessing the injury must have resulted in actua physical harm and the parent must actually be present or at lea: suffer shock "fairly contemporaneous" with the injury.[5]

---

2. Daley v. LaCroix, 179 N.W.2d 390, 384 Mich. 4 (1970); Frishett v. State Far Mutual Ins. Co., 143 N.W.2d 612, 3 Mich.App. 688 (1966).
3. Toms v. McConnell, 207 N.W.2d 140, 45 Mich.App. 647 (1973).
4. *Id.* This case involved damages claimed by a mother who watched her chi be hit and killed by a car as she was crossing the street after getting off school bus. Though the mother was in no danger of being hurt herself, t court ruled she was entitled to damages for mental anguish as a result viewing the accident.
5. Mary v. William Beaumont Hosp., 448 N.W.2d 497, 180 Mich.App. 7: (1989).

(C) Emotional Distress as an Element of Damages

Both of the foregoing claims require the presence of emotional distress. There are other claims, however, that do not require emotional distress to prove liability (e.g., a suit by a plaintiff who was physically injured by a defendant's negligence). Such a suit may include emotional distress as an element of damages. Psychological problems that are causally connected to the defendant's acts may be considered by the jury when assessing the amount of damages, even when there is no underlying organic basis for the complaints. Finally, there are other claims that invoke, directly or indirectly, some measure of emotional distress, such as false imprisonment, slander, or invasion of privacy. These are referred to as dignitory torts (i.e., an injury to the person's reputation or personal sense of worth), yet it is clear that the damage is largely to one's emotional well-being. Although these claims do not require evidence of emotional harm to the plaintiff in order to prove liability, the size of the damage award may hinge on such proof.

5.5

Insanity of Wrongdoers and Civil Liability

A person's mental status may affect whether he or she is liable under civil law for injurious behavior caused to another, whether the person can sue another for wrong caused to him or her, or whether any special procedural rights will be provided to ensure a fair trial. Furthermore, and potentially more important, a party's mental status at the time of the conduct may determine whether the person is covered under a liability insurance policy. MHPs may therefore be asked to evaluate the person and testify as to that person's mental status when the injuries occurred and at the time of trial.

(A) The Liability of an Insane Person

In Michigan, all persons are required to exercise ordinary care, including using all their faculties to avoid negligent actions. However, case law indicates that when considering the degree of diligence required, the court must take into account the level of mental competency of the person and must require no higher degree of diligence than a person at this level of competence would be likely to exercise under the circumstances.[1] In *Clemens*, an 8-year-old boy threw a toy that caused a car accident and the question was whether the boy had the capacity to have done this negligently. The court ruled that in deciding the degree of diligence to be required of children, or other persons more or less incompetent, only that judgment or caution naturally to be expected from persons of the same age or capacity may be expected.

---

1. Clemens v. City of Sault Ste. Marie, 286 N.W. 232, 289 Mich. 254 (1939).

(B) Insanity and Liability Insurance

An insane person cannot be held liable for intentional injuries or voluntary property damage in which the insanity was a causal factor. In Michigan, the issue of an insured's insanity in relation to insurance issues is a question of fact to be decided in each case.[2] In *Blackstone*, an insurance company was trying to deny benefits to the wife of a man who committed suicide. Blackstone's sanity was thus at issue and the court ruled that every person is presumed sane, and the burden is on the party asserting to the contrary to establish insanity.

(C) Procedural Rights of Insane Persons

If an individual has been adjudicated legally incompetent, his or her guardian is responsible for responding to or initiating legal actions on his or her behalf. If not guardianship proceedings may be instituted (see chapter 4.2).

---

2. Blackstone v. Standard Life & Accident, 42 N.W. 156, 74 Mich. 592 (1889).

Competency to Contract

A person wishing to buy or sell property must have a minimum mental capacity. This is a passive requirement in that everyone is expected to possess it. It can become an issue if one of the parties to the contract (or that person's legal representative, such as a guardian) wishes to be relieved from executing his or her part of the agreement. An MHP may be asked to evaluate the competence of the person and to testify as to the mental status either before or at the time the person entered into the contract.

(A) Legal Test of Competency to Contract

The test of a person's competency to contract is whether they possess sufficient mind to understand in a reasonable manner, the nature and the effect of what they are doing by signing the contract.[1] The burden of proof is on the party attempting to void the contract. Mental illness alone will not automatically render a person incompetent to contract.[2] In a divorce case, the husband petitioned to set aside the property settlement because he agreed to it when he was under duress because of physical and mental health problems. The court ruled that even if a person is suffering from a mental illness, it must also be proven that the mental illness was of such an extent or nature that the person had no reasonable perception of the terms of the contract. Thus the hus-

---

1. Star Realty, Inc. v. Bower, 169 N.W.2d 194, 17 Mich.App. 248 (1969).
2. Van Wagoner v. Van Wagoner, 346 N.W.2d 77, 131 Mich.App. 204 (1983).

band had to abide by the original settlement. However, a contract made by a person who is under guardianship is invalid.[3]

B) Determination of Competency to Contract

The determination of competency is a factual issue for the jury, or for the judge if there is no jury. Although a party may present evidence of longstanding behavior indicating inability to understand the nature and consequences of a contract, the most important consideration concerns the person's behavior at or around the time the contract was signed.

---

3. Acacia Mutual Life Ins. Co. v. Jago, 273 N.W. 599, 280 Mich. 360 (1937).

5.7

Competency to Sign A Will

Persons who make wills or amend existing ones (*testators*) must meet minimum mental status requirements. If it is later shown that the person did not have the requisite testamentary capacity, the testator's estate will be distributed according to the terms of a previous valid will, if any, or by the intestacy (i.e., without a will) statutes of Michigan.

Mental health consultation or testimony may be used where an MHP treated or evaluated the testator (but see chapters 3.3 and 3.4 for limitations on the release of such information). Sometimes MHPs are asked by testators or their representatives to certify as to their testamentary capacity at the time of the making of the will in order to prevent future challenges to its validity. Alternatively, an MHP may be asked after the testator's demise to provide an opinion of the person's mental status at the time the will was signed, based on reports of other witnesses and any other relevant information.

(A) Legal Test of Testamentary Capacity

Any person 18 years of age or older who is of sound mind may make a will. The right of testamentary disposition is protected carefully by the courts, who are loathe to overturn a reasonable will. There is often considerable flexibility regarding the amount of mental capacity required. Case law has defined testamentary capacity as the individual's ability to comprehend the nature and extent of his or her property, to recall the extent and value of his or her property, and to understand how he or she wishes to dispose of it.[1] Persons have testamentary capacity if they can keep these facts in mind long enough to dictate their will without prompting from others.[2]

Illiteracy,[3] forgetfulness,[4] eccentricity,[5] or intoxication[6] at the time of the execution of a will do not in and of themselves invalidate it if the person demonstrated the requisite capacity. A will cannot be set aside on the grounds that the testator has insane delusions unless it appears that the person's mental problems had bearing on the framing of the will.[7] In one case, suicide was not seen as sufficient evidence of insanity to authorize the rejection of a will.[8]

B) Proving Testamentary Incapacity

There is a presumption in Michigan law that a person is competent to make a will.[9] The party who objects to the admission of the will to probate must prove that the decedent (a testator who has died) was not of sound mind at the signing of the will. The determination of whether the decedent lacked this capacity is a factual issue, and the decision will not be reversed absent significant error.

1. Vollbrecht's Estate v. Pace, 182 N.W.2d 609, 26 Mich.App. 430 (1970).
2. *In re* Beiter's Estate, 106 N.W.2d 166, 361 Mich. 661 (1960).
3. *In re* Cummins' Estate, 259 N.W. 894, 271 Mich. 215 (1935).
4. *In re* Grow's Estate, 299 N.W. 836, 299 Mich. 133 (1941).
5. *In re* Thayer's Estate, 15 N.W.2d 712, 309 Mich. 473 (1944).
6. Pierce v. Pierce, 38 Mich. 412 (1878).
7. *In re* Walker's Estate, 258 N.W. 206, 270 Mich. 33 (1935).
8. *In re* Walkey, 229 N.W. 485, 249 Mich. 653 (1930).
9. M.C.L. § 600.2152.

5.8

Competency to Vote

Although voting is a basic right, the Michigan Constitution allows the legislature to exclude by law people who are mentally incompetent or incarcerated.[1] MHPs may be asked to evaluate a person whose competency to vote is questioned. While there is no statute or case law that defines competency to vote, it is assumed that the legal considerations would be similar to other competency definitions discussed in this book (see chapter 4.2).

---

1. MICH. CONST. art. 2, § 2.

5.9

Competency to Obtain a Driver's License

The secretary of state has the authority to suspend, revoke, or refuse to grant a license to a person if he or she has reason to believe that the person has a physical or mental disability that would prevent the person from exercising reasonable and ordinary control over their vehicle.[1] While some states have specific laws for disorders such as epilepsy, Michigan does not. The license cannot be suspended for more than 1 year, but the person must be re-examined in a manner prescribed by the secretary of state before it can be restored.[2] An individual whose license has been suspended, revoked, or restricted can petition for a review hearing in circuit court, where he or she can present evidence as to why the license should be restored.[3] MHPs may be asked to evaluate persons whose competency to drive is questioned.

1. M.C.L. § 257.303.
2. M.C.L. § 257.320c.
3. M.C.L. § 257.323.

5.10

Product Liability

Product liability is a legal term that describes a theory (claim) for personal injuries or property damages arising from the use of a product. Although a product liability claim may be based on principles of negligence[1] or warranty,[2] this chapter is limited to the third basis, strict tort liability. The central element of such a claim is that the product was unreasonably dangerous to the user because of a manufacturing defect, a design defect, or inadequate warning. MHPs who have special expertise in human factors may be asked to evaluate the safety of a product and testify in court as to the results. MHPs may also be asked to evaluate claims of emotional damages resulting from a product liability claim.

(A) Elements of a Product Liability Claim

A product liability action is an action based on the death or injury of a person who uses the product or damage to property caused by or resulting from the production of a product.[3] The burden is on the plaintiff to prove that (a) the product was not reasonably safe at the time it left the control of the manufacturer or seller, or (b) that a practical and technically feasible alternative production practice was available that would have prevented the harm without significantly impairing the usefulness or desirability of the

---

1. *Negligence* means that the wrongdoer's conduct fell below what would be expected of a reasonably prudent person in the particular circumstances.
2. A warranty claim alleges that the product did not work as promised or represented by the seller or manufacturer.
3. M.C.L. § 600.2945.

product and without creating equal or greater risk to others.[4] The alternative production practice must have been developed, available, and capable of use in the production of the product and economically feasible for the manufacturer to use.

B) Defenses to a Product Liability Claim

The law provides several defenses to a product liability claim. The manufacturer or seller is not liable if[5]

1. the product was altered or misused in a manner that was not reasonably foreseeable;
2. the purchaser was aware that the use of the product created an unreasonable risk of harm and voluntarily exposed him- or herself to the risk;
3. there was a failure to provide an adequate warning if the product is provided for use by a sophisticated user;[6] and
4. the harm was caused by an inherent characteristic of the product that cannot be eliminated without substantially compromising the product and is recognized by a person with ordinary common knowledge.

However, the above criteria do not apply if the court decides that the manufacturer or seller had actual knowledge that the product was defective and that there was a substantial likelihood that the defect would cause the injury and willfully disregarded this.[7]

C) Limitations on the Award of Damages

Michigan law limits the amount of non-economic damages that can be awarded to a plaintiff to $280,000, unless death or the permanent loss of a vital body function has occurred. In that case the award is limited to $500,000.[8]

---

4. M.C.L. § 600.2946.
5. M.C.L. § 600.2947.
6. A *sophisticated user* is defined as someone who by virtue of their training, experience, profession, or legal obligation is expected to be knowledgeable about a product, including potential hazards and adverse effects.
7. M.C.L. § 600.2949a.
8. M.C.L. § 600.2946a.

5.11

Unfair Competition

Business competitors may engage in fierce battles to win a share of the market. They cannot, however, use tactics that do not serve the public interest or have been legally declared to be unfair, unconscionable, or deceptive such as defaming competitors or their goods, stealing trade secrets, or starting a business with an ex-employer's customer lists.[1] A large area of unfair competition of interest to MHPs, particularly psychologists, is a type of marketing that attempts to confuse the consumer into believing that one business's products or services were produced by another. MHPs may be asked to conduct consumer surveys to determine whether the defendant's business practices resulted in such confusion, and to testify in court as to their findings.

(A) Business Confusion

Business confusion is essentially a form of fraud. It is an attempt to conduct business or sell a product that is very similar to that of a competitor. For instance, a business could be accused of unfair trade practice if it packaged its product in a very similar way as a competing business, or uses similar initials. Confusion can also be created by false advertising. One business was cited because it advertised in a manner that led consumers to believe its product was associated with a particular research study conducted at a local university.[2]

---

1. M.C.L. § 445.903.
2. Janda v. Riley-Meggs Indus., Inc., 764 F.Supp. 1223 (E.D.Mich. 1991).

B) Trademark Infringement

A trademark is any word, name, symbol, or device, or any combination thereof, adopted and used by a person to identify goods made or sold by him or her and which distinguishes them from similar goods made or sold by others.[3] Similarly, a service mark is a mark used by a person in the sale or advertising of services to identify his or her services and distinguish them from similar services of others. Michigan law prohibits the use or reproduction of any reproduction, counterfeit, copy, or colorable imitation of a registered mark without the consent of the person who registered it if its use is intended to cause confusion or mistake or to deceive someone as to the source or origin of the goods or services. Anyone doing so is liable to civil action.[4]

---

3. M.C.L. § 429.31.
4. M.C.L. § 429.42.

5.12

Employment Discrimination

The law prohibits employers from engaging in discriminatory employment practices. In 1992, Congress enacted the American With Disabilities Act (ADA), which prohibits discrimination on the basis of mental and physical disability.[1] The ADA applies to professionals who have employees, as well as to management consultants who advise employers concerning personnel selection, discharge, and promotion. MHPs should be aware of this law as it pertains to industrial consulting and test construction. MHPs may be consulted about what would constitute a "reasonable accommodation" that the employer could make to permit a mentally or emotionally impaired employee to work in spite of a disability. MHPs may also be asked to evaluate individuals who maintain that they have been discriminated against because of a disability and who have sustained emotional damages from such discrimination.

(A) Elliott-Larsen Civil Rights Act

In Michigan, the statute governing employment discrimination is known as the Elliott-Larsen Civil Rights Act.[2] The law states that[3]

> The opportunity to obtain employment, housing and other real estate, and the full and equal utilization of public accommodations, public service, and educational facilities without discrimination because of religion, race, color, national origin, age, sex,

---

1. 42 U.S.C. §§ 12101-12213.
2. M.C.L. § 37.2101 et seq.
3. M.C.L. § 37.2102.

height, weight, or marital status as prohibited by this act, is recognized and declared to be a civil right.

Discrimination on the basis of sex includes sexual harassment, which is defined as unwelcome sexual advances, requests for sexual favors, and other verbal or physical conduct or communication of a sexual nature when[4]

1. submission to such conduct is implicitly or explicitly made a term or condition of employment;
2. submission to or rejection of the harassment is used as a factor in decisions affecting the person's employment; or
3. the conduct has the purpose or effect of substantially interfering with the person's employment, or of creating a hostile, intimidating, or offensive environment.

The statute defines an employer as any person who has one or more employees.[5] It prohibits discriminatory practices by employment agencies, labor organizations, and public service agencies, such as public facilities, departments, agencies, boards, and commissions that are operated on behalf of the state, as well as tax-exempt private agencies that provide services to the public.[6] It also bans discrimination by both public and private educational institutions. Private clubs that allow use of their facilities by one or more adults per membership (e.g., private golf or yacht clubs) are considered places of public accommodation and are thus not exempt from this statute.[7] The law does exempt religious institutions that limit admission or give preference to people who are of that religion,[8] and private schools that are single sex organizations.[9]

(B) Unlawful Employment Practices

Unfair employment practices under Michigan law include[10]

1. failing or refusing to hire or recruit, or discharging, or otherwise discriminating against an individual with respect to employment, compensation, or a term, condition, or privilege of

---

4. M.C.L. § 37.2103.
5. M.C.L. § 37.2201.
6. M.C.L. § 37.2301.
7. M.C.L. § 37.2302a.
8. M.C.L. § 37.2403.
9. M.C.L. § 37.2404.
10. M.C.L. § 37.2202 et seq.

employment, because of religion, race, color, national origin, age, sex, height, weight, or marital status;

2. limiting, segregating, or classifying an employee or applicant in a way that deprives or tends to deprive the person of an employment opportunity because of the statuses noted above;

3. an employment agency failing to refer, recruit, or place a person for employment because of the statuses noted above;

4. a labor organization excluding or expelling from membership, or otherwise discriminating against a protected person or limiting, segregating, or classifying its membership by protected categories;

5. a labor organization failing to adequately represent a member in a grievance process because of the status noted above;

6. an employer, labor, organization, or joint employer–labor committee discriminating in training because of the above status;

7. discriminating in advertising for employment; and

8. inquiring as to an applicant's religion, race, color, national origin, age, sex, height, weight, or marital status.

Employers may apply for an exemption if religion, national origin, age, height, weight, or sex is a bona fide occupational qualification reasonably necessary to the normal operation of the business.[11] However, race is not included because discrimination based on race is always prohibited.[12] It is not considered an unfair practice for an employer to reward employees with compensation or privileges under a bona fide seniority or merit system.[13]

---

11. M.C.L. § 37.2208.
12. U.S. CONST. amend. XIV.
13. M.C.L. § 37.2211.

Civil and Criminal Trial Matters

6.1

Jury Selection

Jury selection is an area of importance to attorneys because the process allows them, to a degree, to select a jury. In actuality, potential jurors are rejected from serving rather than selected. MHPs may be involved in this process by conducting pretrial surveys, constructing questions to ask potential jurors, and evaluating jurors on the basis of the results of pretrial surveys and/or of in-court observations of them.

(A) Juror Qualifications

The jury selection process begins by a random selection of names from the current voter registration lists, the driver's license list, and the personal identification cardholder list.[1] By statute,[2] to qualify as a juror a person must be a citizen of the United States, at least 18 years of age, and a resident in the county for which the person is selected, or in the case of district or municipal courts, a resident in the district or municipality. The person must also be conversant in the English language, and be physically and mentally able to carry out the functions of a juror. A temporary disability shall not be considered a disqualification; a person over age 70 may claim exemption from jury service. The person must not have served as a petit or grand juror in a court of records during the preceding 12 months, and must not be under a sentence for a felony at the time of jury selection.

---

1. M.C.L. § 600.1304.
2. M.C.L. § 600.1307a.

(B) Criminal Trials

(B)(1) When a Jury Is Allowed

The state (and federal) constitution provides that criminal defendants have a right to a trial by jury in every criminal prosecution.[3] A defendant may elect to waive the right to a jury trial (in favor of a bench trial, in which the judge decides the verdict) if the prosecutor consents and the court approves[4] (see chapter 7.2).

(B)(2) Jury Size

Juries in criminal cases typically consist of 12 persons. However, a jury may have fewer than 12 if the crime is a misdemeanor punishable by not more than 1 year in prison.[5] The judge may also impanel alternate jurors, if it is appropriate.[6] Alternate jurors, if necessary, may replace members of the trial jury, as ordered by the court.

(B)(3) Unanimity Requirement

The jury must reach a unanimous verdict in all criminal trials.

(B)(4) Change of Venue

Criminal defendants may request to move the place of trial to another county within the state if good cause is shown.[7] The decision to change venue is at the court's discretion.[8] For change of venue to be granted, the defendant must show that there is a pattern of strong community feeling or bitter prejudice against him or her, and pretrial publicity must be so extensive and inflammatory that jurors, if exposed to it, could not remain impartial.[9]

(B)(5) Voir Dire

In order to ensure a fair and impartial verdict, jurors may be examined as to their qualifications for serving and any potential biases they might have. The purpose of voir dire is to provide the attorneys with enough information to decide whether to exclude jurors for cause or by peremptory challenge.[10] The examination is

---

3. Mich. Const. art. 1, § 20.
4. M.C.L. § 763.3 and M.C.R. § 6.401.
5. Mich. Const. art. 1, § 20.
6. M.C.R. § 6.411.
7. M.C.L. § 762.7.
8. People v. Ranes, 227 N.W.2d 312, 58 Mich.App. 268 (1975).
9. People v. Prast, 319 N.W.2d 627, 114 Mich.App. 469 (1982).
10. Krzysiak v. Hinton, 304 N.W.2d 823, 104 Mich.App. 134 (1981).

usually conducted by the judge, who may also permit attorneys to ask questions of the jurors.[11]

The parties may make an unlimited number of challenges *for cause*, alleging that a juror is unqualified. Grounds for such disqualification include the fact that the prospective juror[12]

1. is not qualified to be a juror;
2. has been convicted of a felony;
3. is biased for or against a party or attorney;
4. shows a state of mind that will prevent the person from rendering a just verdict, or has formed a positive opinion on the facts of the case or what the outcome should be;
5. has opinions or scruples that would improperly influence the verdict;
6. has been subpoenaed as a witness at the trial;
7. has already sat on a trial based on the same action;
8. is related to one of the parties or attorneys;
9. is the guardian, conservator, employer or employee, partner or client of a party or attorney;
10. has complained of or been accused by the party in a criminal or civil action; and
11. has a financial or other interest in the outcome.

Both the defendant and state are also each entitled to a number of peremptory challenges, by which an attorney can strike a juror from the panel for any reason, except if the state uses peremptory challenges in a discriminatory manner to eliminate people of a particular race.[13] The parties are entitled to 5 peremptory challenges, unless an offense charged is punishable by life imprisonment. In this case, 12 challenges are allowed if the defendant is tried singly; when two defendants are tried jointly by a single jury, 10 challenges are permitted, with a decrease of an additional challenge for each additional defendant tried jointly up to 5 or more, in which case 7 challenges are permitted.[14]

---

11. M.C.R. § 37.1.
12. M.C.R. § 2.511.
13. People v. Barker, 446 N.W.2d 549, 179 Mich.App. 702 (1989).
14. M.C.R. § 6.412(E)(1).

(C) Civil Trials

(C)(1) When a Jury Is Allowed

Either the plaintiff or the defendant can request a jury trial in most civil proceedings.[15]

(C)(2) Jury Size

A jury in a civil case consists of six people.[16]

(C)(3) Unanimity Requirement

The verdict is reached when five of the six jurors agree, except in civil commitment cases, where the verdict must be unanimous.[17]

(C)(4) Change of Venue

The law on change of venue is the same as that for criminal trials (see section (B)(4)).

(C)(5) Voir Dire

The procedures governing the voir dire examinations in civil suits are similar to those in criminal trials. Civil parties may make an unlimited number of challenges for cause using the same criteria as those noted in section (B)(5). After these challenges are completed, each party is generally entitled to 3 peremptory challenges, and the court may permit more in multiparty suits.[18]

---

15. MICH. CONST. art. 1, § 14.
16. M.C.L. § 600.1352.
17. MICH. CONST. art. 1, § 14.
18. M.C.R. § 2.511.

Expert Witnesses

MHPs may testify as expert witnesses if they can provide testimony on a topic that is beyond the trier's competence and if this information will permit the trier to rationally decide the case before it. MHPs are frequently called to testify as expert witnesses on a wide variety of issues.

(A) Qualifying as an Expert Witness

Michigan Rules of Evidence, which in this instance closely follows the identically numbered Federal Rules of Evidence, provide that:[1]

> If the court determines that recognized scientific, technical, or other specialized knowledge will assist the trier of fact to understand the evidence or to determine a fact at issue, a witness qualified as an expert by knowledge, skill, experience, training, or education, may testify thereto in the form of an opinion or otherwise.

(B) When an Expert Witness May Be Called to Testify

Mental health experts may be called on to offer testimony about a wide variety of issues. Generally, the determination of whether a proposed expert witness is qualified to testify is left to the discre-

---

1. M.R.E. § 702.

tion of the trial judge.[2] For expert testimony to be admitted, there must be a call for knowledge that goes beyond that of the common layperson.[3] If the matter at hand is one in which all relevant facts can be introduced without an expert, and the jury is competent to draw reasonable inferences from the facts, opinion testimony would not be received.[4] However, expert testimony is required when specialized knowledge is needed to understand evidence or make a factual determination.[5] Medical malpractice is one such case; there, expert testimony is required to establish both the standard of practice or care that applied, and a breach of that standard.[6] An important limitation on the qualifications of expert witnesses in medical malpractice actions was legislatively enacted in 1993 as a reform measure.[7] The statute was changed to require, among other things, that in the year preceding the event in question, an expert must have devoted the majority of his or her professional time to either active clinical practice in the same profession and, if applicable, the same specialty as the person being sued, or in teaching that profession or specialty in an accredited institution or program. This statute also prohibits testimony provided by experts on a contingent fee basis.

(C) Form and Content of Testimony

A witness qualified as an expert, in contrast to other witnesses, may testify on the basis of information that is hearsay or other nonrecord evidence.[8] Hearsay evidence includes statements made out of court, other than by a testifying witness. Expert witnesses, in contrast to lay witnesses, may testify in the form of opinions. As in federal courts, an expert witness may testify to an opinion or inference that embraces the *ultimate issue*, the matter that is to be decided by the judge or jury.[9] In contrast to the Federal Rules of Evidence, Michigan Rules of Evidence do not prevent the court from requiring that the underlying facts or data essential to an opinion or inference be in evidence.[10] In civil cases,

---

2. Wilson v. W.A. Foote Memorial Hosp., 91 Mich.App. 90, 284 N.W.2d 126 (1979); Accetola v. Hood, 7 Mich.App. 83, 151 N.W.2d 210 (1967).
3. Syrowik v. City of Detroit, 119 Mich.App. 343, 326 N.W.2d 507 (1982); Blackwell's Estate v. Hare, 50 Mich.App. 204, 213 N.W.2d 201 (1973).
4. Dudek v. Popp, 373 Mich. 300, 129 N.W.2d 393 (1964).
5. Baldwin v. Williams, 104 Mich.App. 735, 306 N.W.2d 314 (1981).
6. Waati v. Marquette Gen. Hosp., 122 Mich.App. 44, 329 N.W.2d 526 (1982).
7. M.C.L. § 600.2169, as amended by 1993 P.A. No. 288.
8. Swanek v. Hutzel Hosp., 115 Mich.App. 254, 320 N.W.2d 234 (1982); Tiffany v. Christman Co., 93 Mich.App. 267, 287 N.W.2d 199 (1979).
9. M.R.E. § 704.
10. M.R.E. § 703.

contrary to federal rules governing discovery or the disclosure of information to opposing attorneys, a pretrial deposition (sworn and recorded testimony given in response to attorneys' questions outside a courtroom) of any expert witness expected to be called to testify at trial can be taken without either a court order or the agreement of all the attorneys.[11] However, in common with the federal rules, unless the court does require it, expert witnesses may testify in terms of opinions or inferences and give the reasons for them without prior disclosure of the underlying facts or data, although the expert may be required to disclose them in the course of cross-examination.[12] Opposing counsel may use textbooks or other publications during cross-examination of the expert in order to impeach, i.e., discredit the witness, providing that the expert recognizes the work as authoritative[13] or if the trial court takes judicial notice, or rules, that it is authoritative.[14] Expert witnesses may testify by responding to hypothetical questions, provided they are not irrelevant to an issue involved in the case, do not assume facts that are not in evidence or which are contrary to the record, and that they are not misleading.[15] In regard to two particular issues, courts have specifically prevented or limited expert testimony. The Michigan Supreme Court has held[16] that the "sexual abuse accommodation syndrome," or a theory of behavior patterns of sexually abused children, is not a reliable indicator of sexual abuse, and that the evidence in that regard is admissible only for the narrow purpose of rebutting an inference that an alleged victim's behavior following an incident was inconsistent with the behavior patterns of actual victims of sexual abuse, but not for showing that this behavior is evidence of actual sexual abuse (see also chapter 6.7). Similarly, expert testimony has been restricted on the battered spouse syndrome (see chapter 6.6) to testimony describing the syndrome and the symptoms that comprise it; the expert witness is not permitted to offer an opinion that an individual criminal defendant suffers from the syndrome, or acted as she did because of it.[17]

---

11. M.C.R. § 2.302(B)(4).
12. M.R.E. § 705.
13. Ellison v. Wayne County Gen. Hosp., 100 Mich.App 739, *rev'd in part on other grounds*, 411 Mich. 988, 308 N.W.2d 111 (1980); Ravenis v. Detroit Gen. Hosp., 63 Mich.App. 739, 234 N.W.2d 411(1975); Jones v. Bloom, 388 Mich. 98, 200 N.W.2d 196 (1972).
14. Jones v. Bloom, 388 Mich. 98, 200 N.W.2d 196 (1972).
15. West v. Livingston County Road Comm'n, 131 Mich.App. 63, 345 N.W.2d 608 (1983); Serafin v. Peoples Community Hosp. Auth., 67 Mich.App. 560, 242 N.W.2d 438 (1976); Steinberg v. Ford Motor Co.,72 Mich.App. 520, 242 N.W.2d 438 (1976).
16. People v. Beckley, 434 Mich. 691, 456 N.W.2d 687 (1990).
17. People v. Wilson, 194 Mich.App. 599, 487 N.W.2d 822 (1992).

Polygraph Evidence

Polygraph examinations are governed by laws regulating the licensure of polygraph examiners and the submission of test results at trial. These laws apply to all MHPs.

(A) Polygraph Examination Definition

The polygraph examination is not specifically defined in law, but the statutory licensing of polygraph examiners applies to:[1]

> such instrument or device, as minimum standards, shall be capable of recording visually, permanently and simultaneously indications of a person's cardiovascular pattern and changes therein, and a person's respiratory pattern and changes therein. Indications of other psychophysiological changes or bodily responses in addition may also be recorded. . . .

(B) Licensure of Polygraph Examiners

Licensure as a Forensic Polygraph Examiner is required of:[2]

> persons who purport to be able to detect deception, verify truthfulness, or provide a diagnostic opinion of either through the use of any device or instrumentation as lie detectors, forensic polygraphers, deceptographs, emotional stress meters or similar or related devices and instruments. . . .

By statute,[3] no one who has not first secured a license as a Forensic Polygraph Examiner shall:

---

1. M.C.L. § 338.1704.
2. Public Acts of 1972, No. 295, § 1., and M.C.L. § 338.1702.
3. M.C.L. § 338.1708.

use or attempt to use any instrumentation or mechanical device for the purpose of detecting deception, verifying truthfulness or reporting a diagnostic opinion regarding either of these; purport to detect deception or verify truthfulness through instrumentation or mechanical devices. . . .

Exemptions to licensing are not provided for other licensed or certified mental health professionals, although a person would not need to be licensed as a forensic examiner in order to use polygraph equipment solely for the purpose of measuring stress, and not verifying truthfulness[4] (see also chapter 1.12).

C) Admissibility of Polygraph Examinations

Results of polygraph examinations are inadmissible as evidence at trial,[5] and are inadmissible whether the polygraph was administered to the accused or to witnesses.[6] It is inadmissible even if the parties agree or stipulate to its admission.[7] Polygraph examinations and opinions are inadmissible in criminal, civil, and administrative proceedings, in presentence reports, in sentencing proceedings, and in considerations of a motion for a new trial.[8] The fact that a person took a polygraph examination,[9] or offered to take a lie detector test,[10] is also inadmissible. However, a statement made to a polygraph examiner may be admitted if the defendant made it voluntarily, knowingly, and intelligently[11] (see chapter 7.2), and it may be admitted for impeachment,[12] that is, to contradict some other statement by the person. The basis for barring polygraph evidence as such, i.e., the result of a polygraph examination as opposed to statements made to a polygraph examiner, is the lack of scientific recognition of the polygraph's validity and reliability, and the danger that a judge or jury will rely upon polygraph results and otherwise suspend judgment.[13]

---

4. 4855 Op. Att'y. Gen. (1975).
5. People v. Rocha, 110 Mich.App. 1, 312 N.W.2d 657 (1981).
6. People v. Ranes, 63 Mich.App. 498, 234 N.W.2d 673 (1975).
7. People v. Wright, 74 Mich.App. 297, 253 N.W.2d 739 (1977).
8. People v. Liddell, 63 Mich.App. 491, 312 N.W.2d 669 (1975).
9. People v. Wallach, 110 Mich.App.37, 312 N.W.2d 387 (1981).
10. People v. McLaughlin, 3 Mich.App. 391, 142 N.W.2d 484 (1966).
11. People v. Good, 186 Mich.App. 180 (1990).
12. People v. Champion, 97 Mich.App. 25, 293 N.W.2d 715 (1980).
13. People v. Yatooma, 85 Mich.App. 236, 271 N.W.2d 184 (1978).

6.4

Competency to Testify

A witness in a civil or criminal trial must have the mental capacity to testify accurately and reliably in court; any other rule would open the fairness of the trial to question. Thus, whenever there is a reasonable doubt concerning the competency of a witness, the opposing counsel or the court should raise the issue. Child witnesses may be questioned by the court to determine their ability to relate facts accurately and to testify in a truthful manner. To ensure justice, MHPs have been asked to aid in this assessment and to testify as to their findings. In this chapter, the mental status evaluation of rape victims is also discussed.

(A) Determination of Witness Competency

Except as otherwise provided in court rules, unless the court finds after questioning a person that he or she does not have sufficient physical or mental capacity or sense of obligation to testify truthfully and understandably, every person is competent to be a witness.[1] The fact that the proposed witness has a criminal history, has an interest of some sort in the outcome of the matter in question, or has a marital or other relationship with an involved party, cannot lead to the exclusion of that person's testimony.[2] A person cannot be deemed incompetent as a witness because of

---

1. M.R.E. § 601.
2. M.C.L. § 600.2158.

any opinions on the subject of religion, and a witness cannot be questioned about religious opinions either before or after the witness is sworn.[3]

Children are not deemed incompetent simply because of age or immaturity. When a child under the age of 10 is proposed as a witness, the judge must examine the child, either privately or in open court, and be satisfied that the child has sufficient intelligence and sense of obligation to tell the truth.[4] This inquiry by the court is not necessary if the child is over the age of 10, in the absence of evidence that the child lacks intelligence or a sense of obligation to tell the truth.[5] It has been deemed[6] no abuse of discretion to find a 7-year-old witness in a murder case to be competent to testify when he was found by the court to be sufficiently intelligent, to have a sufficient sense of obligation to tell the truth, and to not be unduly influenced in any way by others. It has been held[7] not to be an error even to determine that a 4-year-old witness to a murder was competent to testify, when the court had found that she had a good memory of the events involved, that she actually saw the murder, that she was not merely repeating what she heard from others, and that she understood the importance of telling the truth. In cases in which young children are qualified by the court as competent to testify, the judge may instruct the jury as to the weight to be given to the child's testimony.[8]

B) Competency of Rape Victims to Testify

Unlike some other jurisdictions, the competency of the victim-witness of rape or, in terms of statute, criminal sexual misconduct, is not subject to special challenge in Michigan. No case law raises the issue of the ability of the rape victim as victim to testify. A 6-year-old alleged victim of rape was ruled as properly qualified to testify.[9] A victim of a sexual offense who is 14 years old or younger, or who is developmentally disabled, is not disqualified

---

3. M.C.L. § 600.1436.
4. M.C.L. § 600.1263.
5. People v. Wright, 35 Mich.App. 365, 160 N.W.2d 515 (1971).
6. People v. Harrison, 49 Mich.App. 546, 212 N.W.2d 278 (1973).
7. People v. Washington, 130 Mich.App. 579, 344 N.W.2d 8 (1983).
8. Bravo v. Chernick, 28 Mich.App. 210, 184 N.W.2d 357 (1970).
9. People v. Harris, 158 Mich.App. 463, 404 N.W.2d 779 (1987).

as incompetent to testify, and special provisions may be mad
available for such victims, including but not limited to the pres
ence at testimony of someone to support the victim, and video
taped rather than live testimony.[10]

---

10. M.C.L. § 600.2163a.

Psychological Autopsy

The motivations and mental state of a person prior to death are frequently critical issues in subsequent litigation. For instance, whether a gift was made by a person "in contemplation of death" has significant tax consequences. Similarly, a finding that a person committed suicide rather than died accidentally may determine whether there is insurance coverage. MHPs may contribute in this area by providing a retrospective psychological profile of the decedent.

A) Admissibility of Psychological Autopsies

Court rules[1] provide that if a court determines that recognized scientific, technical, or other specialized knowledge will assist in the determination of a fact at issue, a witness qualified as an expert by knowledge, skill, experience, training, or education may offer testimony, including opinion testimony. No appellate cases in Michigan speak to the admissibility of expert testimony on the question of whether a death was a suicide or an accident.

---

1. M.R.E. § 702.

Battered Woman's
Syndrome

The battered woman's syndrome, discussed in Michigan case law as the *battered spouse syndrome*, attempts to describe the psychological impact on a woman of physical abuse by her husband or paramour on a regular basis over a period of time. In some states, the law recognizes a defense to serious physical injury of a husband on the basis of the battered woman's syndrome. MHPs may provide testimony on the defendant's subjective state of mind and behavior subsequent to the abuse in question.

(A) Legal Test of Battered Spouse Syndrome

In Michigan, while testimony on the battered spouse syndrome may be permitted within certain strictures (see below), it has not been recognized as a formal or defined condition that if present would lead to any certain result, such as a finding that a woman acted in self defense.

(B) Raising the Battered Spouse Syndrome

Evidence regarding battered spouse syndrome may be relevant and helpful to a jury, but the scope of expert testimony in this regard will be limited (see also chapter 6.2). Testimony about this syndrome was offered at the trial of a woman accused of mur dering her husband in order to support a self-defense theory. Consistent with the Michigan Supreme Court rulings in regard to rape trauma syndrome (see chapter 6.7), the Court of Appeals in this case[1] held that a qualified expert may generally describe the syndrome and the symptoms its victims have, and may offer the opinion that certain behavior of the defendant, evidence of which has already been admitted, is characteristic of victims of battered spouse syndrome. However, the expert witness may not offer an opinion as to whether a particular defendant suffers from the syndrome, much less whether she acted as she did under its influence. Importantly, the expert witness cannot testify that the battering of the defendant actually occurred.[2]

---

1. People v. Wilson, 194 Mich.App. 599, 487 N.W.2d 822 (1992).
2. *Id.*

Rape Trauma Syndrome

Rape trauma syndrome describes behavioral, somatic, and psychological sequelae of an attempted or successful forcible rape. In some states, the law allows a party to introduce evidence from MHPs that a rape victim is suffering from rape trauma syndrome to assist in a prosecution where the defendant acknowledges that sexual intercourse occurred but claims that it was consensual. The presence of rape trauma syndrome tends to disprove that the victim consented.

In Michigan, the admissibility of rape trauma syndrome has been addressed only indirectly, and it is uncertain whether an expert witness would be permitted to testify strictly in terms of this syndrome, particularly if it is labeled as a syndrome. However, expert testimony concerning the behavior of child or adolescent sexual abuse victims is clearly permitted for the narrow purpose of rebutting an inference that an alleged victim's behavior following the rape in question was inconsistent with the behavior of a genuine rape victim.[1]

The testimony permitted under *Beckley* would be subject to constraints similar to testimony on battered spouse syndrome (see chapter 6.6). In particular, the expert may testify about the general behavior patterns of child victims of sexual abuse so long as there is no reference to a fixed set of behaviors constituting a syndrome. The syndrome in question (*rape trauma syndrome* or *child sexual abuse accommodation syndrome* were considered), the Michigan Supreme Court held, is merely a therapeutic tool and not a reliable means of detecting abuse; evidence of certain behaviors characteristic of the syndrome does not permit the inference

---

1. People v. Beckley, 434 Mich. 691, 456 N.W.2d 391 (1990).

of actual sexual abuse. The sole purpose of expert testimony in these cases is to provide enough background information about the behavior of the child in question to help the jury dispel any misconceptions they may have about the behavioral reactions to be expected of sexual abuse victims, thereby permitting the jury to make an informed judgment of the child's credibility. The expert may not testify that the complaining witness's allegations are truthful or not, nor offer an opinion as to whether the abuse in fact occurred.

The Michigan Supreme Court clarified its ruling in *Beckley* in *People v. Peterson* in 1995.[2] The court held that prosecution may present expert testimony that a particular child's behavior is consistent with that of a sexually abused child only if the defendant raises the issue of the child's post-incident behavior or attacks the child's credibility.

Beckley and *Peterson* concern children victims of sexual assaults, and although the logic of the holdings may have general application, there is no appellate case specifically addressing adult rape victims. Testimony concerning the alleged rape victim's psychological characteristics and behavior, while thus permitted to shed some light on credibility of her complaints from the prosecution standpoint, cannot be used by the defense against her. Michigan's Rape Shield Law[3] generally prevents the introduction in a prosecution of criminal sexual conduct of any evidence concerning the alleged victim's past sexual conduct or reputation. Likewise, the defendant in such a case is not entitled to a mental health examination of the alleged victim in order to determine her psychological makeup for the purpose of showing that she voluntarily participated in the sexual activity in question.[4]

---

2. 450 Mich. 349, 537 N.W.2d 857 (1995).
3. M.C.L. § 750.520j.
4. People v. Davis, 91 Mich.App. 434, 283 N.W.2d 768 (1979).

Hypnosis of Witnesses

A person who experiences stress or trauma while witnessing a legally important event may be unable to recount the event in sufficient detail to allow the police or attorneys to reconstruct the exact circumstances. Hypnosis induced by MHPs may be used to alleviate the stress or other condition to allow for better recall. A legal issue arises regarding the reliability of the hypnotic memory when it is used for a legal purpose, such as in forming the basis for a search warrant or as evidence at a trial.

(A) Hypnotically Induced Information in a Police Investigation

The use of hypnosis strictly to assist in a police investigation has not been the subject of case law in Michigan. As stated below, however, a witness whose memory has been hypnotically refreshed may not be permitted to testify to anything except what was known prior to hypnosis.

(B) Hypnotically Induced Courtroom Testimony

The Michigan Supreme Court held that hypnosis is not a reliable means of accurately restoring forgotten incidents or repressed memory.[1] Citing the *Frye* rule,[2] the court held that hypnosis has failed to gain general scientific acceptance, and that the technique actively contributes to the formation of pseudomemories and the inability of witnesses to distinguish between those and true memories. In fact, neither the hypnotic subject nor an observer of the process can distinguish between truth and falsehood, and introducing such testimony would deny the defendant the chance to cross-examine the witness adequately.[3]

Although hypnotically-refreshed testimony is considered tainted and inadmissible, a witness may testify at trial based on facts the witness recalled and related before hypnosis and thus is not automatically precluded from testifying.[4] However, the party offering such testimony has the burden of demonstrating its reliability by the relatively rigorous standard of clear and convincing evidence.[5]

Additionally, a witness can testify about an act, such as sexual abuse, that the witness alleged a defendant perpetrated while the witness was undergoing hypnosis. In such a case the danger that hypnosis created a pseudomemory could be minimized by the admission of expert testimony concerning the tendency of hypnotic subjects to confuse fact and fantasy and to confabulate.[6]

1. People v. Gonzales, 415 Mich. 615, 329 N.W.2d 743 (1982), *modified*, 417 Mich. 968, 336 N.W.2d 751 (1983).
2. Frye v. United States, 54 U.S. App. (D.C.) 46, 47, 293 D. 1013, 1014 (1923).
3. People v. Gonzales, 415 Mich. 615, 329 N.W.2d 743 (1982), *modified*, 417 Mich. 968, 336 N.W.2d 751 (1983).
4. People v. Nixon, 421 Mich. 79, 364 N.W.2d 593 (1984).
5. *Id.*
6. People v. Sorscher, 151 Mich.App. 122, 391 N.W.2d 365 (1986).

6.9

Eyewitness Identification

The role of the eyewitness to any event is critical in many trials. Such persons may be parties to the action, victims, or bystanders. Their testimony raises the issue of whether their identification at the time of the event, at a subsequent lineup (or other identifying procedure), or during the trial was valid. MHPs can contribute experimental and clinical expertise to aid the jury or court in evaluating the testimony of eyewitnesses.

In Michigan, neither statute nor case law specifically addresses the admissibility or scope of expert testimony concerning eyewitness identification. The admissibility of the eyewitness identification itself would be subject to rules of evidence, for example on witness credibility,[1] as any proposed expert testimony concerning eyewitness testimony would be subject to rules of evidence.[2]

---

1. M.R.E. § 609.
2. M.R.E. §§ 702, 703.

Criminal Matters

7.1

Screening of Police Officers

Applicants to police departments must satisfy training and selection criteria established by the Michigan Law Enforcement Officers Training Council.[1] Mental fitness is one of the qualifications governing recruitment, appointment, and retention of those personnel. MHPs, namely psychiatrists and licensed psychologists, may provide evaluations and must provide consultation in this process.

(A) Certification Examination

The Law Enforcement Officers Training Council has created selection and employment standards by administrative rule.[2] The Council's Certification Examination, the passing of which is a requirement for selection as a law enforcement officer,[3] by rule[4] is a job-related examination developed in conformance with the professional standards of the American Psychological Association's Division 14 for Industrial and Organizational Psychology, specifically the 1987 *Principles for Validation and Use of Personnel Selection Procedures*, third edition, which was adopted by reference in these rules.[5]

---

1. M.C.L. §§ 16.109, 28.609.
2. R 28.4101–28.4121.
3. R 28.4102(k).
4. R 28.4101(h).
5. R 28.4102(l).

(B) Mental Health Related Standards

The Law Enforcement Officers Training Council medical selection criteria include the requirement that the person selected to be a law enforcement officer be free from mental and emotional instabilities.[6] This necessitates signed certification by a physician or licensed psychologist that the officer candidate is free of psychological and emotional disturbance.

---

6. R 28.102a(e)(v).

7.2

Competency to Waive the Rights to Silence, Counsel, and a Jury

Persons taken into custody by police for a criminal offense can waive their rights to silence and to counsel, which are guaranteed under the U.S. and Michigan constitutions. If they are subsequently charged they may waive these rights as well as the right to a jury trial. MHPs may be asked to examine criminal defendants and testify about their competency to waive their rights in the arrest and investigation stages or at the time of trial.

(A) Right to Silence

In its landmark ruling in *Miranda v. Arizona*[1] the U.S. Supreme Court ruled that persons in police custody must be advised that they have a right to remain silent, that anything they say can be used against them in a court of law, that they have the right to the presence of an attorney, and that if they cannot afford an attorney one will be appointed for them prior to any questioning if they so desire.[2] After these warnings have been given, the Court held, individuals may knowingly and intelligently waive these rights and agree to answer questions or make statements.[3]

In *People v. Conte*[4] the Michigan Supreme Court considered whether promises or inducements could make a confession involuntary. It ruled that this determination can only be made after taking into account the "totality of the surrounding circum-

---

1. 384 U.S. 436, 86 S.Ct. 1602, 16 L.Ed.2d 694 (1966).
2. *Id.* at 479.
3. *Id.*
4. 421 Mich. 704 (1984).

stances," including but not limited to the nature of the inducement, the length and conditions of detention, the physical and mental state of the defendant, the conduct of the police, and how well and how often the defendant was advised of his rights. Two years later, citing the Supreme Court's rulings in *Colorado v. Connelly*[5] as well as in *Moran v. Burbine*[6] and *Colorado v. Spring*,[7] the Michigan Supreme Court in *People v. Cheatham*[8] seemed to close the door on any consideration of a defendant's state of mind in determining whether a confession was voluntary. It held that unless there was police coercion, a defendant's mental state can never render a confession involuntary.[9] The totality of the circumstances of a statement offered by the defendant must be considered, the court held, in determining whether the waiver was "knowing" and "intelligent."[10] Endorsing the language in *North Carolina v. Butler*,[11] it saw the "totality of circumstances" as a term embracing the suspect's age, experience, education, background, intelligence, and the suspect's capacity to understand the warnings given, the nature of Fifth Amendment rights, and the consequences of waiving those rights.[12] A defendant does not need to understand the ramifications and consequences of choosing to waive or exercise the rights that the police have properly explained in order to knowingly waive them. A lack of foresight is not enough to render a waiver invalid. What is needed for a valid waiver is an understanding by the accused of the right not to speak, the right to the presence of counsel, and an understanding that the state could use any statement by the accused at a later trial.[13] Although the court did not identify any particular police conduct that would render a waiver invalid because it was not knowing and intelligent, it did state that any police conduct that could have an effect on a suspect's level of comprehension must be factored into the analysis of whether the waiver was valid.[14] If behavior by police does not exploit an apparent weakness in the defendant that the police knew or should have known about, there would be no *Miranda* violation that leads to the exclusion of the statement as evidence.

5. 479 U.S. 157, 107 S.Ct. 515 (1986).
6. 475 U.S. 412, 106 S.Ct. 1135(1986).
7. 479 U.S. 564, 107 S.Ct. 851(1987).
8. 453 Mich. 1 (1996).
9. *Id.* at 2.
10. *Id.* at 1.
11. 441 U.S. 369, 99 S.Ct. 1755 (1979).
12. 453 Mich. 1, 27 (1996).
13. Adapt 1-2.
14. *Id.* at 3.

B) Right to Counsel

Both the right to be represented by counsel and to waive counsel and defend oneself without an attorney are guaranteed by the U.S. and Michigan constitutions. However, a criminal defendant's stated wish to waive counsel is not automatically granted. Although there is no requirement that the request be made in a timely manner, e.g., prior to the day of trial,[15] pursuant to *People v. Anderson*,[16] a waiver can be considered valid only after a judicial inquiry. After talking to the defendant and advising the defendant of the dangers and disadvantages of self-representation, the judge must determine that the defendant's request was unequivocal and that the right to waive counsel has been asserted knowingly, intelligently, and voluntarily, and that the defendant's self-representation will not disrupt, unduly inconvenience, or burden the court and the administration of the court's business.[17] In addition, the trial court must satisfy Court rule requirements.[18] Under the applicable rule, the trial judge cannot permit a defendant to waive the right to be represented by a lawyer without first advising the defendant of the charge, the maximum possible prison sentence for the offense, any mandatory minimum sentence required by law, and the risk involved in self-representation. Secondly, under the rule the judge must offer the defendant the opportunity to consult with a retained lawyer, or if the defendant is indigent, with an appointed lawyer. In *People v. Adkins*[19] the Michigan Supreme Court clarified the scope of the judicial inquiry required by *Anderson* and M.C.R. § 6.005(D), holding that the particular method of inquiring into the validity of the defendant's waiver is up to the trial court, provided the record showed substantial compliance, and evidence that the defendant made the request unequivocally, understood the right involved, and waived it knowingly, intelligently, and voluntarily; the court did not mandate any examination on this issue by a MHP.

C) Right to Waive a Jury Trial

Michigan statute[20] provides that in all criminal cases the defendant may elect to be tried by the judge rather than by a jury, with

---

15. People v. Rice, 231 Mich.App. 126, 585 N.W.2d 331(1998).
16. 398 Mich. 361, 247 N.W.2d 857 (1976).
17. *Id.* at 367–368.
18. M.C.R. § 6.005(D).
19. 452 Mich. 702 (1996).
20. M.C.L. § 763.3.

the consent of the prosecutor and the approval of the court.[21] The statute requires that except in cases of minor offenses, a waiver of the right to trial by jury must be made in open court, must be in writing, signed by the defendant, and filed in the case as part of the record.[22] The law has been interpreted[23] to require that the record of a trial show that the trial judge has made a finding that, based on information conveyed to the judge in open court by the defendant, or in his or her presence, the defendant has had an opportunity to consult with counsel and has personally, voluntarily, and understandingly given up the right to a trial by jury, and has signed a waiver form prescribed by statute, which has been filed in the case. The law does not require that the form be signed in open court, only that the defendant orally acknowledge in open court that the right has been waived voluntarily and understandingly.

---

21. M.C.R. § 6.401.
22. M.C.L. § 763.3; see also M.C.R. § 6.402.
23. People v. Pasley, 419 Mich. 297 (1984).

7.3

Precharging and Pretrial Evaluations

In some states, the prosecutor may request a mental health evaluation to determine whether to charge a person with a criminal offense or to divert him or her to the mental health system. Michigan does not have such a provision authorized in the statutory or administrative law. However, there are a number of agencies that provide such services on the consent of the prosecutor and defendant. Under the commitment statutes, individuals, including those arrested for crimes, can be examined to determine if they are persons requiring treatment (see chapter 8.4). In some cases, civil commitment may be the basis for a discretionary decision by the prosecutor not to proceed with prosecution.

7.4

Bail Determinations

Most persons charged with a crime have the right to post bail to secure their release from jail pending trial. It cannot be excessive bail, however. The sole purpose of the amount imposed and any other attendant conditions is to ensure that the defendant returns to court when required. MHPs may contribute to the bail determination through consultation with the court or with other personnel advising the court, such as probation officers, regarding the person's mental health and community stability. Note, however, that the law does not require evaluation or consultation.

(A) Determining Whether Bail Is Appropriate

The Michigan Constitution[1] provides that a person may be released on bail pending trial, except when there is strong proof of guilt and under certain circumstances. Bail may be denied if the person has been convicted of two violent felonies, stemming from two separate incidents, within the previous 15 years.[2] Bail may be denied if the person is charged with murder or treason.[3] It may be denied if the person is charged with first-degree criminal sexual conduct, armed robbery, or kidnaping unless the court finds by clear and convincing evidence that the defendant is not likely to flee or present a danger to another person.[4] Bail may be denied to

---

1. MICH. CONST., art. 1, § 15.
2. Id. (a).
3. Id. (b); see also Love v. Ficano, 19 F. Supp. 2d 754 (1998).
4. MICH. CONST., art. 1, § 15 (c).

anyone charged with a violent felony committed while the person was on bail.[5]

Following conviction, a person is no longer entitled to the presumption of innocence or to release on bail, and bail becomes a matter of discretion by the court, and is not a matter of right.[6]

(B) Determining the Amount and Conditions of Bail

Michigan law provides that in fixing the amount of bail the court must consider the seriousness of the offense charged, the protection of the public, the previous criminal record and the dangerousness of the person accused, and the probability or improbability of the person accused appearing at trial.[7] In cases of arrest for ordinance violations or misdemeanors, the court may require, in addition to other bond or security arrangements, the surrender of the defendant's driver's license.[8] Release on bail may be subject to conditions reasonably necessary for the protection of one or more named persons, provided the judge imposing the protective conditions makes a finding of the need for such conditions and informs the defendant of them and of the penalty for violating the conditions.[9]

---

5. *Id.* (d).
6. People v. Tate, 134 Mich.App. 682, 352 N.W.2d 297 (1984).
7. M.C.L. § 756.6(1).
8. M.C.L. § 756.6(2).
9. M.C.L. § 765.6b.

Competency to Stand Trial

Justice requires not only that a criminal defendant be *sane* at the time of the offense (see chapter 7.9), but that the defendant be aware of and able to participate in any criminal proceedings against him or her. This right, originating in common law (case law), is guaranteed under the U.S. Constitution. MHPs may be appointed to conduct competency evaluations in Michigan.

(A) Legal Determination of Competency to Stand Trial

(A)(1) Test of Competency

In Michigan, a defendant to a criminal charge is presumed to be competent to stand trial, and is determined incompetent "only if he is incapable because of a mental condition of understanding the nature and object of the proceedings against him or of assisting in his defense in a rational manner."[1] The defendant who is being given psychotropic or other medication is not determined to be incompetent even if without that medication the defendant might be incompetent to stand trial.[2]

(A)(2) Raising the Competency Issue

The issue of incompetency to stand trial may be raised by the defense, the judge, or the prosecution,[3] by evidence of incompe-

---

1. M.C.L. § 330.2020(1).
2. M.C.L. § 330.2020(2).
3. M.C.L. § 330.2024.

tency.[4] The trial judge has the duty of raising the issue once facts are brought to the judge's attention which raise bona fide doubt as to the defendant's competency,[5] although the question of whether a bona fide doubt exists is at the judge's discretion.[6] The issue can be raised at any time during the proceedings against the defendant, including in district court, or after trial at sentencing, and it can be raised by any court before which proceedings are pending or are being held.[7] Unless the issue of incompetency manifests itself during the course of court proceedings, in which case the court may adjourn the proceedings and order a competency examination on its own initiative or the motion of the defense or the prosecution, the party that raises the issue, either the defense or the prosecution, must do so in writing.[8] Once raised, the issue must be addressed by the trial court.[9]

(B) Competency Evaluation

Once there has been a showing that a defendant may be incompetent to stand trial, the judge must order that the defendant be examined by personnel of the Center for Forensic Psychiatry (Forensic Center), or by another facility certified by the Department of Community Health to perform competency evaluations by statute.[10] Facility certification follows administrative rules.[11] Currently, the only facility other than the Forensic Center is the Third Circuit Criminal Court (formerly Recorder's Court) Psychiatric Clinic. By administrative rule[12] examinations of defendants for competency to stand trial at certified facilities must be performed by a certified forensic examiner, who is a qualified social worker, psychiatrist, or psychologist who has undergone the requisite training and supervision. There is no bar to independent examinations of the defendant's competency to stand trial, whether requested by the defense or the prosecution or ordered by the court, but by law an examination at a certified facility must be ordered in any case.

The Forensic Center or other certified facility conducting a competency examination must consult with the defendant's attorney, and may consult with the prosecutor or other persons, for the

---

4. People v. Blocker, 393 Mich. 501, 227 N.W.2d 767 (1975).
5. People v. Harris, 185 Mich.App 100, 460 N.W.2d 239 (1990).
6. People v. Groeneveld, 54 Mich.App. 424, 221 N.W.2d 254 (1974).
7. M.C.R. 6.125(B).
8. Id.
9. People v. Thomas, 292 N.W.2d 523 (1980).
10. M.C.L. § 330.2026.
11. R 330.10058.
12. R 330.10056.

purpose of gathering information pertinent to the defendant's incompetency to stand trial.[13] The defendant's lawyer need not be permitted to be present at the examination of the defendant.[14] The mandatory examination and consultation with defense counsel must be completed within 60 days, and a written report submitted to the court.[15] Ordinarily, the examination is completed in a single day, without an inpatient admission, with the defendant making him- or herself available for the examination at an appointed time, and with defendants in custody transported to the examination by sheriff's deputies.[16] If the defendant is admitted to the Forensic Center for an inpatient examination, the examination, though permitted 60 days from the date of the order, must be performed as expeditiously as possible; during that time psychotropic medication can only be administered with the defendant patient's consent or as otherwise provided by administrative rules.[17]

The report of the competency examination must contain[18] (a) the clinical findings of the examiner, (b) the facts, in reasonable detail, upon which the findings are based, as well as other germane facts that may be requested by the judge or attorneys, and (c) an opinion on the issue of the defendant's competency to stand trial. If the examiner's opinion is that the defendant is incompetent, an opinion must be offered on the likelihood that the defendant, if provided treatment, will attain competency to stand trial within the statutory[19] time limit of one-third of the maximum sentence to which the defendant would be subject if convicted, or 15 months, whichever is less. Whether the examination was performed at the Forensic Center or at the Third Circuit Court Psychiatric Clinic, if the examiner's opinion is that the defendant is incompetent and is likely to attain competency if afforded treatment, the Forensic Center must make a recommendation to the court regarding the need for the defendant to be treated in an inpatient facility at the Forensic Center or elsewhere, or the appropriateness of outpatient treatment.[20]

13. M.C.L. § 330.2028(1)
14. People v. Martin, 386 Mich. 407, 192 N.W.2d 215 (1971).
15. Id.
16. R 330.10059.
17. R 330.10059(6), (7).
18. M.C.L. § 330.2028(2).
19. M.C.L. § 330.2034(1).
20. R 330.10079(a).

(C) Competency Hearing

A hearing on the question of the defendant's competency to stand trial is supposed to be held within 5 days of the receipt of the evaluation report by the court.[21] The examination report may be admitted as evidence in regard to the issue of competency per stipulation, or agreement, by the defense and the prosecution, but either may offer additional evidence.[22] The judge at a competency hearing must determine the defendant's competency to stand trial. If the court finds the defendant incompetent, it must determine whether there is a substantial probability that the defendant, if provided treatment, will attain competency to stand trial within the statutory time limit.[23] The court may find that a defendant who is currently taking medication is not incompetent, and it may order the defendant to continue taking the medication to maintain competency.[24]

(D) Confidentiality and Privileged Communications

Disclosures of communications by defendants who are examined for competency at the Forensic Center or at the Third Circuit Court Psychiatric Clinic are subject to Michigan's privileged communications statute;[25] as such, they may be made only with respect to the purpose for which the examination was ordered. This applies as well to any statements made by the defendant in the course of treatment to restore competency. The examiner's opinion concerning competency to stand trial is not admissible as evidence in any proceeding other than a competency hearing.[26] In particular, neither statements made by the defendant during a court-ordered competency examination nor the results of a competency examination may be used at trial as evidence of guilt.[27] However, testimony by an MHP regarding background information gathered in the course of a competency examination is admissible at trial, when that testimony does not apprise the jury of the prior competency hearing. Further, an examiner performing a

---

21. M.C.L. § 330.2030; M.C.R. § 6.125(E).
22. M.C.L. § 330.2030(3).
23. M.C.L. § 330.2030(2).
24. M.C.L. § 330.2030(4).
25. M.C.L. § 330.1750.
26. M.C.L. § 330.2028(3).
27. People v. Stevens, 386 Mich. 579, 194 N.W.2d 370 (1972); People v. Wright, 431 Mich. 282, 430 N.W.2d (1988).

court-ordered evaluation of a defendant's sanity at the time of the offense or other court-ordered evaluation may use and present information gathered in the course of a prior examination of competency in forming an opinion.[28] This may include information concerning the defendant's inpatient admission to the Forensic Center.[29] Testimony at trial about previous records and reports by an expert who was hired to perform an examination of the defendant but who did not perform an examination under a court order has been ruled inadmissible.[30]

(E) Disposition of Defendants Found Incompetent to Stand Trial

If the court determines that the defendant is incompetent to stand trial, and that there is a substantial likelihood that, if provided a course of treatment, the defendant will attain competency within the statutory time limit of one-third of the maximum sentence or 15 months, whichever is less, the court must order the defendant to undergo treatment to render him or her competent to stand trial.[31] If commitment is necessary for effective treatment, the court may commit the defendant to the custody of the Department of Community Health, to be treated at the Forensic Center or another state facility, or it may commit the defendant to the custody of another inpatient mental health facility, but in any case the court must appoint a medical supervisor of the course of treatment.[32] The medical supervisor of treatment must file reports with the court every 90 days regarding the defendant's competency, progress toward competency, or lack of substantial probability that the defendant will attain competency within the statutory time limit.[33] Unless defense waives it, a hearing is held to redetermine the defendant's competency to stand trial on receipt of the report by the treatment supervisor by the court.[34]

If the court finds that the defendant is incompetent to stand trial but that there is not a substantial likelihood that the defendant will attain competency within the statutory time limit even if afforded treatment, it may direct the prosecutor to file a civil commitment petition asserting that the defendant is a person

---

28. M.C.L. § 4330.2028(3).
29. People v. Ashford, 91 Mich.App. 693, 283 N.W.2d 830 (1979).
30. People v. Dobben, 187 Mich.App. 462, 468 N.W.2d 527 (1991).
31. M.C.L. § 330.2032.
32. Id.
33. M.C.L. § 330.2038.
34. M.C.L. § 330.2040.

requiring treatment, or meets the criteria for judicial admission[35] (see chapter 8.4). In such a case, the charges pending against the defendant are dismissed; they are similarly dismissed when the prosecutor notifies the court of an intention not to prosecute the case, or if 15 months have gone by since the defendant was determined incompetent to stand trial and no determination has been made that the defendant has attained competency.[36] If charges are dismissed because the 15-month period has expired, they may be filed again against the defendant, with the court's permission, within a period of time equal to one-third of the maximum possible sentence to which the defendant would be subject if convicted, or at any time in the case of any crime charged which is punishable by life in prison. Before granting permission to re-file charges, the court would need to determine at a hearing that the defendant is competent to stand trial, and may order an examination of the defendant for this purpose.[37]

---

35. M.C.L. § 330.2031.
36. M.C.L. § 330.2044.
37. *Id.*

7.6

Provocation

The law in some states provides that persons who have been charged with second-degree murder may offer an affirmative defense of *extreme emotional disturbance*. Such a defense will be a bar to a conviction on second-degree murder charges, but will be grounds for a conviction on charges of manslaughter. MHPs may provide testimony on this issue. This is not a defense option in Michigan. Instead, second-degree murder is established where the defendant inflicted death with malice, and without provocation.[1] Malice in this regard is the intent to kill, the intent to do great bodily harm, or the intent to do an act in wanton and willful disregard of the likelihood that a natural tendency of that behavior is to cause death or great bodily harm.[2] Homicide is reduced to voluntary manslaughter if the circumstances surrounding the killing show that malice was negated by adequate and reasonable provocation, and that the killing took place in the heat of passion.[3] Provocation is not an element of voluntary manslaughter in the sense that it needs to be established beyond a reasonable doubt; there need only be a modicum of evidence of provocation for the jury to consider the lesser charge of voluntary manslaughter.[4] No provisions are made in Michigan law for testimony by MHPs in regard to the presence of provocation. An argument that the

---

1. People v. Spearman, 195 Mich.App. 434, 491 N.W.2d 606 (1992), *rev'd in part by* People v. Rush, 443 Mich. 870, 504 N.W.2d 185 (1993).
2. People v. Baker, 216 Mich.App. 687, 551 N.W.2d 195 (1996), *rev'd*, 457 Mich. 442, 579 N.W.2d 868 (1998).
3. People v. Harris, 190 Mich.App. 652, 476 N.W.2d 767 (1991).
4. People v. Moore, 189 Mich.App. 315, 472 N.W.2d 1 (1991).

defendant was not a reasonable person because of any special traits the defendant had may not be considered.[5]

5. People v. Sullivan, 231 Mich.App. 510, 586 N.W.2d 578 (1998).

7.7

Mens Rea

The criminal code prescribes that the minimum requirement for criminal liability is a voluntary act (or omission to perform a duty) that caused the criminal result, plus the necessary *culpable mental state*, formerly referred to as *mens rea*. The purpose of determining a mental state is to distinguish between inadvertent or accidental acts and those that are performed with a *guilty mind*. MHPs are legally entitled to testify on this issue (see chapter 6.2). They most frequently do so when a defendant argues that, because of mental illness, mental retardation, intoxication, or some other mental impairment, he or she lacked the culpable mental state required as an element of a crime (see chapter 7.8).

Michigan law recognizes two categories of *mens rea* or intent: general intent and specific intent. Only specific intent offenses are susceptible to the intoxication and diminished capacity defenses (see chapter 7.8). The difference between general and specific intent is not defined by Michigan statute, and while case law has not addressed the nature of intent in respect to all crimes, it has recognized the difference in some instances. Traditionally, specific intent has been seen to involve an intention that goes beyond the lesser-included general intent.[1] For example, in the crime of burglary (in Michigan breaking and entering with intent to commit larceny) the specific intent is larceny. Larceny, when it is an element of an offense, is seen as a specific intent element, for example in car theft or "unlawfully driving away an automobile."[2] A seemingly similar crime without the traditional

---

1. People v. Depew, 215 Mich. 317, 183 N.W.750 (1921); Roberts v. People, 19 Mich. 401(1870).
2. People v. Lerma, 66 Mich.App. 566, 239 N.W.2d 424 (1976).

larcenous intent to permanently deprive an owner of property, such as joyriding or unlawfully taking and using an automobile, is only a general intent offense.[3] Case law recognizes first-degree murder, which requires premeditation, as a specific intent offense,[4] and has established that the malice required for second-degree murder is only a general intent element.[5] Typically, crimes denoted by the term *with intent* are treated as specific intent offenses, such as assault with intent to commit murder.[6] Felonious assault is seen as a specific intent offense[7] but carrying a concealed weapon is not.[8] Rape or first-degree criminal sexual conduct is not a specific intent offense,[9] nor is the lesser third-degree criminal sexual conduct.[10] The designation of rape offenses as general intent reflects the logic of the general/specific intent distinction: rape is an act that is viewed as an end in itself, and not a crime that presumes or requires some further specific aim or intention.

3. People v. Laur, 128 Mich.App. 11, 300 N.W.2d 717 (1980).
4. People v. Garcia, 398 Mich. 250, 247 N.W.2d 547 (1976).
5. People v. England, 164 Mich.App. 370, 416 N.W.2d 425 (1987); People v. Biggs 202 Mich.App. 450, 509 N.W.2d 803 (1993).
6. People v. Mangiapane, 83 Mich.App. 379, 271 N.W.2d 240 (1978).
7. People v. DeLong, 128 Mich.App. 1, 339 N.W.2d 659 (1983).
8. People v. Lane, 102 Mich.App. 11, 300 N.W.2d 717 (1980).
9. People v. Langworthy, 416 Mich. 630, 331 N.W.2d 171 (1982).
10. People v. Davis, 102 Mich.App. 403, 301 N.W.2d 871 (1980).

7.8

Diminished Capacity

There are two primary versions of diminished capacity law that have been used in the United States. In some jurisdictions, a defense termed diminished capacity (more properly diminished responsibility) has been used to reduce the degree of a crime for which the defendant may be convicted, even if the defendant's conduct satisfied all of the formal elements of a higher offense. However, in most states, including Michigan, the diminished capacity concept allows a criminal defendant to introduce evidence of mental abnormality at trial to negate a mental element, the "specific intent" element needed for the crime charged (see chapter 7.7), thereby completely exonerating the defendant of that charge, although not necessarily of a lesser included offense that does not incorporate that specific intent element.

(A) Legal Test of Diminished Capacity

Diminished capacity only applies to crimes that have a specific intent element, and not simply a general intent element (see chapter 7.7). A defendant had diminished capacity only when his or her impairment rendered him or her unable to formulate the specific intent element; it is not enough that the defendant could not fully appreciate the consequences of his or her acts.[1] The

---

1. People v. Fields, 64 Mich.App. 166, 235 N.W.2d 95 (1975); People v. Denton, 138 Mich.App. 568, 360 N.W.2d 245 (1984); People v. Jones, 151 Mich.App. 1, 390 N.W.2d 189 (1986).

mental capacity needed to formulate specific intent generally is not defined. However, first-degree murder, a specific intent offense, is differentiated from general-intent second-degree murder by premeditation, which necessitates sufficient time to allow the defendant an opportunity for a second look prior to the killing.[2] Testimony by MHPs may be helpful to an inquiry about a defendant's capacity to form specific intent, but the determination of diminished capacity is to be made by the trier of fact, the judge, or the jury.[3]

B) Raising the Diminished Capacity Issue

Evidence bearing on specific intent is admissible even if it falls short of supporting a finding of insanity.[4] *People v. Mangiapane*[5] brought diminished capacity within the ambit of the insanity defense, in the sense that it made diminished capacity subject to the notice and examination procedures that apply to the insanity defense. (See chapter 7.9).

C) Standard of Proof

As an element of the crime charged, specific intent must be proven beyond a reasonable doubt. As with any other element or fact alleged, the prosecution has been seen as bearing the burden of proof.[6]

D) Intoxication and Diminished Capacity

In Michigan, although intoxication at the time of an offense does not preclude a finding of insanity,[7] voluntary intoxication cannot be the sole basis for a finding of insanity.[8] An exception exists

---

2. People v. Berthiaume, 59 Mich.App. 451, 229 N.W.2d 497 (1975).
3. People v. Denton, 138 Mich.App. 568, 360 N.W.2d 245 (1984).
4. People v. Lynch, 47 Mich.App. 8, 208 N.W.2d 656 (1973).
5. People v. Mangiapane, 83 Mich.App. 379, 271 N.W.2d 240 (1978).
6. People v. Denton, 138 Mich.App. 568, 360 N.W.2d 245 (1984); People v. Jones, 151 Mich.App. 1, 390 N.W.2d 189 (1986).
7. People v. Chapman, 165 Mich.App. 215, 418 N.W.2d 658 (1987).
8. M.C.L. § 768.21a(3).

when voluntary use of mind-altering substances results in a se
tled condition equivalent to insanity,[9] one not limited merely 1
periods of intoxication.[10] Involuntary intoxication may be th
basis for a claim of insanity,[11] and that defense, like diminishe
capacity, is included within the ambit of insanity, and is subject 1
its notice and examination requirements.[12]

Voluntary intoxication may be a defense to a charge of
crime that requires specific intent,[13] and its logic is identical 1
that of diminished capacity. The intoxication defense used in th
manner in fact preceded the somewhat broader diminished c.
pacity approach in Michigan, and is the origin in the state's law
on the distinction between general and specific intent.[14] Th
intoxication defense seeks to establish that the defendant was s
intoxicated as to be incapable of entertaining the specific inter
involved in the crime charged.[15] The defense does not have th
burden of proof, however; as with any other element of a crim
the prosecution has the burden of proving specific intent beyon
a reasonable doubt.[16] Unlike the defenses of diminished capacit
and involuntary intoxication, the intoxication defense aimed 4
negating specific intent falls outside the ambit of insanity, an
does not require notice of intent to claim insanity, or submissio
of the defendant to a mandatory court-ordered examination at
certified forensic examination facility.[17]

9. People v. Caulley, 197 Mich.App. 177, 494 N.W.2d 853 (1992).
10. People v. Conrad, 148 Mich.App. 433, 385 N.W.2d 277 (1986).
11. People v. Caulley, 197 Mich.App. 177, 494 N.W.2d 853 (1992).
12. People v. Wilkins, 184 Mich.App. 443, 459 N.W.2d 57 (1990).
13. People v. Kelley, 21 Mich.App. 612, 176 N.W.2d 435 (1970).
14. Roberts v. People, 19 Mich. 401 (1870).
15. People v. Savoie, 419 Mich. 118, 439 N.W.2d 139(1984).
16. People v. Belanger, 158 Mich.App. 522, 405 N.W.2d 405 (1987).
17. People v. Wilkins, 184 Mich.App. 443, 459 N.W.2d 57 (1990).

7.9

Criminal
Responsibility

An early, yet still controversial, contribution of MHP expertise in the courtroom has been the evaluation of criminal defendants who plead not guilty by reason of insanity because of their mental state at the time of the offense. MHPs may evaluate a defendant and testify as to his or her psychological functioning at the time the criminal behavior occurred. Once the defendant files notice to claim insanity, an examination is ordered to be performed by the Center for Forensic Psychiatry or by other qualified personnel. Aside from the mandatory state examination, the defense or the prosecution has the right to retain its own expert to perform an independent evaluation.

A) Legal Determination of Insanity

In Michigan, an individual is legally insane if, as a result of mental illness or mental retardation as defined in the Mental Health Code, that person lacks substantial capacity either to appreciate the nature and quality or the wrongfulness of his or her conduct or to conform his or her conduct to the requirements of the law.[1] The statute further provides that an individual who was under the influence of voluntarily consumed or injected alcohol or controlled substances at the time of his or her alleged offense is not considered to have been legally insane solely because of being under the influence of the alcohol or controlled substances.[2]

---

1. M.C.L. § 761.21a(1).
2. M.C.L. § 761.21a(2).

The two conditions that are threshold requirements for insanity, mental illness and mental retardation, are explicitly defined by statute. *Mental illness* is defined as a substantial disorder of thought or mood that significantly impairs judgment, behavior, capacity to recognize reality, or ability to cope with the ordinary demands of life.[3] *Mental retardation* is defined as significantly subaverage general intellectual functioning that originates during the developmental period and is associated with impairment in adaptive behavior.[4]

(A)(1) Burden of Proof

The defendant has the burden of proving the defense of insanity by a preponderance of the evidence.[5]

(B) Mental Examination

Once the defendant in a felony case has filed notice of intent to assert the defense of insanity, the court must order the defendant to undergo an examination relating to the claim of insanity by personnel of the Center for Forensic Psychiatry (Forensic Center) or by other qualified personnel within 60 days.[6] Qualified personnel for the purposes of performing the court-ordered examination are defined by administrative rule[7] as consulting forensic examiners. Defense and prosecution may also obtain independent examinations by a clinician of their own choice on the issue of insanity.[8] If the defendant fails to cooperate fully in the court-ordered examination or in the independent examinations for the defense or prosecution, the defendant may be barred from presenting testimony at trial relating to insanity.[9]

Following the court-ordered or independent examination, the examiner must prepare a written report, and that report must be submitted to both the defense and prosecuting attorneys. The report must contain (a) the examiner's clinical findings, (b) the facts, in reasonable detail, on which the findings were based, and (c) the opinion of the examiner as to whether the defendant was mentally ill or mentally retarded at the time the alleged offense

---

3. M.C.L. § 330.1400(a).
4. M.C.L. § 330.1500(h).
5. M.C.L. § 761.21a(3).
6. M.C.L. § 768.20a(2).
7. R 330.1005(e), 330.10057.
8. M.C.L. § 768.20a(3).
9. M.C.L. § 768.20a(4); *see also* People v. Hayes, 421 Mich. 271, 364 N.W.2d 635 (1984).

was committed.[10] At trial, expert witnesses may testify in the form of an opinion on the ultimate issue, that is whether or not the defendant was legally insane.[11]

(C) Confidentiality and Privileged Communications

Disclosure of communications by defendants who are examined for competency at the Forensic Center or at the Third Circuit Court Psychiatric Clinic is subject to Michigan's privileged communications statute;[12] as such, they may be made only with respect to the purpose for which the examination was ordered. If a defendant elects not to assert the defense of insanity or diminished capacity, statements made during a court-ordered examination are not admissible,[13] and in any case statements by the defendant in the course of an examination are not admissible on issues other than the defendant's mental illness or insanity.[14] A defendant pleading insanity who has voluntarily released medical records cannot assert privilege and prevent testimony by former treating doctors regarding the defendant's mental state at the time of the offense.[15]

(D) Commitment of Defendants Found Not Guilty by Reason of Insanity

By administrative rule,[16] an individual acquitted of a criminal charge by reason of insanity, though not guilty of the offense, must be admitted to the Forensic Center for 60 days to be examined in respect to whether he or she is civilly committable as a person requiring treatment (see chapter 8.4). Pending the completion of the examination and the clinical certificates, psychotropic medication and physical treatment is voluntary and subject to

---

10. M.C.L. § 768.20a(5).
11. M.R.E. § 701.
12. M.C.L. § 330.1750.
13. People v. Jacobs, 138 Mich.App. 273, 360 N.W.2d 593 (1984).
14. M.C.L. § 768.20a(5); *see also* People v. Williams, 162 Mich.App. 542, 414 N.W.2d 139 (1987).
15. People v. Sullivan, 231 Mich.App. 510, 586 N.W.2d 578 (1998).
16. R 330.10086–330.10097.

administrative rules governing emergency treatment.[17] On completion of the examinations and certificates, the director of the Forensic Center prepares a summary report to be sent to the trial court and to the defense and prosecuting attorneys that indicates the examiners' opinions as to the acquittee's status as a person requiring treatment, with recommendations for treatment and placement as appropriate.[18] If at the end of the 60-day examination period a petition is not to be filed recommending that the acquittee be committed for treatment, the individual is discharged.[19] When the person is ordered to be hospitalized, admitted to a facility, or otherwise receive treatment, that person is not to be discharged or placed on leave without prior consultation with the Forensic Center, which may respond and object to the proposed discharge or leave; in cases of dispute between the treating agency or facility and the Forensic Center, the matter may be submitted to the director of the Department of Community Health for approval or disapproval of the plan.[20]

(E) Guilty But Mentally Ill

In Michigan, a defendant may be found to have been mentally ill at the time of the alleged offense, but criminally responsible and not legally insane[21] when it is determined that the defendant did commit the alleged offense, but when it does not determine that mental illness resulted in a lack of substantial capacity either to appreciate the nature and quality or the wrongfulness of his or her conduct, or to conform his or her conduct to the requirements of the law. Before accepting a plea of guilty but mentally ill, the court must establish a factual basis for the plea, and must examine the evaluation reports and hold a hearing that establishes that the defendant was mentally ill, but not legally insane.[22] If demanded by the defendant, a hearing may be held after the verdict to determine if appropriate treatment can be provided by the Department of Corrections,[23] and a mental health examination of the individual may be ordered for that reason. Although the purpose of the law in part was to assure that someone found guilty but mentally ill would be provided mental health treatment, such a

---

17. R 330.10089.
18. R 330.10087(5).
19. R 330.10095.
20. R 330.10097.
21. M.C.L. § 768.36.
22. M.C.R. § 6.303.
23. People v. McLeod, 407 Mich. 632, 288 N.W.2d 909 (1980); People v. Mack, 104 Mich.App. 560, 305 N.W.2d 264 (1981).

convict is only entitled to whatever treatment is psychiatrically indicated,[24] and those found guilty but not mentally ill may receive the same treatment.[25] A periodic report to the court on the mental condition of an individual found guilty but mentally ill but sentenced to probation may be required.[26]

24. People v. Toner, 125 Mich.App. 439, 336 N.W.2d 22 (1983).
25. People v. Darden, 132 Mich.App. 154, 346 N.W.2d 915 (1984).
26. *Id.*

7.10

Competency to Be Sentenced

Any time, before the imposition of the sentence, that the court believes a defendant may be an incapacitated (incompetent) person, a mental status evaluation for fitness to proceed must be ordered (see chapter 7.5). If the defendant is found to be incapacitated, the plea is generally vacated. All judicial proceedings begin again after the defendant regains competency. Michigan does not make specific provision for the determination of competency to be sentenced, but the issue may be raised at any time in proceedings, including at sentencing.[1] At that time the provisions for examination and determination described in chapter 7.5 would apply.

---

1. M.C.R. § 6.125(B).

7.11

Sentencing

After a finding of guilt, many states, including Michigan, permit the court to request a mental health evaluation prior to reaching a sentencing decision. This information may function as a supplement to the pre-sentence report by a probation officer. Mental health pre-sentence evaluations are not mandated by Michigan law, however, or otherwise regulated. While a sentencing court may look into available psychiatric treatment resources, there is no requirement that it do so.[1]

---

1. People v. Linzey, 112 Mich.App. 374, 315 N.W.2d 550 (1982).

7.12

Probation

A sentencing court may place a defendant on probation or conditional discharge following conviction. When imposing such a sentence, the court may require that the defendant, among other conditions, undergo available medical or psychological treatment, remain in a specified institution, participate in an alcohol or substance abuse program, and satisfy any other stipulations reasonably related to rehabilitation. If the defendant fails to meet the conditions of probation, the conditions may be modified and probation may be revoked.

A court may impose a sentence of probation under the supervision of a probation officer in all felony and misdemeanor cases other than murder, treason, criminal sexual conduct in the first or third degree, armed robbery, and certain major drug offenses, if the court determines that the defendant is not likely again to engage in an offensive or criminal course of conduct, and if the public good does not otherwise require the ordinary punishment.[1] Probation may be revoked, and the individual resentenced, if a condition of probation is violated.[2]

Before the court sentences a person to probation, a probation officer must investigate the antecedents, character, and circumstances of the person, and provide the court with a report; in the course of a pre-sentence investigation, a mental health evaluation may be performed, but such an evaluation is not mandatory.[3] A report of a pre-trial examination of the defendant relative to

---

1. M.C.L. § 771.1.
2. M.C.L. § 771.4
3. M.C.L. § 771.14.

insanity or criminal responsibility may be referred to in a pre-sentence report, if the criminal responsibility report contains information that may be useful to the sentencing judge in fashioning an individualized sentence.[4]

---

4. People v. Protrafka, 140 Mich.App. 749, 366 N.W.2d 35 (1985).

7.13

Dangerous Offenders

In some states, the criminal sentencing law has provisions for increasing the term of imprisonment of defendants who pose special risks or who are determined to be dangerous offenders because of a propensity for future criminal activity. The legal determination of whether a defendant fits this category may depend on psychological characteristics that could be assessed by an MHP. Michigan currently has no such statutory provisions. If, however, a prisoner is to be paroled or discharged from prison, and the Correctional Mental Health Program(see chapter 7.17) considers that the prisoner should be civilly committed as a person requiring treatment as defined in the Mental Health Code (see chapter 8.4), the director of the Program may file a petition in probate court asserting that belief.[1]

---

1. M.C.L. § 330.2006(3).

7.14

Habitual Offenders

In some states, the criminal sentencing law has provisions for increasing the term of imprisonment of defendants who have a history of criminal offenses. The determination of whether a person is likely to commit additional offenses in the future may depend on psychological characteristics that could be assessed by an MHP. In Michigan, however, decisions to sentence an individual as a habitual offender, when the individual has committed and been convicted for two or more successive felonies[1] are made on the basis of the record of the individual's prior convictions.

---

1. M.C.L. §§ 769.10, 766.11.

7.15

Competency to Serve a Sentence

The law in several states provides that a criminal defendant must be competent to serve a sentence. Michigan does not have such a statute. If an inmate suffers from mental illness, his or her problem would typically be covered by the laws governing the treatment of inmates and the transfer of inmates from prisons to mental health facilities (see chapters 7.17 and 7.18).

7.16

Mental Health Services in Jails and Prisons

Mental health services in prisons and jails are a vital part of an overall health care program for incarcerated persons. MHPs may provide services as employees of these institutions or in a consulting capacity.

(A) Prisons

The Corrections Mental Health Program (CMHP), authorized by statute,[1] is a program operated by the Michigan Department of Community Health for the Michigan Department of Corrections. It includes hospital-based programs, as well as outpatient services and crisis stabilization services in individual correctional facilities (see chapter 7.17).

(B) Jails

There are no statutory provisions for mental health services in Michigan county jails. Mental health services in those facilities are variously provided by jail personnel, county community mental health services, or contracted mental health providers.

---

1. M.C.L. § 330.2003.

Transfer From Penal to Mental Health Facilities

An inmate of a state-operated correctional facility who is mentally disordered may be eligible for mental health treatment provided by the Correctional Mental Health Program (CMHP).[1] Commitment of correctional inmates or prisoners to hospitals is analogous to the civil commitment of non-prisoner adults (see chapter 8.4), with the finding that the prisoner requires mental health services substituting for findings that the person is dangerous to self or others.

(A) Mentally Ill Inmates

Prisoners who are mentally ill may be admitted to the CMHP for inpatient or outpatient services either involuntarily or voluntarily. Mental illness is defined as a substantial disorder of thought or mood that significantly impairs judgment, behavior, capacity to recognize reality, or ability to cope with the ordinary demands of life.[2]

(A)(1) Procedures

A person such as a corrections officer may file a written notice with the officer in charge of a state correctional facility that a prisoner is mentally ill and requires treatment. The officer in charge must have that prisoner examined by an MHP as soon as possible. The examiner completes a certificate specifying whether in the opinion of the MHP the prisoner is mentally ill and if so,

---

1. M.C.L. § 330.2003.
2. M.C.L. § 330.1400(a).

what treatment is recommended.[3] A prisoner may initiate a referral, or may agree with the findings and recommendations of the examiner, and may enter the CMHP voluntarily.[4]

If the prisoner refuses treatment or services recommended by an examiner who has determined that the prisoner is mentally ill and requires mental health services, or if a prisoner wishes to terminate voluntary services when the CMHP has concluded that the prisoner is still mentally ill and requires mental health services, a hearing is held before a committee or panel consisting of a psychiatrist, a psychologist, and another mental health professional.[5] The prisoner is entitled to review documents 24 hours before the hearing, to be present at the hearing, to present evidence, confront and cross-examine witnesses (unless precluded from doing so because of security and safety considerations), and to have the assistance of a recipient rights advisor or a mental health professional.[6] If the hearing committee or panel determines that the prisoner is mentally ill and requires mental health services, it may order the prisoner into treatment; the prisoner may appeal this decision to the director of the CMHP within 2 days. An initial order for treatment is for 90 days; if prior to the expiration of that order the treating MHP believes that the prisoner continues to be mentally ill and requires mental health services, a report to this effect may be filed with the director of the CMHP. A second 90-day period of treatment may then be ordered by a hearing committee, as well as a third 180-day treatment period under the same circumstances. At the end of that 180-day period, if it is the opinion of the treating MHP that the prisoner is still mentally ill and requires mental health services, the process must start from the beginning with a request for admission to the CMHP *de novo*.[7]

(B) Mentally Retarded Inmates

Mental retardation is defined as significantly subaverage general intellectual functioning that originates during the developmental period of the fetus and is associated with impairment in adaptive behavior.[8] The provisions for the voluntary and involuntary treatment of mentally retarded prisoners are the same as for mentally ill prisoners (see Chapter 1.17(A)).

---

3. M.C.L. § 330.2003a.
4. M.C.L. § 330.2003b.
5. M.C.L. § 330.2003c.
6. *Id.*
7. M.C.L. § 330.2005d.
8. M.C.L. § 330.1500(h).

7.18

Parole Determinations

Parole is a conditional release from imprisonment that entitles the parolee to serve the remainder of the term outside of the confines of the prison. It differs from probation in that the convicted person must first serve a period of time in a Michigan Department of Corrections institution. Although a parole determination is made by the Parole Board, MHPs in or out of the system may provide information for the parole hearing.

(A) Parole Board

The Michigan Parole Board consists of 10 appointed members who are not state civil service employees.[1]

(B) Eligibility for Parole

Convicts, or prisoners, may be released on parole only when the Parole Board has considered all of the facts and circumstances and has a reasonable assurance that the prisoner will not become a menace to society or to the public safety.[2] Conditions to be met by the parolee during the period of parole may be imposed.[3] Parole is discretionary with the Parole Board, but an action by the Board in granting or denying parole may be appealed by the prisoner, the prosecutor of the county from which the prisoner

---

1. M.C.L. § 791.231a.
2. M.C.L. § 791.233.
3. M.C.L. § 791.236.

was sent to prison, or the victim of the crime for which the prisoner was convicted; the appeal is by leave, rather than by right, to the circuit court in the county from which the person was sent to prison; that court may deny permission to appeal.[4]

At least 90 days before the prisoner first becomes eligible for parole, the correctional staff must prepare a parole eligibility report, which must contain, among other information, the results of any physical, mental, or psychiatric examinations of the prisoner that may have been performed.[5] The Parole Board may request a psychological evaluation, which may be performed by the same person who provided the prisoner with treatment, unless the prisoner or Board requests someone else.[6]

---

4. M.C.L. § 791.234(8).
5. M.C.L. § 791.235(7).
6. *Id.*

7.19

Competency to Be Executed

A person who has been convicted of first-degree murder and sentenced to death must be legally competent at the time of execution. The rationale for this law is that the convict must be able to communicate with his or her attorney about the possibility of appeal until the moment of death. MHPs may be involved in the evaluation of these persons. Michigan has no death penalty, and thus this issue does not arise in the state's jurisdiction.

7.20

Pornography

The law prohibits promoting, or possessing with intent to promote, any obscene material; or producing, directing, presenting, or participating in an obscene performance. MHPs may be asked to evaluate and testify whether the dominant theme of a work taken as a whole appeals to a prurient interest in sex, whether a work is patently offensive because it affronts contemporary community standards regarding sexual matters, or whether a work is utterly without redeeming social value. However, expert testimony is not necessary for a conviction on any obscenity charge, and proof cannot be based on such testimony alone.

Michigan obscenity law does not make any provision for testimony from MHPs. Material is defined as obscene if it meets these criteria: (a) the average individual, applying contemporary community standards, would find that the material taken as a whole appeals to the prurient interest; (b) the reasonable person would find that the material taken as a whole lacks serious literary, artistic, political, or scientific value; and (c) the material depicts or describes sexual conduct in a patently offensive way.[1]

---

1. M.C.L. § 752.362(5).

7.21

Services for Sex Offenders

In some states, the law provides specialized services for sex offenders through commitment or sentencing to a treatment program. MHPs are involved in evaluating the individual, testifying in court, and providing treatment. Michigan has a criminal sexual psychopath law[1] (the first such in the nation, enacted in 1939) that permits the examination, hospitalization, and parole of sex offenders, but this law, and the administrative rule implementing it[2] are not in current use. Michigan does have mandatory sex offender registration,[3] but this law makes no provision for treatment.

1. M.C.L. § 330.1942.
2. R 330.10099.
3. M.C.L. §§ 28.721–28.731.

7.22

Services for Victims of Crimes

Some states, including Michigan, have enacted laws that provide services for victims of crimes from MHPs and others. Michigan provides crime victims with a number of services,[1] including the right to make a victim impact statement, the right to be notified of the disposition of a criminal case or of a prisoner who has been convicted for the crime involved, the right to a speedy trial of the defendant in certain cases, such as sexual offenses, and restitution by an individual who has been convicted of the crime. In cases of felonies committed by adults,[2] serious misdemeanors,[3] or crimes committed by juveniles,[4] the court may, if a crime results in physical or psychological injury, order restitution to a victim that includes paying the cost of professional services related to physical and psychological care, and paying the cost of psychological and medical treatment for members of the victim's family that has been incurred as a result of the crime.

---

1. M.C.L. §§ 780.753–780.834.
2. M.C.L. § 780.766(4).
3. M.C.L. § 780.826(4).
4. M.C.L. § 780.794(4).

Voluntary or Involuntary Receipt of State Services

8.1

Medicaid

Medicaid[1] is the federally supported program whereby the states provide direct payments to suppliers of medical care and services (including MHPs) for individuals receiving cash payments in programs such as old-age assistance, aid to needy families with dependent children, aid to the blind, and aid to the permanently and totally disabled. In Michigan, the program is administered primarily by the Family Independence Agency (FIA), in conjunction with other departments.[2] Mental health care is a benefit available to those who qualify for Medicaid.[3]

---

1. 42 U.S.C. § 1396.
2. M.C.L. § 400 et seq.
3. M.C.L. § 400.109.

8.2

Health Care Cost Containment System

Some states have health care cost containment systems that administer medical and other services to indigent persons. In Michigan, the Medicaid program is administered primarily by the Family Independence Agency (FIA), in conjunction with other departments (see chapter 8.1). Counties can set up a patient care management system, which establishes rates of reimbursement for services and appropriate lengths of inpatient treatment for eligible persons.[1] The county can contract with hospitals and other health care providers to provide these services. Payment can be denied for services that are not medically necessary or could be provided at lower cost at another facility.[2]

---

1. M.C.L. § 400.66j.
2. M.C.L. § 400.66k.

8.3

Voluntary Admission of Mentally Ill Adults

The law provides for the voluntary admission of mentally ill persons to state-operated facilities. MHPs are involved in this process both in evaluating the person for admission and in providing services within the facility.

A) Differences Between Voluntary and Involuntary Hospitalization

In Michigan, no person can be retained as a patient in any facility that treats mental illness without his or her permission and informed consent, unless they are involuntarily committed. Thus, a person may choose to request admission to a facility if they feel they are in need of care or treatment. However, it is much more common for those with serious mental illness to fail to recognize or resist the need for treatment. Under carefully proscribed circumstances, the state may move to retain and treat such people against their will, or involuntarily. Unlike voluntary admission, this process requires a specified legal procedure that safeguards the rights of the person being considered for involuntary admission (see chapter 8.4).

B) Evaluation and Admission

Anyone 18 years of age or older seeking voluntary admission to a hospital must first be screened by a community mental health services preadmission screening unit.[1] If hospitalization is authorized, the person may be admitted in one of two ways:

1. They may apply to be admitted to a hospital as an informal voluntary patient, although most hospitals typically do not accept this type of admission. They must request hospitalization as such, agree to be treated, and the hospital director must consider the person to be clinically suitable for that form of hospitalization.[2] Anyone over the age of 18 can also be admitted as a formal voluntary patient if he or she or their guardian makes a formal written application to be admitted and the hospital director considers him or her to be clinically suitable for admission.[3]

2. If a person who is in the process of being committed involuntarily is considered by a hospital to be suitable for voluntary admission, that person can be offered the chance to request this.[4]

(C) Discharge

An informal voluntary patient is free to leave the hospital any time during the normal day shift hours.[5] If a formal voluntary patient gives written notice of intent to leave the hospital, they must be released within 3 days.[6] However, if the hospital determines that the individual is a person requiring treatment (that is, committable, see chapter 8.4), it may apply for a court order authorizing involuntary retention.[7] The retention procedure is similar to the regular involuntary commitment process.

---

1. M.C.L. § 330.1410.
2. M.C.L. § 330.1411.
3. M.C.L. §§ 330.1415, 330.1416.
4. M.C.L. § 330.1406.
5. M.C.L. § 330.1412.
6. M.C.L. § 330.1419.
7. M.C.L. § 330.1420.

8.4

Involuntary Commitment of Mentally Ill Adults

The law pertaining to involuntary civil commitment concerns mentally ill adults as well as minors (see chapter 4.19). MHPs are involved in this process in evaluating and certifying the person for admission, in testifying in court as to their findings, and in providing services within the facility to which the person is committed. Two physicians, including at least one psychiatrist or a psychiatrist and a licensed psychologist, must be involved in the certification process, although other MHPs may assist.

A) Definitions

To understand the law concerning involuntary commitment, MHPs should be familiar with the following terms and their legal meanings:[1]

Mental illness means a substantial disorder of thought or mood that significantly impairs judgment, behavior, capacity to recognize reality, or ability to cope with the ordinary demands of life.

Person requiring treatment means an individual who has a mental illness and (a) who as a result of that mental illness can reasonably be expected within the near future to intentionally or unintentionally seriously physically injure himself or herself or another person, and who has engaged in an act or acts or made significant threats that are substantially supportive of the expectation, (b) who as a result of that mental illness is unable to attend to his or her basic needs such as food, clothing, or shelter that must be

---

1. M.C.L. § 330.1400–1401.

attended to in order for the person to avoid serious harm in the near future and who has demonstrated that inability by failing to attend to those basic physical needs, and (c) whose judgment is so impaired that he or she is unable to understand the need for treatment and whose continued behavior can reasonably be expected, on the basis of a competent clinical opinion, to result in significant physical harm to himself, herself, or others.

Competent clinical opinion means the clinical judgment of a physician, psychiatrist, or licensed psychologist.

Clinical certificate means the written conclusion and statements of a physician or licensed psychologist that an individual is a person requiring treatment, together with information and opinions, in reasonable detail, that underlie the conclusion.

(B) Admission

Each area community mental health center (CMHC) may contract with any local hospital that is able to receive and detain persons requiring civil commitment.[2] Each CMHC must also establish one or more preadmission screening units that provide 24 hour assessment and screening services for potentially committable persons.[3] An individual may be taken to the screening unit for examination for involuntary hospitalization if there is reason to believe he or she is a person requiring treatment (see section (A) above). Involuntary admission, on an emergency basis or otherwise, may be initiated in one of two ways shown in the next sections.

(B)(1) Admission by Application and Certification

In order to commit a person by this method, two actions that must be taken are:

1. an application must be made that asserts that the person requires treatment, and
2. a physician (who may be a psychiatrist) or licensed psychologist must examine the person and file a clinical certificate that also concludes that the individual is a person requiring treatment.

Any person over the age of 18 can present an application for hospitalization of an individual to a hospital or screening unit.

---

2. M.C.L. § 330.1422.
3. M.C.L. § 330.1409.

Applications can be obtained from any public mental health facility and from the probate court. The application must assert that the individual is a person requiring treatment, give facts that form the basis of the assertion, provide a list of witnesses to the facts, and provide the name and address of the person's nearest relative (or if none, a friend). The application must be made within 10 days of screening for admission.[4] A person can then be held involuntarily for 72 hours if, after examination, a physician or licensed psychologist files a clinical certificate.[5]

An application or clinical certificate can also be given to a police officer, who is then authorized to take the person into protective custody and transport him or her to the screening unit or hospital.[6] In addition, a police officer observing behavior that he or she reasonably believes makes the individual a person requiring treatment may take the person into protective custody without any other application or certification.[7]

If for some reason, a person who has executed an application is unable to obtain a clinical certification, the application can be brought directly before the probate court, which may order the person to be taken into protective custody or to be examined by the screening unit.[8] A person cannot be held for more than 24 hours without an examination being conducted and a clinical certificate completed. However, the law requires that unless there are extenuating circumstances, the screening unit must complete the certification examination within 2 hours.[9]

Once the person is hospitalized, he or she cannot be held unless a psychiatrist performs an examination within 24 hours and also certifies that he or she is a person requiring treatment. At this point the person can be held until a court hearing.[10] Thus, involuntary hospitalization under this procedure requires an application and two clinical certificates.

B)(2) Admission by Petition

A person can also be involuntarily hospitalized by petition to the court (as opposed to being filed at the treating facility which is done with an application). The same form is used for a petition as for an application. The petition must be accompanied by a clinical certificate of a physician or licensed psychologist who has examined the person within 72 hours of the petition. If a certificate

---

4. M.C.L. § 330.1424.
5. M.C.L. § 330.1425.
6. M.C.L. § 330.1426.
7. M.C.L. § 330.1427.
8. M.C.L. § 330.1428.
9. M.C.L. § 330.1429.
10. M.C.L. § 330.1430.

cannot be obtained, an affidavit giving reasons why must be filed.[11] Persons requiring treatment who meet the impaired judgment criterion (see section (A) above), can only be admitted by petition.[12] A case begun by application can only rely on the first two criteria: danger to self of others or inability to care for self. Upon receiving the petition, the court then orders any necessary examinations and certificates.[13] Involuntary hospitalization under this procedure also requires two certificates, at least one by a psychiatrist and one by any physician or licensed psychologist. Unless the court determines that the person needs to be taken into protective custody because of being a danger to self or others, the person can remain at home until the examinations are conducted.[14]

(C) Commitment Proceedings

Once the court receives an application or petition and two certificates, it must schedule a hearing within 7 days.[15] Persons have a right to request an adjournment, or postponement of the hearing for good cause.[16] Hearings are typically adjourned only with the patient's consent. Adjournments are granted if an independent medical evaluation is requested or if a jury trial is demanded. If a hearing is held, the community mental health center must prepare a report for the court that assesses the availability and appropriateness of alternatives to hospitalization.[17] The person must be given notice of the hearing,[18] the right to counsel,[19] the right to a jury,[20] and of the opportunity to waive a hearing.[21] Within 72 hours of the court's receipt of the commitment documents, a meeting of the person, his or her attorney, a treatment team member and a community mental health worker must be held. At this meeting the person is informed of his or her treatment plan, the nature and possible consequences of the commitment procedures, and the proposed discharge plan that must consist of either an alternative to hospitalization or a combination of hospitalization of no more than 60 days and alternative com-

---

11. M.C.L. § 330.1434.
12. M.C.L. § 330.1400–1401.
13. M.C.L. § 330.1435.
14. M.C.L. § 330.1437.
15. M.C.L. § 330.1452.
16. M.C.R. § 5,735.
17. M.C.L. § 330.1453a.
18. M.C.L. § 330.1453.
19. M.C.L. § 330.1454.
20. M.C.L. § 330.1458.
21. M.C.L. § 330.1455.

munity treatment thereafter. After this meeting, the person can request to defer a hearing for 60 days if he or she chooses to remain hospitalized or for 90 days if he or she chooses alternative treatment or a combination of hospitalization and alternative treatment. At this point they are given status as a voluntary patient. However, if they at any time refuse treatment, a commitment hearing can be held.[22]

If a hearing is held, it must be proven by clear and convincing evidence that the individual is a person requiring treatment.[23] The person has a right to have his or her own evaluation done.[24] If the person is found to be committable, the court can order (a) hospitalization for not more than 60 days, (b) alternative community treatment for not more than 90 days, or (c) a combination of the two. In a combined order, the hospitalization part cannot exceed 60 days. If the initial order has expired and the individual is still a person requiring treatment, the court can (a) order hospitalization for not more than 90 days, (b) alternative treatment for not more than one year, or (c) a combination of both. After this, continuing orders for not more than 1 year can be issued.[25] The person's status must be reviewed at least every 6 months.[26]

D) Discharge

The director of the hospital must discharge a person if he or she no longer meets the criteria for involuntary hospitalization.[27] If a person is hospitalized under a combined order of hospitalization and alternative treatment, he or she can be released to the alternative treatment program on the decision of a designated psychiatrist.[28] The person can be rehospitalized under this order if necessary, but can object and request a hearing.[29] He or she can be discharged from alternative treatment by the person responsible for providing that treatment.[30]

22. M.C.L. § 330.1455.
23. M.C.L. § 330.1465; Matter of Wagstaff, 287 N.W.2d 339, 93 Mich.App. 755 (1979).
24. M.C.L. § 330.1463.
25. M.C.L. § 330.1472a.
26. M.C.L. § 330.1482.
27. M.C.L. § 330.1476.
28. M.C.L. § 330.1474.
29. M.C.L. § 330.1475, 1475a.
30. M.C.L. § 330.1477.

(E) Patient (Recipient's) Rights

No person may be deprived of any civil right solely because he or she meets the criteria for involuntary hospitalization.[31] Patients are guaranteed (a) the right to mental health services suited to his or her condition, (b) safe, sanitary, and humane treatment in the least restrictive setting available, and (c) the right to be treated and have family members treated with dignity and respect.[32] They also have the right to be able to communicate privately by mail, telephone, or visit with whomever they wish, unless it is not authorized by their treatment plan.[33]

Each facility must have an officer of recipient's rights and the rights must be made easily available to patients. Patients must also be informed of the procedure for filing a complaint with the recipient's rights officer. The officer is responsible for making sure any complaint is investigated thoroughly.[34]

Patients have a right to an individualized treatment plan and must be informed periodically of their progress in treatment.[35] Each person must receive a comprehensive physical and mental examination within 24 hours of admission and be re-examined at least yearly.[36] The patient must give informed consent for surgery or shock therapy.[37] Psychotropic medication cannot be given before the initial court hearing unless the patient consents.[38] Michigan law does not address whether a patient has a right to refuse medication after the hearing is held. Restraints or seclusion may be used only when necessary to prevent a patient from seriously injuring him- or herself or others or causing substantial property damage. It may be applied only if less restrictive techniques have been considered first. A person can be temporarily restrained for no more than 30 minutes without an order; after this, restraint can continue only by order of a physician who has personally examined the patient.[39]

Patient records are generally confidential and may be released only in specified situations.[40] Records established after March 28, 1996, must be disclosed to the patient at his or her request within 30 days (there was no specified time period for disclosure before this). Exceptions to the confidentiality require-

---

31. M.C.L. § 330.1702.
32. M.C.L. § 330.1708, 1711.
33. M.C.L. § 330.1726.
34. M.C.L. § 330.1755.
35. M.C.L. § 330.1714.
36. M.C.L. § 330.1710.
37. M.C.L. § 330.1716, 1717.
38. M.C.L. § 330.1718.
39. M.C.L. § 330.1740, 1742.
40. M.C.L. § 4330.1748 et seq.

ment include the release of information to the following: (a) the court, (b) prosecuting attorneys, (c) the Department of Community Health if required by law, (d) the auditor general's office, or (e) a surviving spouse if the information is needed for applying for benefits. Information may be disclosed without consent if it is necessary for the patient to receive benefits, and for research or statistical purposes only if identification of the person is essential and it is not likely to be harmful to the patient. Finally, information can be released to a public agency or to providers of mental health services if there is a compelling need based on the substantial probability of harm to the patient or others.

(F) Civil Liability

The Department of Community Health and its employees, as government workers, are generally immune from civil suits for injury or damages due to patients injuring themselves or others while the employee was discharging a governmental function.[41] Discharging a governmental function includes caring for and treating residents of a state facility.[42] The government employee is immune when he or she is acting within the scope of his or her authority and does not engage in conduct so reckless as to demonstrate a substantial lack of concern for whether an injury results.[43]

---

41. Ross v. Consumers Power Co., 420 Mich. 567, 363 N.W.2d 641 (1984).
42. Perry v. Kalamazoo State Hosp., 406 Mich. 1118, 273 N.W.2d 421 (1978).
43. M.C.L. § 691.1407.

8.5

Voluntary Admission and Involuntary Treatment of People With Substance Abuse Problems

In 1973, the Michigan legislature established the Office of Substance Abuse Services in order to provide prevention, treatment, and rehabilitation services for alcoholics and drug abusers.[1] Facilities that provide assessment and treatment of substance abusers must be licensed by the state as approved service centers. MHPs may be part of a multidisciplinary evaluation and treatment team under this law.

(A) Voluntary Admissions

Any person who wishes to enter treatment for substance abuse may voluntarily seek admission at an approved program or emergency room.[2] They must be examined by a licensed physician or his or her designee and may undergo a blood test. If the medical examiner finds the person to be incapacitated[3] they can be referred for treatment and someone the person designates is notified. The person may leave at any time.

(B) Involuntary Admissions

A person who appears to be incapacitated in a public place can be taken into protective custody by law enforcement personnel and

---

1. M.C.L. § 6201 et seq.
2. M.C.L. § 333.6506.
3. Unfortunately, the law does not define *incapacitated*.

taken to a service program or emergency room.[4] This does not mean that the person cannot also be charged criminally. Once at the approved service program, the person in protective custody must be examined by a licensed physician or his or her designee within 8 hours.[5] A blood test can be ordered at the request of the physician or the person. If the person is found to be incapacitated they can be detained for up to 72 hours and released when no longer incapacitated. If they have been charged with a misdemeanor and are still incapacitated after 72 hours they must be discharged to a law enforcement officer unless they agree to remain in the program longer or the physician believes it is more appropriate for the person to stay longer.[6]

4. M.C.L. § 333.6501.
5. M.C.L. § 333.6502.
6. M.C.L. § 333.6503.

8.6

Voluntary Admission and Involuntary Commitment of Drug Addicts

Michigan has no separate law for the treatment of individuals addicted to drugs (see chapter 8.5).

8.7

Services for Persons With Developmental Disabilities

The law provides various residential and outreach services to persons with developmental disabilities and retardation. These include (a) inpatient, (b) outpatient, (c) partial hospitalization, (d) day care, (e) emergency, (f) rehabilitative, and (g) other appropriate treatments and services. MHPs aid in the provision of evaluation and treatment.

(A) Definitions

To understand fully the law regarding developmental disability services, MHPs should understand the following terms and their legal meanings:[1]

1. *Mentally retarded* means significantly subaverage general intellectual functioning that originates during the developmental period and is associated with impairment in adaptive behavior.

2. *Developmental disability* means an impairment of general intellectual functioning or adaptive behavior that meets all of the following criteria:

   a. it originated before the age of 22;

   b. it has continued since its origination and can be expected to continue indefinitely;

   c. it constitutes a substantial burden to the person's ability to perform normally in society; and

---

1. M.C.L. § 330.1500.

d. it is attributable to one or more of the following:

    i.   mental retardation, cerebral palsy, epilepsy, or autism;

    ii.   any other condition found closely related to mental retardation because it produces similar impairment and requires similar service; or

    iii.   dyslexia resulting from either i. or ii.

3. *Facility* means any place that is operated by or under contract with a public agency or is licensed by the state that regularly admits persons with developmental disabilities and provides residential and other services.

4. *Private facility* means an adult foster care home.

(B) Voluntary Admission to Services

Voluntary admission is known as *administrative admission,* and is the preferred form of admission to services for all people age 18 or over.[2] An application for admission can be made by the person him- or herself, if competent to do so, or by the parent, guardian, or person acting in loco parentis (in the place of a parent). Suitability for an administrative admission is determined only by referral to and evaluation by a community mental health services program (CMHP).[3] The CMHP must conduct a preadmission examination performed under the supervision of a registered nurse or other mental health professional who has at least a master's degree. Evaluation of the person's mental, physical, social, and educational needs must be made and a report must be written. If admitted to a facility, the developmentally disabled person must be examined at least once a year to determine whether he or she continues to be suitable for admission.[4] Unfortunately, the law is silent on the definition of "suitable for admission."

Objections to admission can be made by the person, if at least 13 years of age, or by any person found suitable by the court. Objections can be made not more than 30 days after admission or at any 6-month interval following admission. A hearing must be held within 7 days. The hearing requirements are similar to those for involuntary admission and will be discussed below.[5] If a resident wishes to leave a facility, he or she can only be held for 3

---

2. M.C.L. § 330.1503.
3. M.C.L. § 330.1509.
4. M.C.L. § 330.1510.
5. M.C.L. § 330.1511.

days, unless it is determined within this time that involuntary admission is necessary.[6]

(C) Involuntary Admission

Involuntary admission is known as *judicial admission*, and is prohibited for minors under 18.[7] The criteria for judicial admission of a developmentally disabled person age 18 or over are that he or she: (a) has been diagnosed as an individual with mental retardation, and (b) can reasonably be expected within the near future to intentionally or unintentionally seriously physically injure him- or herself or another person, and has overtly acted in a manner substantially supportive of that expectation.[8] Any person found suitable by the court may file a petition and if the court deems it sufficient, it must order the person to be examined by a qualified professional. If the person will not voluntarily comply with the evaluation, the court may order that they be placed in protective custody by the police. The examination must be conducted at least in part by either a physician and a licensed psychologist or two physicians, who must both conclude that the person meets the criteria for judicial admission. The examination must (a) include evaluations of the person's mental, physical, social, and educational condition, (b) list available alternative forms of care and treatment, and (c) make a recommendation as to the most appropriate living arrangement for the person.[9]

A hearing must be conducted within 7 days of the receipt of the report of the examination. Notice of a hearing must be given to (a) the person, (b) his or her attorney, (c) the petitioner, (d) the prosecutor, (e) the CMHP, and (f) the person's spouse, guardian, or any other appropriate relatives. The person must also be given a copy of the report of the examination, and be notified that they have (a) a right to a hearing, (b) the right to be present at that hearing, (c) the right to be represented by counsel, (d) the right to demand a jury trial, and (e) the right to have an independent clinical or psychological evaluation. The developmentally disabled person is entitled to require an examining physician or licensed psychologist to testify at the hearing and be cross-examined.[10]

The court must determine whether the person meets admission criteria, and must release the person, or order the person (a)

6. M.C.L. § 330.1512.
7. M.C.L. § 330.1503.
8. M.C.L. § 330.1515.
9. M.C.L. § 300.1516.
10. M.C.L. § 300.1517.

to be admitted to a facility recommended by the CMHP, (b) be admitted to a licensed hospital at the request of the person or his or her family if private funds are used to pay, or (c) be treated for 1 year in a recommended alternative program.[11] Preference for facilities is given to the one that offers the least restrictive environment that meets the person's needs and is located nearest to his or her home.[12]

The person's status must be reviewed every 6 months. The person may petition for discharge once within each 12-month period after admission. The petition must be accompanied by the report of a physician or licensed psychologist that states the MHP's reasons why the person no longer meets the criteria for judicial admission and a hearing must be held.[13]

(D) Rights of the Mentally Retarded and Developmentally Disabled

Mentally retarded and developmentally disabled people who reside in facilities have substantially the same rights as patients in psychiatric centers (see chapter 8.4(E)). If an individual is judged to be incompetent, a guardian can be appointed to manage his or her affairs and protect his or her rights.[14]

---

11. M.C.L. § 300.1518.
12. M.C.L. § 300.1521.
13. M.C.L. § 300.1532.
14. M.C.L. § 300.1600 et seq.

8.8

Hospice Care

Hospice care is a program of psychological and physical support offered to terminally ill persons. The emphasis is on increasing the quality of a person's last days or months through active participation by the family in caring for the person and openly facing the meaning and importance of death. There is continued medical assistance in such matters as the control of pain and other symptoms so as to allow the person to concentrate on other aspects of life. A complete program may consist of three phases: home care with nursing, emotional and religious support; inpatient care with overnight facilities for the family; and bereavement services for the family. MHPs may be involved in all three phases as a member of the support team.

There is a strong federal interest in hospice care, especially as it pertains to health insurance coverage and the quality of services. Individual states are also considering laws pertaining to hospice care. Michigan is committed to the hospice concept and has enacted legislation to incorporate the hospice as a permanent component of the health care system.[1]

In Michigan, a *hospice* is defined as follows:[2]

> *Hospice* means a health care program which provides a coordinated set of services rendered at home or in outpatient or institutional settings for individuals suffering from a disease or condition with a terminal prognosis.

---

1. M.C.L. § 333.21401 et seq.
2. M.C.L. § 333.20106

A person cannot be cared for by a hospice unless they have a terminal prognosis, which is defined as having 6 months or less to live in the opinion of a physician.[3]

Hospices must be licensed by the Department of Health, and may provide inpatient services or services delivered to people who choose to stay at home.[4] The services must address the physical, psychological, social, and spiritual needs of the terminally ill person, as well as the needs of his or her family during the time of the illness and bereavement. These services must be provided through an interdisciplinary team that can also include trained volunteers.[5]

---

3. M.C.L. § 333.21417.
4. M.C.L. § 333.21411.
5. M.C.L. § 333.21415.

Appendix

Table of Cases

Table of Statutes

Table of Rules of Court

Table of Administrative Rules and Regulations

Table of References to Constitution

Table of Cases

References are to page numbers in this book.

P

R

S

T

Table of Statutes

References are to page numbers in this book.

Michigan Public Acts

United States Code

Table of Rules of Court

References are to page numbers in this book.

Table of Administrative Rules and Regulations

References are to page numbers in this book.

Opinions of Attorney General

Revenue Rulings

Table of References
to Constitution

References are to page numbers in this book.

Index

References are to chapters.

COMPETENCY
   Admission and commitment of
      alcoholics and drug abusers, 8.5
   To be executed, 7.19
   To be sentenced, 7.10
   Of children to stand trial, 4.16
   Conservatorships for adults, 4.3
   To contract, 5.6
   Diminished capacity defense, 7.8
   To execute a will, 5.7
   Guardianship for incapacitated
      adults, 4.2
   Involuntary commitment of
      mentally ill adults, 8.4
   To marry, 4.1
   To obtain driver's license, 5.9
   Pretrial evaluation, 7.3
   To serve sentence, 7.15
   To stand trial, 7.5
   To testify, 6.4
   Voluntary admission of mentally ill
      adults, 8.3
   To vote, 5.8
   To waive legal rights, 7.2
CONDITIONING
   Avoidance/aversion, 3.8
CONFIDENTIALITY
   Adult abuse reporting, 4.7(E)
   Child abuse reporting, 4.8(E)
   Competency examination, 7.5(D)
   Consent for minor's abortion, 4.22
   Generally, 3.3
   Insanity defense examination, 7.9(C)
   Privileged communications, 3.4
   Public records, 3.6
   Search and seizure of records, 3.5
CONSERVATORSHIP
   For adults, 4.3
   For minors, 4.12
CONTRACT LAW
   Competency issues, 5.6
   Professional liability, 3.11(B)(2)
COUNSELORS
   Licensure and regulation, 1.10
   Privileged communications, 3.4(C)
CRIMINAL LAW
   Bail determinations, 7.4
   Competency to be sentenced, 7.10
   Competency to serve sentence, 7.15
   Competency to stand trial, 7.5
   Competency to waive rights, 7.2
   Dangerous offenders, 7.13
   Diminished capacity defense, 7.8
   Habitual offenders, 7.14
   Insanity defense, 7.9

   Jury selection, 6.1(B)
   Mens rea determination, 7.7
   Pornography, 7.20
   Pretrial evaluations, 7.3
   Probation, 7.12
   Professional liability, 3.12
   Provocation defense, 7.6
   Sentencing, 7.11
   Sex offenders, 7.21
   Victim's services, 7.22
   See also JUVENILE JUSTICE

D

DANGEROUS OFFENDERS
   Generally, 7.13
DEFAMATION OF CHARACTER
   Professional liability, 3.11(A)(1)
DELINQUENCY
   Generally, 4.15(A)
DEVELOPMENTAL DISABILITIES
   Services for people with, 8.7
DIMINISHED CAPACITY DEFENSE
   Generally, 7.8
DISABLED PERSONS
   Vocational disability, 5.3
DISCRIMINATION
   Employment, 5.12
DIVORCE
   Annulment of marriage, 4.4
   Child custody, 4.6
   Generally, 4.5
DOMESTIC VIOLENCE
   Adult abuse, 4.7
   Battered woman's syndrome as legal
      defense, 6.6
DRIVER'S LICENSE
   Competency issues, 5.9
DRUG ABUSE. *See* SUBSTANCE ABUSE

E

EDUCATIONAL SYSTEM
   Services for gifted and handicapped
      children, 4.20
EMOTIONAL DISTRESS
   As personal injury, 5.4
EMPLOYMENT DISCRIMINATION
   Generally, 5.12
EMPLOYMENT SCREENING
   Police officer, 7.1
EXPERT WITNESSES
   On eyewitness identification, 6.9
   Provocation defense, 7.6

Licensed professional counselors (LPC), 1.10
Marriage and family therapists, 1.9
Mental status of professionals, 5.1
Polygraph examiners, 1.12, 6.3(B)
Psychiatric nurses, 1.3
Psychiatrists, 1.2
Psychologists, 1.4
School counselors and social workers, 1.8
School psychologists, 1.7
Social workers, 1.6
Subdoctoral/limited license psychologists, 1.5
Sunset laws, 1.14
Unlicensed mental health professionals, 1.13
See also CERTIFICATION AND REGULATION

M

MALICIOUS PROSECUTION
Professional liability, 3.11(A)(2)
MALPRACTICE
Generally, 3.10
Statute of limitations, 3.10(A)
MANDATED REPORTING
Adult abuse, 4.7
Child abuse, 4.8
MANSLAUGHTER/MURDER
Criminal liability, 3.12(C)
Provocation defense, 7.6
MARRIAGE
Annulment, 4.4
Competency to marry, 4.1
Voiding, 4.4
See also DIVORCE
MARRIAGE THERAPISTS
Confidentiality issues, 3.3(C)
Licensure and regulation, 1.9
Privileged communication, 3.4(E)
MEDICAID
Generally, 8.1
MEDICAL CARE
Admission and commitment of alcoholics and drug abusers, 8.5
Conservatorship for adults, 4.3
Cost containment, 8.2
Decision-making for minors, 4.21
Guardianship for incapacitated adults, 4.2
Hospice care, 8.8
Mental health services as tax medical deduction, 2.11(A)

Quality assurance, 3.9
Rights of noncustodial parent, 4.23
Right to refuse treatment, 3.7
MEDICAL PROFESSIONALS
Mental status, 5.1
MENS REA
Generally, 7.7
MENTAL HEALTH PROFESSIONALS
Civil liability, 3.11
Confidentiality issues, 3.3
Criminal liability, 3.12
Hospital staff privileges, 2.7
Licensure and regulation, 1.1, 1.10
Malpractice liability, 3.10
Mental status, 5.1
Records maintenance, 3.2
Unlicensed, 1.13
See also SPECIFIC PROFESSION
MENTAL ILLNESS
Competency to stand trial, 7.5
Competency to testify, 6.4
Conservatorship for adults, 4.3
Diminished capacity criminal defense, 7.8
Evaluation of licensed professionals, 5.1
Guardianship for adults, 4.2
Guardianship for minors, 4.11
Involuntary commitment of mentally ill adults, 8.4
Legal liability and, 5.5
Services for people with developmental disabilities, 8.7
Services for prisoners, 7.16
Transfer of incarcerated persons, 7.17
Vocational disability, 5.3
Voluntary admission/commitment of minors, 4.19
Voluntary admission of adults, 8.3
Worker's compensation, 5.2(B)

N

NEGLIGENCE
Professional liability, 3.11(B)(3)
NONRESPONSIBILITY DEFENSE
Generally, 4.17

P

PARENTAL RIGHTS
Consent for minor's abortion, 4.22

SENTENCING
Competency to be executed, 7.19
Competency to be sentenced, 7.10
Competency to serve sentence, 7.15
Of dangerous offenders, 7.13
Generally, 7.11
Of habitual offenders, 7.14
SEXUAL ASSAULT
Competency of rape victim to
testify, 6.4(B)
Professional liability, 3.12(A)
Rape trauma syndrome, 6.7
Registration of offenders, 7.21
Treatment of offenders, 7.21
SEXUAL ASSAULT COUNSELORS
Privileged communications, 3.4(E)
SOCIAL WORKERS
Confidentiality issues, 3.3(C)
Licensure and regulation, 1.6
Privileged communication, 3.4(B)
School, 1.8
SOLE PROPRIETORSHIPS
Regulation, 2.1
SUBPOENA
For search and seizure of records,
3.5(B)
SUBSTANCE ABUSE
Admission and commitment of
alcoholics and drug abusers, 8.5,
8.6
Diminished capacity defense, 7.8(D)
Treatment of minors, 4.21(B)
SUNSET LAWS
Generally, 1.14

T

TAX LAW
Deductions for mental health service
payments, 2.11

V

VICTIM'S SERVICES
Generally, 7.22
VOCATIONAL DISABILITY
Evaluation for, 5.3
VOTING
Competency for, 5.8

W

WARRANTS
For search and seizure of records,
3.5
WILLS
Competency of testator, 5.7
WORKER'S COMPENSATION
Generally, 5.2

Z

ZONING
For community homes, 2.8

About the Authors

Beth K. Clark, PhD, ABPP, received her doctorate in clinical psychology from Long Island University in 1980. She has been in private practice in Ann Arbor since 1982. She has an extensive practice in the area of forensic psychology, with a concentration in the areas of civil and family law, and has been involved in evaluations and consultations on a variety of related issues throughout the country. Her publications and her presentations have focused on psychological testing, child custody, the forensic assessment of children, risk management, and ethical practice. She is a Forensic Diplomate of the American Board of Professional Psychology, a former president of the Michigan Psychological Association, and currently is the vice president of the American Academy of Forensic Psychology. She is immediate past-chair of the American Psychological Association's Committee on Legal Issues and is chairperson of its working group to establish a joint ABA/APA Institute on Marriage, Family and Divorce and chair of its subcommittee to facilitate APA/ABA Relations. She is currently secretary of the Michigan Society of Forensic Psychology and is an associate member of the American Psychological Association Ethics Committee.

Charles R. Clark, PhD, ABPP, is a clinical and forensic psychologist in private practice in Ann Arbor, Michigan. He received his doctoral degree in clinical psychology from Long Island University in 1978. He is a 1986 American Board of Professional Psychology diplomate in Forensic Psychology. For 10 years he held positions in Michigan's Center for Forensic Psychiatry, including that of Director of Psychology; while there he performed pretrial evaluations of criminal defendants and provided expert testimony in courts in that state. Since 1988 Dr. Clark's independent practice has focused on evaluations and consultations with prosecution, defendant and plaintiff attorneys on state and federal criminal matters, and on a number of civil and administrative law issues, especially those involving personal injury, malpractice, discrimination, sexual abuse, and sexual harassment. He was a founding member in 1981 of the Michigan Society of Forensic Psychology, served as the president of the Michigan Psychological Association in 1991, and served on the American Psychological Association's Ethics Committee, of which he was chairperson in 1993–1994. His publications focus on forensic assessment, on criminal law, particularly criminal responsibility and intent, and on ethics. Most recently he is the author of the chapter on specific intent and diminished capacity in the 1999 *Handbook of Forensic Psychology*, edited by Allen K. Hess and Irving B. Weiner.